THE BIRD & THE FEATHER

BY GRAEME STRACHAN

Caniggia and Ravanelli's
Dundee Adventures

Foreword

IT was the best of times, it was the worst of times. It can't be claimed those words were written with Dundee FC in mind, but the opening line of Dickens' classic A Tale of Two Cities are just about spot-on when describing the events of the three years from the start of the millennium at Dens Park.

It was the period when Dark Blues fans saw their team make a plethora of big-name signings and be linked with many more. But it was also an episode that led to financial disaster and took the club to the edge of oblivion.

Taking the good first, the biggest of the signings came early on when, in October 2000, Argentine World Cup hero Claudio Caniggia was snapped up.

A chance meeting with Dundee's Italian manager Ivano Bonetti in, of all places, a Tesco supermarket, was how I learned of the news, though it was only after a nervous few days for me that Ivano agreed I could run with the story.

For all the great players who'd turned out for Dundee, not since Billy Steel in the early 1950s had they pulled off anything like a signing coup of that magnitude. We weren't just talking about a world-class player, a decade earlier Caniggia had been one of the stars of Italia 90 when his semi-final goal was instrumental in his country reaching the final for a second World Cup running.

And he just happened to be a close friend of the legendary Diego Maradona and his favourite strike partner for the Argentines.

So close were the two that when Maradona and Pele were named FIFA world players of the 20th Century, Dundee had to give Caniggia time off to attend the awards ceremony.

And if he was a class act on the pitch, those who were lucky enough to cross his path during his brief stay at Dens would learn he was just

By Tom Duthie
Lead Football Writer
The Evening Telegraph

as impressive off it. Quiet-spoken, humble and courteous, he was a gentleman and just as popular in the dressing room as he was with fans.

Lucky enough to be granted an interview with him during a winter break trip to Italy, Caniggia talked football to me long after the formal part of our sit-down was over.

He even took great delight in recalling his first memory of a World Cup was when Scotland took part in the finals in his own Argentina. When told the Tartan Army travelled under Ally MacLeod thinking there was a chance of winning the trophy, he laughed out loud before, in typical fashion, apologising profusely for what he felt was his rudeness, but was not more than a natural reaction.

After Caniggia, other notable names such Temuri Ketsbaia and Scotland international Craig Burley would follow. The likes of Edgar Davids, Attilio Lombardo and Angelo Peruzzi were also linked with moves. It meant that when Italian superstar Fabrizio Ravanelli was signed up in September 2003, for many fans such sensational news had become the norm.

His stay at Dens would be brief and end painfully when his contract was cancelled as the consequences of three years of the kind of extravagant spending needed to secure such names became apparent and Dundee were plunged into administration because of massive debts.

Showing his class, incidentally, Ravanelli insisted that his should be one of the contracts cancelled in the hope of saving the jobs of younger players whose careers lay ahead of them.

His departure, along with many others who'd served the club well both on the field and behind the scenes, was a sad end to a remarkable period.

Tom Duthie

This book was first published in Great Britain in 2019 by DC Thomson
Media, Meadowside, Dundee, Scotland, DD1 9QJ.

Edited by Steve Finan.
Internal design by Steve Finan.
Cover design by Chris Hudson.

The main text of this book is set in 10.5pt Times New Roman Regular.

ISBN: 978-1-84535-786-3

Thanks to

Sylwia Jackowska
Jacqui Hunter
Chris Hudson
Barry Sullivan
Catriona MacInnes
David Lord
Pat Kelly
John 'Blether with' Brown
Peter McDonald
Norman Wisdom's Albanian interpreter
Tom Duthie
Steve Smith
Graham Smith
Catriona Strachan
Rachel Lonie
Ruth Lonie
Esmée Strachan
Steve Finan

Contents

Contents

CHAPTER ONE

Rising Up From The Ashes Of The Past

Some days will stay a thousand years, Some pass like the flash of a spark, Who knows where all our days go?

Lyrics from 'East of Eden' by Big Country

THESE days, Dundee is a city transformed. Named the UK's first City of Design by the United Nations, Dundee's new billion-pound waterfront development with the Victoria and Albert Museum at its heart is bringing visitors from far and wide. There's a change in the city. There's fire in the belly in the way people talk about Dundee. People are standing tall in a city which is now a citadel of science. It's also a world leader in the computer games industry. Genes, games and joysticks now share the same status as jute, jam and journalism.

But the end of the 19th century was markedly different. Dundee had developed into the world centre of the jute trade, having received its first consignment of "Indian grass" in 1822 when it was stored in a warehouse because a buyer couldn't be found. William Anderson, a linen manufacturer who was an expert in hemp, experimented on it but it was found to be brittle and lacking strength. In 1832, Dundee merchants, Thomas Neish and James Watt, received a consignment, which they took to a local company. The material was woven into sacking and sold to Dutch companies for the shipment of coffee beans. At that time, manufacturers were obtaining supplies from London and Liverpool, but in 1840 the first consignment arrived direct from Calcutta when the barque Selma sailed into Dundee harbour with 850 bales.

India's jute output brought prosperity to the city. There were 40,000 workers toiling in appalling conditions amongst a forest of factory chimneys which spewed dirty smoke across the city. Satirical postcards of the time showed Dundee from across the water at Newport as a thicket of chimneys with smoke belching out.

Ever-present was the risk of accident and injury. Conditions were dreadful and the workers lived in appalling squalor. The mills were mainly staffed by women and girls, cheaper to employ than men. The boys got chucked out once they reached the age where they'd earn a man's wage. Children regularly suffered missing limbs and horrific disfigurement after being caught in machinery. Many workers went deaf due to the noise from the machines. The heat, grease and oil fumes made bronchitis and breathing problems a work-related hazard. Jute was very flammable and fires were common. The smell of the jute mills was also a physical presence in the city.

Camperdown Works was the largest factory in Europe, boasting 820 power looms, 150 hand looms and more than 5,000 workers. Smoke from about 60 furnaces spewed across Lochee from the 282-foot high brick chimney Cox's Stack, built by James MacLaren in 1866 and modelled on Italian bell towers. The Cox family built it to ensure smoke from the furnaces was carried well above the nearby workers' houses.

While their factories in Dundee were driving industry, many jute barons set up home in Broughty Ferry – then outside of the city boundaries and part of Angus – which meant they were able to avoid paying Dundee's higher tax rates on the money earned from their factories. They built extravagant homes and created what was at one stage the richest square mile in Europe – including Carbet Castle, owned by the Grimond jute barons, and Castleroy mansion house, which had stables and vineries. Dundee was once home to more millionaires than any other British city.

The impact of jute attracted more and more people to the city. Irish workers started to arrive to join the endless rows of women, men and children who made the bobbins fly and the mills bustle. They came mainly from the Irish counties where linen and yarn were produced, such as Donegal, Londonderry, Monaghan, Sligo and Tyrone. The population increased six-fold, from 26,084 in 1800 to 160,000. But overcrowding became a serious problem with Dundee's stone-built tenement dwellings filled a dozen to a room. Crime and ill-health became by-products of the vigorous growth. Tory Judge Lord Cockburn condemned Dundee as "a sink of atrocity which no moral flushing seems capable of cleansing".

Horse-drawn trams were still running in the streets when Dundee was given city status by Queen Victoria in 1889. It was Dundee's reward for surviving an era of industrial change. Just two years earlier the new double-track Tay Bridge had opened, built next to the stumps of the original doomed structure which perished during a terrible storm and sent a train carrying 75 passengers plunging into the icy firth. Queen Victoria herself had bestowed a knighthood upon the designer of the first bridge, just after it opened in 1878, as an acknowledgment of his skills as an engineer.

Life was tough in Dundee. Drunkenness among jute mill workers and factory workers had become rife, with no less than 453 houses licensed for the sale of alcohol. One commentator spoke of "wretched men and women" and "very young children in dirt and rags" who streamed in and out of public houses at all hours, 8am until 11pm.

Against this backdrop of concerns over binge drinking, women adopting masculine drinking patterns, and debates over legislation to restrict alcohol consumption, Dundee Football Club's own story, ironically, started in a temperance hotel. At the time, professionalism had just been legalised in Scotland. Football was becoming popular in Dundee and it was the desire of two ambitious local outfits which craved a challenge at a national level which led to Dundee's founding. Andrew Buttar, president of the Dundee Charity Football Association and an official of Our Boys, wanted to join forces with rivals East End and apply for admission to the Scottish League. The clubs met at the Mathers Hotel on May 20, 1893, within a month of Mr Buttar publicly airing the idea. They put together an application and were admitted to the league on June 12. Dundee FC's peaks and troughs over the coming years would coincide with the peaks and troughs of the city.

Hopes of playing at Carolina Port at the city docks were thwarted. Another team, Strathmore, obtained the lease, so Dundee instead started life at Our Boys' home ground, West Craigie Park, located just off Albert Street to the north of Arbroath Road. It required a substantial amount of renovation to get it ready for the national league. At the same time the committee set about putting together a team capable of competing at a higher level. Most of the squad was pulled together from the two amalgamated teams but Scotland international outside-left Sandy Keillor, and a team-mate from Montrose – goalie Billy McKie – were also brought in to strengthen the ranks.

On August 12, 1893, Dundee ran out to face Rangers at West Craigie on the first day of the new Scottish League season. There was a healthy attendance of 5,000 for the game, and many fans made their way on foot. Those with more money took a tram to the ground. Rangers were already a well-established league outfit. They had secured their first title just two years earlier, but Dundee battled from two goals down to earn their first league point with a 3-3 draw. They went down 4-1 to eventual champions Celtic the following week, before a first win came against Renton, followed by a 5-3 victory over Leith. Strathmore then amalgamated with Johnstone Wanderers and began playing at Clepington Park. That allowed Dundee to move to their first choice home, where a steaming rubbish dump on the neighbouring gas works at Carolina Port regularly gave hundreds of fans a free view of the game.

The 18-game first season campaign would yield an acceptable eighth-place finish and, although that meant Dundee had to apply for re-election, the bid was successful. But the club was racking up vast debts as a result of diminishing crowds because Carolina Port was simply too isolated with no public transport links. The club was eventually saved from liquidation in 1898.The new executive committee took the decision after the Harbour Trustees "intimated their intention of acquiring Carolina Port for other purposes than that of sport".

They upped sticks and moved to a new ground where it was said "a large contingent of the sporting public of the city reside". Discussions were resolved with the trustees of the late Mr James Neish. They agreed the lease, for 10 years, of a piece of ground of about five acres and bounded on one side by the Clepington Spinning Company's works and by Provost Road on the other.

Dens Park officially opened in 1899 and Fred McDiarmid was awarded a medal for scoring the first goal on the new ground against St Bernard's. Crowds started to flock to the more accessible venue.

The city was going through a period of change with hard times ahead for the jute industry, which by now employed almost half of all workers in the town. Dundee jute barons and the British East India Company began to set up mills in India and by 1900 the Calcutta jute industry had captured much of the world trade. The reality was that

Calcutta had overtaken Dundee's trade. There was a great deal of poverty in Dundee in the early 20th Century and the men were slightly shorter than their counterparts in Glasgow. Infant mortality was also higher than normal. Whaling, which had employed large numbers and brought great prosperity to communities, given the requirement for whale oil as a source of lighting, was starting to decline. Ships would sail to the Arctic in search of the mammals which, once detected, were harpooned then gutted – the precious oil being found within the blubber. After the mid-1880s Dundee was the only whaling port in the UK but the industry was fading. Dundee's shipyards continued to thrive, however. Captain Robert Falcon Scott's Antarctic exploration ship was built for £50,000 in the Panmure Yard of Dundee Shipbuilders Ltd.

Scott was a decorated naval officer. He entered the race to the pole following a chance encounter with Clements Markham, president of the Royal Geographical Society, who commissioned the RRS Discovery for her southern voyage. The Discovery Expedition left British shores on July 31, 1901. It returned to the UK in 1904 after being stuck in the Antarctic ice for more than two years. As they waited for the ice to thaw, or a rescue ship to release them from their frozen prison, Scott and the sailors and scientists with him made the most of their extra time in Antarctica. They discovered the first Emperor penguin colony, travelled closer to the pole than anyone had managed previously, mapped hundreds of miles of formerly unknown coastline and explored the vast wastes of ice where no man had ever dared to walk. Discovery's stay in Antarctica made newspaper headlines around the world. Once the ship had finally been blasted free of the ice, Captain Scott returned to the UK to discover he had become a national hero.

Dundee FC's own solo voyage was also about to come to an end. The club had had it all their own way for 16 years before the Irish community in the city formed a club called Dundee Hibernian in 1909. The driving force behind the move was bicycle trader Pat Reilly. Reilly was born in Belfast in 1873 and his family arrived in Dundee in the late 1870s to work in the jute mills. After he left school, Reilly also worked in the mills before he started making bikes. Reilly was in his 20s when he opened a cycle shop in Perth Road. While the jute industry began to decline in the 20th century, Reilly's business was flourishing after women started taking up cycling. He was the biggest frame builder in Dundee and would build mainly roadster-type bikes which were very well constructed. Reilly also sold cars and motorbikes and opened branches in Perth and Edinburgh where he developed an interest in Hibernian FC.

He was active in the Catholic church and the Irish business community and wanted his home city to have a football club with similar links. Reilly wasn't put off by the fact that a previous attempt to provide a focus of sporting interest for the city's Catholic community had failed. Dundee Harp originally played at Magdalen Green and won the Forfarshire Cup three times, but they dissolved in 1894 after being unable to pay their bills. Reilly was the driving force behind the formation of Dundee Hibernian after getting together with other local businessmen with Irish origins. Reilly became secretary and was also the fledgling club's first manager. The club played in green and white and Reilly set to work putting a squad together for the new season. Reilly approached the landlord of Clepington Park which was home to Northern League side Dundee Wanderers and across the road from Dens Park. Reilly's offer exceeded what the Wanderers were paying and the lease was transferred to Dundee Hibs. Wanderers were infuriated and dismantled the ground before they left. The new tenants started rebuilding and changed the name to Tannadice Park after one of the surrounding streets.

Another arrival in Dundee that summer was Harry Houdini, who leapt (bound, gagged and handcuffed) into the harbour. Houdini arrived carrying 200 documents signed by prison governors certifying he had broken out of the safest cells in their jails. In characteristic daredevil style Houdini jumped into Earl Grey Dock on Sunday, June 20, in handcuffs and shackles to attract audiences. A few seconds later he appeared on the surface free from the irons which had bound him.

Dundee FC were proving just as big a star turn. The club had finished second in the league three times during the decade before Captain Scott set sail again for Antarctica on a scientific mission, aboard an ex-whaling ship Terra Nova, in 1910. This was the same year the Dark Blues won the Scottish Cup with a victory over Clyde at Ibrox. The appropriately named John "Sailor" Hunter scored the winning goal.

Captain Scott and his men were hoping to achieve similar success when they started their 800-mile trek to the South Pole, which ultimately ended in catastrophic failure. Scott and his four fellow explorers arrived at the South Pole on January 18, 1912, to be met by the sight of a Norwegian flag. They had been beaten by more than a month. Captain Scott wrote in his diary: "A terrible disappointment. This is a terrible place." The long march back to base camp proved even more testing than the inward journey. By March, two of the team were dead, while Captain Scott, Dr Edward Adrian Wilson and Birdie Bowers sought refuge in their tent and huddled together for warmth when a terrible storm struck. Almost a year later a search party found their frozen bodies in a snow-buried tent.

Arctic whaling came to a close in Scotland just before World War 1, which also provided a boost to industry in Dundee. The town gave an astonishing 63% of its eligible men to the forces, leaving barely a street, house or tenement in the city unaffected. Dundee paid a blood price too – the city's casualty rate was more than 16%, double that of Glasgow and one of the highest of any British city. Back home, Dundee's shipyards continued to churn out ships for the war effort but the slump which followed eventually saw the closure of the Dundee Shipbuilding Company yard in 1920. During the war, demand for jute had soared as the need for sandbags increased and the industry was protected by a government ban on jute products being processed in Calcutta. After the war, the ban was lifted and jute prices fell, along with demand for jute products. By the armistice, more than 4,000 Dundee men had lost their lives to the war while many more came home with terrible physical and mental scars.

The General Election of November 1922 saw Winston Churchill, Colonial Secretary in Prime Minister Lloyd George's coalition government, sensationally lose his Dundee seat to Britain's only Prohibitionist MP Edwin Scrymgeour. His elevation to the Commons helped, no doubt, by Dundee urchins chanting "Vote, vote, vote for Neddy Scrymgeour, he's the man tae gie ye ham and eggs".

In 1923, Dundee Hibernian changed its name to Dundee United to widen its appeal following a failed attempt to change their name to Dundee City. The hand-written minute book from the boardroom proved "Dundee City" had actually been registered before a complaint from Dundee FC meant another transition to Dundee United.

Dundee were also establishing their superiority on the pitch. They again contested a Scottish Cup Final in 1925 but went down 2-1 to Celtic. The directors reduced Dundee's playing staff to 13 and scrapped the reserve team in 1938, before Dundee emerged as a major force in the Scottish game after World War 2.

The infrastructure of the city had escaped largely unscathed during the conflict with Nazi Germany. Dundee's worst incident was on November 5, 1940, when a stick of four bombs came down in a random attack by a German raider. One crashed all the way through a four-storey tenement in Rosefield Street, killing two people and destroying the property. Another of the bombs missed the Forest Park Picture House, which was packed with children at the time, by just 20 yards.

Until 1946, normal competitive football was suspended. Many footballers had signed up to fight in the war and as a result teams were depleted, and fielded guest players instead, including Stanley Matthews at Airdrie. The league got back under way after the guns fell silent but there was further heartbreak in season 1948-49 when Dundee reached the semi-finals of both the League Cup and the Scottish Cup and finished second in the league after a last-day defeat to Falkirk.

The city entered the 1950s with jute processing in Dundee in rapid decline. There were only 39 jute firms left out of a total of 150 at the industry's peak. Inner city overcrowding also meant the housing emphasis in Dundee shifted from central areas to peripheral sites such as Downfield, Dryburgh, Fintry, Clement Park and Douglas.

One man who was also moving was one of Scotland's greatest inside forwards. Dundee paid £23,500 to Derby County for Billy Steel in 1950. Nicknamed "The Pocket Dynamo", Steel had already developed into one of the first football superstars. Dundee paid a Scottish record fee to bring him back to Scotland. Two days after he signed, 34,000 fans (around 8,000 more than usual) watched his debut against Aberdeen. A year later, in 1951, he set up skipper Alfie Boyd for the winner with just 30 seconds to go when Dundee beat Rangers 3-2 to lift the League Cup at Hampden. Dundee became the first club to retain the trophy the following year. Steel scored six goals on the road to Hampden, where a double from Bobby Flavell was enough to defeat Kilmarnock 2-0 and take the trophy back to Dens again.

Dundee undertook a two-month tour of South Africa at the end of that season which included winning a three-game test series against the South African national

The Bird & The Feather

team. Those matches were played to sell-out crowds, which was something Frank Sinatra was missing when he performed twice at the 3,300-capacity Caird Hall in Dundee in July 1953. Just 600 turned up to the first show and 1,189 to the second house with the 15-shilling seats at the front left empty because his largely teenage following couldn't afford such prices. The singer was bitten by the golf bug and had been lured across the Atlantic to watch American Ben Hogan at the 1953 Open at Carnoustie and he did a few gigs to earn some pocket money. Ol' Blue Eyes had the fans who did turn up at the Caird Hall in raptures, with a 45-minute set which included a pause for a cup of tea. The release of the film From Here to Eternity just a few months later would lead to a best supporting actor Oscar and mark the beginning of a remarkable career revival for Sinatra.

That was in stark contrast to Dundee's fortunes for the rest of the decade, which included embarrassing defeats in the Scottish Cup to Berwick Rangers in 1954 and Fraserburgh in the first round in 1959 – arguably the greatest shock in Scottish Cup history to that point. The Broch became the first Highland League club to eliminate a top-tier team. The scorer of their winner was Johnny Strachan, a gas board clerk.

Dundee's trams era was a distant memory by the time the swinging 60s brought the Beatles, Rolling Stones and David Bowie to Dundee. Much of the city's pre-war architecture was also lost for ever when a number of old buildings were torn down in favour of modern developments.

But it was also a golden age for the Dark Blues, who enjoyed their most successful era under manager Bob Shankly. The greatest day in the club's history came on April 28, 1962. Dundee were crowned champions of Scotland with a team which legendary football historian and broadcaster Bob Crampsey described as "the best footballing side to emerge in Scotland since the war, even better than the Lisbon Lions". Shankly's Dundee side clinched the title with a 3-0 victory over St Johnstone at Muirton Park in front of 26,000 fans, thanks to a double from Scotland's top scorer Alan Gilzean and a third from Andy Penman. The greatest team in Dens Park history then embarked on a hugely successful European Cup campaign which saw wins over Cologne, Sporting Lisbon and Anderlecht. If it wasn't for a cruel semi-final draw, Dundee might have been the first British club to lift the European Cup. But AC Milan ended that dream amongst shattering flash bulbs. They won the first-leg 5-1 in front of 73,000 fans in the San Siro. Dundee memorably won the second leg 1-0 under the floodlights at Dens but the damage was already done. It was later revealed that the referee for the tie in Milan, Vincente Caballero, was found guilty of being wined, dined and accepting extravagant gifts from the Milan officials. He was banned from officiating any other games. There was also a complaint made against the Italian press photographers who gathered behind Dundee goalkeeper Bert Slater's goal. When a high ball came over, it appeared as if they were all flashing their bulbs at the same time in an effort to temporarily blind the Dens keeper. One local journalist suggested afterwards that Dundee should fit a searchlight at the side of the AC Milan goalkeeper's post in the return leg.

There was further misery in 1964 when Dundee went down 3-1 to all-conquering treble winners Rangers in what many believe was one of the best Scottish Cup Finals of all time.

England had just won the 1966 World Cup when the city of Dundee conquered Europe. It entered a new era of its history with the opening of the longest road bridge on the continent. Proposals for a road bridge had first been mooted in 1918 when the city engineer, James Thomson, suggested a road bridge could be built on the old piers of the first rail bridge. The idea was rejected by the Ministry of Transport but numerous campaigns were launched over the years to have a bridge built, before finally a Tay Road Bridge Committee was set up. Previously, workers had to take the train, hop aboard the Fifies – the ferries which sailed between Newport and Dundee – or embark on a lengthy road journey if they wanted to get across the water.

The bridge carried 70,000 vehicles that first weekend, averaging out at 6,000 per day thereafter. Construction required the demolition of Dundee's Royal Arch, where Queen Victoria had entered the city on a royal visit

The ferry boats then returned to Victoria Dock shortly after the bridge opened to await their fate. Things had been just as grim for Dundee United until the club finally made a return to the top flight for the first time in 28 years following the arrival of Jerry Kerr as manager. A fifth-place league finish in 1966 meant that United not only finished above their great rivals, but also qualified for Europe for the first time. The club famously defeated Barcelona in 1966 and their 2-1 away win was the first victory by a Scottish club on Spanish soil. The opposition were by no means the best side in Barcelona's history. Third in La Liga the previous season, Barca were in the midst of a barren run of six years without a league title. However, as defending Fairs Cup champions, they were expected to progress to the third round with a minimum of fuss.

Dundee went down 5-3 to Celtic in the League Cup Final the following year, which would also be remembered in the city for a senseless act of evil in a school classroom which sent shockwaves across the country. Robert Mone, a former pupil of St John's High School who was serving in the Gordon Highlanders at the time, walked into the building carrying a shotgun and killed 26-year-old teacher Nanette Hanson.

Dundee reached their second European semi-final during the 1967-68 season. The Dark Blues had qualified for the Inter City Fairs Cup by a twist of fate. Clyde had been the original qualifiers, but only one team per city was allowed to enter and Rangers were the first qualifiers from Glasgow. That meant Clyde had to forfeit their place which went to Dundee. The Dark Blues cruelly missed out on the final after going down 2-1 on aggregate to Don Revie's Leeds United who would go on to win the trophy and confirm their status as a new power in the footballing galaxy.

Things didn't get much better off the park. Dundee was a city in decline in the 1970s. There was a new decimal currency, new postcodes and new telephone numbers. Football hooliganism was rampant, Britain was struck by an IRA bombing campaign and the decade brought militant strikes, power cuts and the three-day week. But against the backdrop of a fuel crisis during the blackout winter of 1973, Dundee won their third League Cup. Tommy Gemmell lifted the trophy after Gordon Wallace's winner had beaten a formidable Celtic side in a final which had to be played at 1.30pm because the use of floodlights was banned. The game almost didn't go ahead following driving snow and sleet which made for a poor attendance of just 27,924. Emergency measures also included a 50mph speed limit on all roads. It took the team bus three hours to reach Glasgow, where respective managers Jock Stein and Davie White declared the Hampden playing surface unplayable. Referee Bobby Davidson surprisingly gave the go-ahead despite the pitch being half frozen and half flooded. Wallace's winner lifted the gloom and the lights were back on by the time the Scottish Premier League was formed in 1975-76. But Dundee's board took a side that had begun to look capable of emulating the celebrated 1960s heroes and shredded it, selling its stars one by one with the inevitable consequence of relegation.

Punk emerged in the mid-70s and its birth was helped by a gig cancellation in Dundee that was to change the face of music history in the UK.

John Lydon's Sex Pistols had already played Dundee's bowling alley in October 1976 as a young punk band intent on shaking up the establishment just days after signing with EMI Records. The band's first single, Anarchy in the UK, was due for release on November 26. Manager Malcolm McLaren put together a tour to promote the record which was to include a second gig in Dundee on December 1. But the Caird Hall date became the gig that never was. Rock giants Queen pulled out of an appearance on Thames Today, which was the live London evening TV show presented by Bill Grundy. Their plugger suggested the Pistols as a substitute. McLaren thought the publicity generated by live TV was too good to turn down and a limousine was duly sent for the band. The Caird Hall gig was hastily rescheduled for later in December. The Pistols appeared on Grundy's show and the infamous performance made "Filth and fury" front page headlines. Steve Jones responded to Bill Grundy's dare that he should say "something outrageous" and responded with a four-letter word. EMI immediately withdrew the single and shortly afterwards fired the band.

The infamy that surrounded the Pistols turned the group into stars. McLaren later said the interview was a "pivotal moment that changed everything" and "punk became the most important cultural phenomenon of the late 20th century".

Despite the anti-establishment attitude of punk, Dundee put the economic woes and industrial unrest behind it with a street party to celebrate the Queen's Silver Jubilee in 1977. Things were slightly less upbeat at Dens Park, where Dundee were finding life hard in the second tier. They went back up in 1978-79 as champions of the First Division before going back down again the following season.

Dundee's topsy-turvy existence continued when the club were promoted again the next season and also reached a League Cup Final against United. The two sides decided there would be a greater attendance at a ground in Dundee rather than having to play at Hampden and the game was played at Dens after a coin toss. Home advantage didn't matter though as United effortlessly ran out 3-0 winners in front of 24,466 fans, thanks to a Davie Dodds goal and a double from Paul Sturrock. The showpiece was nicknamed the Jute Cup Final which appeared a cruel joke given the industry's spiralling decline.

By this stage the net was closing in on the Yorkshire Ripper following a five-year reign of terror, but there was panic in Dundee whose residents feared a serial killer was walking amongst them. The naked strangled body of 20-year-old nursery nurse Elizabeth McCabe was discovered in Templeton Woods on the outskirts of Dundee in 1980 – just 150 yards from where the corpse of Carol Lannen, 18, was found almost a year before. The part-time prostitute was also found naked and strangled. The deaths would become the city's most notorious unsolved murders. The city's great shipbuilding tradition finally ended with the closure of the Robb Caledon yard in 1981, just as Dundee began to embrace the technological revolution of the 1980s.

Clive Sinclair launched his home computer in 1982. The ZX Spectrum was assembled in Dundee's Timex factory which was the UK's largest supplier of watches and the city's biggest employer at its height, with 5,000 workers. The computers would be responsible for creating a generation of programmers. At the time, Timex was seen as the future. It was a workforce which had skilled, nimble fingers perfect for watch manufacture – women who'd worked in weaving. The work was safer, healthier and better paid than the traditional industries such as jute processing. But just 12 months later Timex management revealed they were bringing to an end their traditional mechanical watch-making operations which had made the company world famous.

News that 1,900 people were to lose their jobs in what would be the biggest single redundancy blow ever for Dundee, was accompanied by a grim warning that the future of the surviving 2,300 employees was also at risk. In 1983, workers at the Milton plant held a six-week sit-in in an attempt to save the 1,900 jobs – and they won. But the sun was setting on Timex.

Things didn't get much better at Dens which became the scene of United's greatest triumph. Jim McLean's side held its nerve to beat Dundee 2-1 in the final game of the season and win the 1982-83 league championship title on their turf. McLean had moved to Tannadice as manager in 1971 after spending 18 months as a coach at Dens. But, despite that allegiance, he would become the tactical genius behind the Tannadice club's unimaginable success throughout the 1980s at home and abroad.

Dundee spent almost the entirety of that decade in the top flight but were firmly in the shadows of their great rivals who reached the European Cup semi-final in 1984. Dundee did stop another title party on their own turf in 1986 when Albert Kidd turned party-pooper and scored two goals to defeat Hearts on the final day, which handed Celtic the championship. There was little to cheer a year later when United became the first Scottish club to reach the final of the UEFA Cup in 1987 which included again defeating the mighty Barcelona home and away. They eventually went down to Swedish side IFK Gothenburg in the two-legged final.

Dundee also played one of Europe's best sides in 1987 but it was a testimonial. Kenny Dalglish brought his star-studded Liverpool team to Dens Park to honour Dark Blues defender George McGeachie. Liverpool played their first team and won 4-0.

By that time Captain Scott's Discovery had just arrived back in the city which built her and her journey from London brought with it a whole new image for Dundee.

Liverpool returned to Dundee in February 1989 for a Sunday afternoon testimonial match for goalkeeper Bobby Geddes in front of 10,000 fans. Liverpool won 3-1 this time, although victory appeared to do little for team harmony and goalkeeper Bruce Grobbelaar broke team-mate Steve McMahon's nose following an altercation in a Tayside hotel after the match.

Grobbelaar and McMahon would be united in grief just a few months later. Tragedy unfolded on the terracing just yards from them during the FA Cup semi-final match against Nottingham Forest at Hillsborough in which 96 Liverpool fans went to a football match and never came home. The sound of people screaming from within the pens would never leave them.

Back in Dundee, things were looking up in the newly-titled City of Discovery, but the 1990s brought more years in the second tier wilderness for the Dark Blues following relegation in season 1989-90. Dundee slipped out of the league with a miserable -24 goal difference. But lower league football brought silverware. The Dark Blues were the first winners of the Centenary Cup in 1990, when a hat-trick from striker Billy Dodds was enough to see off Ayr United 3-2 at Fir Park in Motherwell.

A year later, Dundee owner Angus Cook hit the front and back page headlines. Cook boldly declared plans to buy Dundee United after failing to reach a deal over a merger or ground sharing. But after a summer of hostile squabbling, in which it became clear that both sets of supporters were dead against the move, Cook announced he was putting his bid on ice. But it didn't stop some of his successors in the boardroom from coming up with equally daring ideas.

The club won the First Division title in 1992 after being saved from closure by millionaire Canadian businessman Ron Dixon who brought in big-money foreign signings. Dixon was first connected with Dundee when he made a bid for its ice rink and ice hockey team. He then became attracted to Dundee FC and immediately declared his intention to challenge Rangers and Celtic. Dixon appeared to have a chequebook to match his mouthy ambitions. Denmark international Morten Wieghorst joined and Dariusz Adamczuk was signed for a club record fee of £250,000. Adamczuk signed on the same day that his fellow Poland internationalist Piotr Czachowski put pen to paper for the same amount of money from Legia Warsaw.

While things were looking up at Dens, Dundee's biggest employer was winding down. An order from IBM was cut back in 1992 and Timex management asked for 110 people to be laid off. The timing of the announcement – Christmas Eve – was deemed heartless. The unions tried to negotiate but agreement wasn't reached and on January 29, 340 workers, many with decades of service, went on strike. They offered to return on February 15 but wouldn't accept reduced wages. Everyone thought the next step would be more talks. But when people turned up for work they found the gates locked. Workers organised a picket at the factory gates which drew thousands, but things turned ugly when the American company started bussing in replacement workers a few days later. There was violence, arrests and injuries as the angry dispute escalated. It went on for months but, in August 1993, the factory shut. Timex's time in Dundee was up. It had been part of the fabric of Dundee for decades and the closure affected thousands of families.

Ron Dixon hoped to restore the mood of a fragile city when he unveiled extravagant plans for a super-stand on the south side of Dens Park. The proposal included an ice rink, office accommodation and a large car park. None of it happened. What did emerge was an ill-fated greyhound track around the pitch. Dog racing had taken place at Dens from 1932 to 1936 and it started up again in October 1994 before ending just as quickly in December 1996 as gates dried up.

Dixon also dreamed up big plans of taking over United and amalgamating the two teams. He dropped the bombshell when he called the whole club together for a meeting one day. He boldly told them: "Right, that's us, we're going to buy that lot down the road. Let's have some pizzas and champagne."

Dixon felt the city could sustain only one team but it was never going to happen and he got no backing from Tannadice, which killed it stone dead. Back on the pitch, there was a changing of the guard. Jim Duffy had taken over as player/manager and guided the club to its first top-flight cup final in 15 years, the 1995 League Cup against Aberdeen. But Dundee didn't perform well on the day and went down 2-0.

Dixon didn't return to Scotland after that final and paid little attention to matters at Dens Park. Before he left he even tried to get Duffy to take over the club. He told the media out of the blue that his manager was buying Dundee and told Duffy he "should just go along with it and we'd sort it out later". Duffy reeled out some cliches for the TV cameras and afterwards Dixon did try to sell the club to Duffy and some others. But in the end it wasn't viable and the idea drifted away. Duffy had actually paid wages out of his own pocket a couple of times just to keep things going, with Dixon on the verge of selling all the players, bolting the doors and walking away.

Lifelong fans Peter and Jimmy Marr – well-known figures in the city's pub industry, who had spent five years in the junior ranks running St Joseph's – raised £1 million against their nightclub to stop him shutting the club.

From rags to riches, the Marr family would bring glamour to Dundee. Peter and Jimmy grew up in Fintry and were inspired by their father who was a grafter. He ran mobile shops north of the Kingsway and made enough to buy a supermarket through nothing but hard work.

Jimmy worked as a painter and decorator before getting into the licensed trade to make a better future for himself. The Hawthorn Bar in Hilltown was his first establishment, and he eventually took over more businesses and built an empire of pubs, nightclubs and hotels. Peter got a break when he ended up taking on a club with a friend, which they called The Venue. After a couple of years, he also branched out into shops, and from there into pubs. He had a solid career building businesses up from next to nothing and making them profitable. They had a combined turnover running to millions of pounds and employed several hundred people.

The brothers eventually took control in 1997 with the Dark Blues back where they were when Dixon arrived – out of cash and in the First Division. With the Marrs firmly at the helm, they gave manager John McCormack money for signings before ruthlessly sacking him in February 1998 after deciding he wasn't the right man for the job. Dundee were five points clear at the top of the First Division at the time but they replaced McCormack with former player and manager Jocky Scott, who delivered promotion. Scott had a fantastic career as a player at Dundee after making his debut in 1964. He turned out 433 times for the Dark Blues and scored 154 goals. He picked up winners' medals in the League Cup with Dundee and Aberdeen during the 1970s and was one of many British players who had a taste of the glamour of football in the USA. He was famously part of the Seattle Sounders team that, despite being underdogs, came close to upsetting Pele's farewell party at the 1977 Soccerbowl. Scott first took the Dundee job from 1986-88 before returning to replace McCormack after management spells with Aberdeen, Dunfermline, Arbroath and Hibernian.

If McCormack's future had reached the point of no return, it was a similar situation for Britain's jute industry which had shaped the city of Dundee and seen it dubbed "Juteopolis". The end, when it finally came in October 1998, was without ceremony. A cargo ship, the Banglar Urmi, arrived at Dundee docks from Bangladesh. It discharged a few bales of raw jute which were the last to ever come ashore in the city.

That was it. Once the consignment was spun into yarn for carpet backing, all that was left of an industry that employed 50,000 people in its heyday, was a heritage museum and bitter-sweet memories. Tay Spinners, the last jute spinner in Europe, closed shortly before Christmas with the loss of 80 jobs.

Just as well travelled was Giovanni di Stefano, who made a takeover bid for Dundee in March 1999, by which time the Dark Blues were finally back in Scotland's top flight. But the board declined after his links with Serbian warlord Arkan became public. Di Stefano was known as "the Devil's Advocate" for his history representing high-profile criminals including Harold Shipman, Ronnie Biggs, Jeremy Bamber and Slobodan Milosevic.

Di Stefano's parents had moved from Italy to Northampton when he was five and he earned a fortune importing video tapes from Hong Kong. Reports at the time suggested he had offered to assist the club financially with numbers from £800,000 to more than £2 million put forward. A statement from his office in Belgrade indicated he was ready to turn his attention to any other Scottish club which might welcome his investment following the disappointment.

The statement read: "Mr di Stefano has been in contact with Mr Peter Marr and accepts fully the interim decision taken by the current owners of the club. Mr di Stefano always stated that in the possible majority ownership of the club there were no deadlines and that it was entirely a matter for the Marr family, the current majority shareholders. Mr di Stefano from the outset had the benefit of the Dundee community and Scotland at heart, seeking to make a substantial further investment in the club so that Dundee FC could challenge Celtic and Rangers next season for the Scottish Premier League title. That position remains the same and he is convinced his input would be beneficial for the whole Dundee community. Out of his deep respect for the Marr family there will be no legal challenges to their decision since, if the Marr family believe the interest of the Dundee community is best served under their leadership, then that decision must be respected. Mr di Stefano will thus look for different investment possibilities within Scotland at the same level as the investment that would have been made in Dundee FC and welcomes the input from the Scottish business community on this matter. The Marr family and Dundee FC will always have strong support from Mr di Stefano and he looks forward to watching their progress in the remaining games, and the following seasons, and requests the supporters of Dundee FC to maintain a strong support to the club and to the Marr family who have made many personal and unrecognised sacrifices for the good of the club."

Jocky Scott soon found that "unrecognised sacrifices" rarely count for anything. He retained top flight status before taking Dundee above their city rivals into fifth place the following season. But rumours that the end was nigh had been growing since the Dark Blues board signed six players without telling their manager and failed to offer him a new deal. The involvement of Steve Archibald in bringing some of the foreign players to Dundee prompted rumours he would take charge with his former Barcelona team-mate Berndt Schuster. Scott's reward for the club's highest league position in 25 years was the exit door. He was sacked at the end of the 1999-2000 season.

His replacement strutted through the Dens Park entrance like a peacock. Amidst the economic doom and gloom, former Juventus and Sampdoria midfielder Ivano Bonetti turned up in a designer leather jacket and jeans. He pledged big-name signings and attractive football. Chairman Jimmy Marr said: "I do think it is a big gamble but decisions we have made in the past have been gambles. You have to live by the decisions you make in football, as in life, and we are prepared to do that. We can't be right all the time, but everything we do, we do because we believe it to be in the best interests of Dundee Football Club. A new broom sweeps clean and we will make every effort to help the manager get the players he wants to bring to the club. We have been in conversation with a number of investors and are hopeful that we will be able to attract a significant amount of money into the club in the near future."

Dundee had gone from being a financially-stricken club to one managed by a former top-flight Italian star promising to bring in a host of exciting exotic imports.

The Dark Blues were living the high life but the Dundee FC soap opera – and the story of the city itself – was set for another twist.

CHAPTER TWO

From Buenos Aires To Broughty Ferry

He is not that old at 33, and played at the very top level for a long time.

Peter Marr, Dundee FC Chief Executive

UNLIKE 100 years before, Dundee's population at the turn of the new millennium was in a state of decline. There were even fears Dundee could lose its city status. Figures from the Registrar General predicted almost 20,000 people would abandon the city over the next 15 years and suggested there would be a 15% population drop to 123,000 by 2016.

Dundee's population might have been crumbling away but the city itself was in the midst of a cultural revolution. Things were slowly changing. Dundee Contemporary Arts – a newly-opened art centre in the Nethergate – was giving the city a social and artistic hub. The Dundee Partnership had started preparations on a masterplan to ultimately transform and reimagine the central waterfront area. A new £6m science centre was being built, while the £50m City Quay development would bring retail units, a four-star hotel and a housing development to one of the most scenic parts of the harbour. World-famous architect Frank Gehry, whose work included Bilbao's Guggenheim Museum – which had turned a struggling industrial town into a cultural metropolis – had just unveiled designs for a cancer care centre at Dundee's Ninewells Hospital.

Fans drinking in the High Corner Bar, in the shadow of Dens Park, in July 2000 were just as impressed by Ivano Bonetti's cosmopolitan revolution which had been gathering pace since his summer arrival. Ivano was engineering a colourful overhaul of his playing squad alongside his brother Dario. Inspiring performances in pre-season – admittedly against the likes of Falkirk and Grimsby Town – were giving the Dark Blues faithful cause for optimism. Season ticket sales had broken the 4,000 barrier for the first time in 15 years.

Ivano and Dario had a collective 21 seasons playing in Italy's top flight. Their management skills were unproven beyond the semi-professional levels in Italy, but it was a flutter the Marr brothers were willing to take.

The Marrs' plan was to recruit talented foreign players then sell them on at a profit. They were no strangers to controversial decisions since taking up the helm at Dens, having already chucked two managers from their posts in just two years.

The charismatic Ivano – who often struggled with early morning starts and referred to the SPL as Serie A – had enjoyed an illustrious playing career. Two Italian league titles and one Intercontinental Cup were among the impressive entries on the CV of a man who once shared a dressing room with Michel Platini.

The 35-year-old might well have played for Juventus and Sampdoria but he was perhaps best known in Britain as the unfortunate victim of Grimsby manager Brian Laws' dressing-room rage at Kenilworth Road in 1996. Grimsby had just been defeated 3-2 by Luton Town and Laws turned on Ivano after the match. He threw a plate of crispy chicken wings in his direction – fracturing the Italian winger's cheekbone in the process. Ivano moved to Tranmere following the spat and struck up an instant friendship with former Chelsea and Scotland international Pat Nevin, who also gave him his first taste of Scottish football when the two attended an Old Firm game in 1997.

His brother Dario was imposing in stature and character, with a resume just as impressive as Ivano's. Dario played for Roma, AC Milan, Juventus and Sampdoria, winning the Italian Cup four times, the UEFA Cup and picking up two caps for Italy. He'd been part of the AS Roma squad which defeated Dundee United over two legs in the semi-final of the European Cup in 1984 before going down to Liverpool in the final.

The only other Bonetti to have previously been anywhere near Tannadice or Dens was former England goalkeeper, Peter, who was running a guest house on the Isle of Mull in 1979 when Dundee United manager Jim McLean persuaded him to come out of retirement after falling out with first choice Hamish McAlpine.

Dario had been the man in the hot seat at Sestrese in Italy's Serie D with Ivano as his deputy, but it was a role reversal when they arrived at Dens. It became evident – fairly quickly – that what they lacked in top-flight managerial experience they would more than make up for with an extensive list of contacts.

The colourful Bonetti brothers weren't entirely strangers to Dundee. They already had links with the club. Their cousin Dario Magri had co-ordinated the signing of Patrizio Billio from Crystal Palace the previous season.

During their conversations Magri suggested Ivano might fancy signing for Dundee. The Dark Blues board had already signed six players without the manager's prior knowledge, including Javier Artero, Jose Mesas Puerta and Francisco Luna. Things didn't go any further until chief executive Peter Marr started the search for a new manager after the board had apparently become unhappy with the style of football being played. Jocky Scott was struggling to deal with the foreign players that had been brought in and Marr flew to Genoa to meet Ivano and Dario. He asked where they could take Dundee.

Ivano sent him a detailed plan of the long-term goal, and was eventually offered the job ahead of former Barcelona midfielder Berndt Schuster who was also in the frame. Ivano and Dario had seen Dundee in action that season when they watched the derby match against United at Tannadice where, ironically, they also met their predecessor. The brothers were there that day on behalf of a consortium that was attempting to buy over an Italian club that was interested in establishing links with Dundee. Ivano had also previously been linked with attempting to buy out the Marr brothers in a deal involving his former Sampdoria team-mates Attilio Lombardo and Roberto Mancini.

So when they finally arrived at Dens Park the Marr brothers were quick to stress that Ivano and Dario were becoming involved on a coaching basis only. They also brought with them a translator, although Ivano's English was understandable if not great.

Ivano said he would look to tap in to the knowledge of friends like Pat Nevin, ex-Hearts midfielder Stefano Salvatori, Paulo di Canio and, especially, Chelsea manager Gianluca Vialli.

"Jocky Scott is a football man and he knows what happens in football," said Ivano. "I think the same things – it is football and what has happened is nothing personal. I know Patrizo Billio well and he has told me Jocky is a really nice person. If we could manage to, I would like to meet and talk to him about the team. I think it is important that you have as many good young players as possible because that is the way ahead. You must also find good experienced players who can help them and teach them. If you look at Manchester United, they have brought in experienced players but also used their young players like Beckham and others, and that is the way to be successful."

No club outside Celtic and Rangers had won the Scottish title since the 1984–85 season, when the Aberdeen side managed by Sir Alex Ferguson won the Premier Division. Ivano insisted his long-term aim was to turn Dundee into Scottish football's third force.

Amongst their list of contacts, Ivano knew the legendary Claudio Caniggia from his time in Italy.

Caniggia was still one of the most famous footballers on the planet. He had been capped 50 times for Argentina and scored 16 goals, including four in eight matches at the 1990 and 1994 World Cups. He was without a club after being released by Italian Serie B outfit Atalanta. Dundee fans who had grown up watching the 1990 World Cup and the golden era of Italian football on Channel 4's Football Italia show could remember a player with rock star looks, breath-taking pace and long blonde hair who could score goals at the highest level.

Born in 1967 in a small town called Henderson in Buenos Aires Province, Caniggia grew up to become an Argentinian football rebel. Before taking up football, the young Caniggia had competed in athletics at provincial level. He could run 100 metres in just under 11 seconds despite a strange running style. He used to begin hunched forward and run on tiptoe, because he thought this would give him a better start. He later admitted he was "lightning on the grass" because he'd already run the 100 and 200 metres which helped him when he had to slow down fast and change direction. Little wonder, then, that he would soon become known as The Bird.

Caniggia was developed in the famous River Plate youth academy. Players were plucked from nearby neighbourhoods and transformed into stars. The Bird burst into the first team as a fresh-faced 18-year-old in 1985. River Plate would make history the following year by winning the league, the Copa Libertadores, the Copa Interamericana and the club's first Intercontinental Cup title.

He was capped in the Argentina squad for the Olympic Games qualifiers in early 1987, before becoming an established part of the senior national team later that year. Caniggia's performances prompted a move to Italy where he joined Hellas Verona in 1988. Playing as a winger at times, he managed 21 appearances and three goals in the No. 7 shirt. He was playing in Serie A at a time when his international strike partner Diego Maradona had almost single-handedly turned Napoli into Italy's outstanding side. After one season in Verona, Caniggia moved to Atalanta. He went on to play 117 games and score 31 goals during two spells at the Stadio Atleti Azzurri d'Italia, but it was his performances in the national side that would make him a household name.

For a man known as The Bird it was perhaps fitting that a flying boot propelled him to that fame. The irony was that it wasn't his boot. But that's where it started, in Milan's space-age cathedral of football in front of 73,000 fans and a record global television audience at the 1990 World Cup in Italy. Against the strains of Luciano Pavarotti's Nessun Dorma, Caniggia started on the bench as defending champions Argentina opened the tournament and their own World Cup campaign against Cameroon in the San Siro.

Dundee had been relegated from the Premier League just weeks before Caniggia lined up against Cameroon in what would become known as the "Miracle of Milan". Winner of two of the past three World Cups, Argentina were football royalty. They were expected to thrash a Cameroon team which were 500/1 outsiders and largely made up of journeymen players from the French lower divisions. Cameroon had a Siberian manager who didn't speak the same language as his players. His team-talks were translated by a driver at the Cameroon embassy in Moscow.

But Argentina struggled to break down Cameroon and The Bird was thrown on at half-time. He was subjected to rough treatment almost immediately. Cameroon went a man down when André Kana-Biyik was sent off for a late challenge on Caniggia on 61 minutes. Just six minutes later Cameroon took the lead when André's brother François Omam-Biyik rose to meet a deflected ball and popped a weak header past Argentine goalkeeper Nery Pumpido.

With two minutes to go, Caniggia picked up the ball inside his own half. The images remain iconic. He drove up the right wing towards goal at blistering pace, hurdled a challenge from Emmanuel Kunde and jumped another tackle from Victor N'Dip. The challenge from N'Dip forced a stumble and he almost lost his balance before Benjamin Massing flew in waist-high with a challenge that sent Caniggia into orbit along with Massing's boot.

Massing was sent off for an incident which would resonate in football folklore. The tackle would become known as one of the most spectacular fouls in World Cup history. It was even recreated in a brick-by-brick video animation by a national newspaper in the run-up to the 2014 World Cup in Brazil.

None of the World Cup's 13 previous opening matches had witnessed a red card. When the international news agency Reuters reported Massing's tragic death, aged just 55, in 2017 the headline stated: "Ex-Cameroon defender who committed World Cup's worst tackle dies".

The African team held on for a shock 1-0 win in Milan but Caniggia picked himself up, dusted himself down, and never looked back. He started the next two games against the Soviet Union and Romania as Argentina made it through the group stages, despite Maradona looking a shadow of his former self.

Maradona was hampered by blisters on his feet going into the tournament. His misery had been compounded when a passenger accidentally stepped on his big toe when the team was flying to Tel Aviv for a warm-up game against Israel. The little magician also suffered a severe ankle injury early in the tournament. But despite his afflictions he still managed to conjure a dazzling run and pass for Caniggia's second-round late winner against Brazil.

It was a goal which would give Caniggia immortality back home. It also knocked out their great rivals and the tournament favourites into the bargain.

In the semi-final against Italy, Caniggia sent a header past goalkeeper Walter Zenga, which was the first goal the host nation conceded in the tournament. The goal sent the match into extra-time. Argentina won on penalties but Caniggia received a yellow card and was forced to sit out the defeat in a dismal and very ill-tempered final against West Germany. To this day, Maradona maintains that Argentina would have won the final had Caniggia been able to play.

The following year Caniggia scored two as Argentina won the Copa America in Chile, where he formed a new strike partnership with legendary sharpshooter Gabriel Batistuta.

Caniggia joined Roma in 1992 but the club finished a disappointing campaign in mid-table. Italian football was very healthy, though, with Serie A continuing to attract the world's best footballing talent. Caniggia also helped Argentina to the 1992 Confederations Cup where he scored in the final against Saudi Arabia in a 3-1 win. In February 1993, he scored in the final of the Artemio Franchi Trophy against European champions Denmark. Argentina was declared intercontinental champions following the penalty shoot-out win.

But while things on the pitch were going well, Caniggia was living the high life away from the training pitch. His world was turned upside down when he was hit with a 13-month ban for taking cocaine following a random dope test after Roma's 1-1 draw with Napoli.

The ban expired just before the 1994 World Cup. Caniggia returned to the Argentina squad as if he'd never been away and scored two in the first round against Nigeria. Argentina were again among the favourites to win the tournament in the USA but it was, sadly, another doping incident which turned everything upside down and also signalled the end of his great friend and team-mate Diego Maradona's World Cup career. A urine test showed Maradona had taken a "cocktail" of drugs and he was sent home in disgrace. It was the first violation uncovered by FIFA's random testing since Scotland winger Willie Johnston was found to have taken a prescribed substance during the 1978 finals in Argentina.

Caniggia and his team-mates weren't that far behind Maradona on the plane home. Argentina lost 2-0 to Bulgaria in the final group game without their captain, before crashing out altogether following a 3-2 second-round defeat to Romania.

Caniggia's time was also up with the national team. He was frozen out for a number of years after refusing to cut his famous blonde locks in defiance of the strict rules of national coach Daniel Passarella whose controversial squad restrictions included "no earrings, long hair or homosexuals".

After the 1994 World Cup Caniggia spent a season with Benfica in Portugal on a year-long loan which was financed by a dairy company. He returned to Argentina to sign for Boca Juniors. Caniggia was reunited with Maradona who had also returned to La Bombonera after serving his 15-month doping suspension.

But there was "trouble at t'mill" when Caniggia's wife refused to return to Argentina for a second season and the striker was heavily linked with top-flight clubs in England. Caniggia then got on a plane for Miami where he was later arrested and spent a night in jail with Mariana for allegedly stealing from a shoe shop. Things got worse when his mother took her own life by jumping from the fifth floor of her building in September 1996, which prompted Caniggia to shun the game for a year following the tragedy. He returned to play for Boca Juniors following a season of inactivity and averaged almost a goal every two games before leaving Argentina for a second time in 1999 to rejoin Atalanta who by now were in Serie B. He left almost as quickly as he joined following a dispute with coach Giovanni Vavassori, despite helping the club gain promotion back to the top flight.

Following his decision to leave Italy at the end of the 1999-2000 season, talks had been held as early as pre-season as Ivano tried to convince him to join his Dark Blues revolution.

"I would say this is only 50-50, but we are talking to him," he said. "It would be a very big thing for a club like Dundee to get a player of his stature, but we must try very hard to persuade him to come."

Caniggia initially declined the approach. He told Ivano he was looking to take a break from the game before heading to America in early 2001 to wind down and finish his career in Major League Soccer. The MLS at the time was a retirement home for ageing stars taking one last pay day. But Ivano persevered. He called Caniggia at his home in Bergomi and urged him to visit Dundee. He told him to at least consider joining the Dark Blues. Amazingly, Caniggia eventually agreed.

"Getting Caniggia would be a big thing for us because we are speaking about a world-class player," said Ivano. "The fact he is coming across to talk is I think a positive sign. But in attempting to convince him to join us, finance will be an important factor so I cannot say for sure that he is going to join the club. Caniggia is the best player I believe we can bring to the club and I hope we can persuade him to join us until May. I have told him he can leave playing in America for another year and pursue his career in Scotland instead."

But all that was firmly in the background as the 2000-2001 season got under way. Dundee spent three weeks of the summer in Italy, based on the top of a mountain, half-an-hour from civilisation. The days of being hammered physically during pre-season appeared to be over. The majority of the work on the training ground was with the ball and focused mainly on shape, with the players getting to know what was expected of them in on-pitch formations.

Ivano also spent the summer snapping up a host of talent from across the globe. Georgian international captain Georgi Nemsadze, Italian left-back Marcello Marrocco and former Juventus defender Marco de Marchi were among those who signed. Argentine strikers Juan Sara and Fabian Caballero had also put pen to paper before their fellow countryman Walter del Rio later joined the ranks from Crystal Palace.

While the cosmopolitan arrivals were being welcomed to the city with open arms, Dundee University students Benni Esposito and Graham Phillips were being told to "emigrate" by furious city councillors after putting on a controversial comedy show at the Edinburgh Fringe. The students – whose stage names were Ben Darcy and Brandon Reed – were already up-and-coming stars on the UK stand-up circuit. The "Road From Dundee" described the city as a "cesspool of filth, corruption, shell-suits, and bad marketing campaigns".

The show was accused of doing untold damage to the city's reputation. It even managed to incur the wrath of church leaders after claiming Knight Rider and Baywatch actor David Hasselhoff was the Second Coming.

Back at Dens, the Bonetti brothers were out to prove they weren't false prophets as they took their place in the dugout for the first game of the campaign. Things started well. Dundee kicked off the season with a 2-0 win against Motherwell. Ivano was sent off five minutes into the second half and offered to buy his team-mates dinner after the match by way of penitence for his red card.

Dundee won again against Dunfermline before a disappointing run of two defeats and a draw was compounded by an early exit from the League Cup at the hands of St Mirren.

Dundee's Jenny Wood-Allen had just been named the oldest female marathon runner by Guinness World Records at the age of 88 when Dundee United took a slightly shorter journey up Tannadice Street for the first city derby of the season under the floodlights at Dens Park.

Dundee got back on track with a 3-0 win but the victory was overshadowed by a serious injury to striker Fabian Caballero in a three-way clash with Jason De Vos and Kevin McDonald. Ivano immediately put in calls around the globe to find a replacement for Caballero and there were rumours that former Italy striker Gianluca Vialli would be arriving as a short-term replacement. Vialli had just been sacked as manager of Chelsea and the dismissal had led to suggestions Ivano would make a move for his old friend, who had retained a high level of fitness despite scarcely kicking a ball for more than a year.

The only arrival in Dundee from London that week, however, was EastEnders star Sid Owen. The actor – who played Ricky Butcher in the popular soap opera – was the unlikely choice to make a special guest appearance at the opening of Dundee's new £7m ice arena. He pulled on his skates and invited people to join him on the ice after former hockey star Marshall Key cut the ribbon to confirm the return of ice sports to Dundee after a gap of more than eight years.

Dundee City Council also decided that week to revisit the issue of introducing a dress code for taxi drivers following movements in Edinburgh where male drivers were being asked to wear a shirt with collar, preferably with a tie, flannel trousers and black dress shoes.

Such formalities were in short supply at Dens Park where Caballero's injury had served to refresh and intensify the talks that were continuing behind the scenes with Claudio Caniggia. Ivano was also targeting Argentina midfielder Beto Carranza who looked the likelier signing and had played alongside Caniggia during a spell at Boca Juniors. The midfielder had won nine international caps for Argentina and his previous clubs also included the likes of Racing Club, Independiente and San Lorenzo.

"In addition to Caniggia we also want Carranza," said Ivano. "And I think the fact Caniggia is coming across will help us convince Carranza to sign. Our pursuit of such a player shows the ambition we have at Dundee. At the moment we are waiting for international clearance but once that comes through we will start serious talks with Carranza. We've been trying for days to get clearance for Beto, but things don't move as quickly in Argentina as they do here."

Dundee chief executive Peter Marr insisted the 1990 World Cup hero's signature would be a major boost for the whole of Scottish football.

"He is not that old at 33, and played at the very top level for a long time," said Marr, who admitted to thinking his leg was being pulled when Caniggia's name was first mentioned. "He has been training with Atalanta and is physically fit enough to play. But we will see about his match fitness. There is no fee involved. It is obviously through Ivano's connections in Italy, and we will be negotiating with him for a deal. It will be short-term, and it is the injury to (Fabian) Caballero which has prompted this. We have been left pretty thin on the ground for strikers."

The news that this potential short-term link up with Dundee might actually happen immediately set the international football world alight. However, the huge media interest that followed the speculation – especially in Caniggia's homeland – almost saw the move go up in smoke. The story of Caniggia's proposed move to Scotland made the front pages of the Argentinian national newspapers and was even the lead item on the TV news. The media attention unsettled Caniggia even further and he failed to get on the scheduled flight to Scotland for expected signing talks at Dens Park at the end of September.

Dens officials at the time put his non-appearance down to the striker being somewhat "taken aback" by the high level of media interest in his proposed move to the Scottish Premier League.

The written word was, however, a cause for celebration in some quarters of Dundee that week. The world's best-known bad poet was honoured with a plaque where he used to live. William McGonagall described how it was in Paton's Lane that he was moved by the "spirit of poetry" which prompted him to devote the rest of his life to becoming a wordsmith and performer. McGonagall, poet and tragedian of Dundee, lived from 1825 to September 1902, and was widely hailed as the writer of the worst poetry ever seen in the English language.

Also putting pen to paper in Dundee was Beto Carranza. Carranza's capture was a statement of intent by the Dark Blues. The signing was announced at the start of October but was immediately trumped when Ivano revealed the club had also reached an agreement with Caniggia.

However – perhaps in relation to what had gone before – Ivano insisted nothing was yet official. "He (Carranza) has signed and will certainly be involved in our next game against Aberdeen at Pittodrie in two weeks' time. I have also reached an agreement with Claudio, although nothing will be official until he actually signs. He also has the chance to play in the North American league. Fortunately, their season doesn't start until April, so we should have him for around seven months."

Having played alongside the 33-year-old striker at Boca Juniors, Carranza said he was convinced Caniggia would prove to be a success at Dens if he did finally arrive. "Claudio is an incredible player, as skilful a footballer as I have ever seen," he said.

"He has fantastic technique and is a very clever man. He uses his brain to hurt opposition teams as much as he uses his feet. I have no doubt he will make a huge impact in Scotland because I have no doubt he would make a huge impact anywhere in the world. The supporters will enjoy him for he is a real personality and, as a Dundee player, I am very excited about the prospect of him joining us."

Eventually, after all the false starts and missed flights, Caniggia jetted into Scotland before making his way to Dens Park to finalise details of his short-term move on October 3.

The audacious capture of Caniggia came just eight years after Dundee had signed gangly defender Garry Paterson for £1,000 and a set of tracksuits. Paterson's arrival from Fife junior outfit Lochore United is part of Dens Park folklore and had long been a cause of embarrassment amongst the Dark Blues legions. The big defender was signed by fedora-wearing manager Simon Stainrod following an injury crisis and was aptly nicknamed "Trackies Paterson" during his short spell at Dundee, which ironically started with a debut goal against Aberdeen at Pittodrie. Dundee fans who could recall Paterson's capture were left pinching themselves when Caniggia turned up in Sandeman Street with his catwalk model wife Mariana who was resplendent outside the rusty and chained up gates of Dens in a leopardskin coat and heels. The South American model was famed for her extravagant lifestyle and there were rumours her dog Bau Bau was only ever washed with expensive Evian water. Mariana wasn't left standing in the cold for too long, however, as the padlock was eventually opened to let the Caniggia family inside and talks followed in the boardroom.

Caniggia eventually agreed to become the highest-paid player in Dundee's history for £10,000 a week. Caniggia said he had arrived in Dundee looking to play as much football as he could after the nomadic path his career had taken in recent years. The contract apparently contained "a million clauses" which would allow him to leave at any time "in case things got really bad".

Meanwhile, however, a more urgent matter for Caniggia's wife was acquiring a Scottish castle to live in for the duration of her family's stay. Mariana was said to be a huge fan of castles. She had made finding one a top priority. Not that the former model would be spending all her time in Scotland as she had declared her intention to spend the next eight months of her husband's contract travelling to and from the fashion capital of Milan.

Castle or no castle, Dundee had finally got their man.

"Dun time, Dun coke, Dun-dee" was one of the more memorable newspaper headlines after Caniggia agreed to join the Dark Blues. Another claimed "the old city of Dundee has not been this mind-boggled since the days when Sinatra and the Beatles arrived in town".

Can't Buy Me Love? Not according to the Dark Blues faithful who had a new terrace hero. After all the waiting, the biggest signing in the club's history could be unveiled.

There was no talk of tracksuits now.

CHAPTER THREE

Blue And White Dynamite In The Granite City

*"It was more than I expected and it makes me
even more determined to do everything I can for
this football club."*

Claudio Caniggia

CLAUDIO CANIGGIA was unveiled at a packed press conference at Dens Park which brought journalists from all corners of the country to Dundee. It was standing room only as the 33-year-old insisted he was ultimately motivated by a desire to be part of the Bonetti blueprint and subsequently force his way into Argentina's 2002 World Cup squad.

Ivano sat shoulder to shoulder with his new signing. He smiled all through the press conference as he told the assembled journalists he had absolutely no doubt that Caniggia would be a success in the SPL. Ivano also predicted Caniggia would achieve his World Cup dream.

He said: "I have dreamed of bringing Claudio to this club and today my dream has come true. He is a great champion, a man with a wonderful reputation as a footballer who can do fantastic things not only for Dundee, but for all of Scottish football. When people like Caniggia play, everyone watches – not just Scotland, not just Europe, but the whole world. For he is one of the very biggest names the sport has. He has come here to help his friends and to help himself. He still has a real desire to play for his country in the next World Cup. I believe he can do it, for at 33 he is more professional than he has ever been. And I think that his bid to win his way back into the national side will be to our very real benefit. There was a similar situation in Italy a few years back when Roberto Baggio went to Bologna at a time when he was out of the side and he produced some beautiful football. Claudio can do likewise and be a teacher to our players at the same time."

The other time in recent memory that a player as decorated as Caniggia had arrived in Scotland to "help a friend" was in 1989. Spanish international Victor left the glamour of La Liga to spend a season in the unlikely setting of Paisley and ended his career with former Barçelona team-mate Steve Archibald at St Mirren.

But the Spaniard was just one in a long list of unexpected arrivals in the Scottish game that had also included George Best turning out for Hibs at the end of the 1970s, Russian international Sergei Baltacha signing for St Johnstone in 1990, Chris Waddle at Falkirk in 1996, and Paul Gascoigne joining Rangers in 1995. There was also an equally famous "what if?" when city rivals Dundee United almost brought a South American World Cup hero to Tayside in 1988 when the rampaging Brazilian full-back Josimar nearly swapped Botafogo for Sandeman Street.

Back at the press conference, Ivano was also quizzed about Caniggia's lively past which had included the cocaine doping ban as well as his night in jail for alleged theft.

Ivano insisted however that those days of high-living and wild excess were in the past. "The drugs thing is behind Claudio and we have to forget about it, just as he has," he said. "Like Tony Adams of Arsenal, he is rehabilitated and that is that. No one wonders whether Tony has a problem any more. Yes, there are drugs in Caniggia's past but that is not nearly as important as the football – two World Cup Finals and play to delight anyone with a love of the game. This is a huge transfer for us and it is a very positive one which I am sure will make our fans as happy as we are at this moment."

Ivano was referring to England international Tony Adams. The defender had admitted he was an alcoholic in 1996 but his recovery also helped to extend his career by several years. He went on to play some of the best football of his life, captaining Arsenal to two English league and FA Cup doubles under Arsene Wenger.

"I am feeling young and strong and I cannot wait to play for the club," Caniggia said through interpreter Dario Magri. "My ambition is to play for Argentina in the coming World Cup so it suits me very well to be part of this project the Bonetti brothers have in Scotland. They play football the way I believe it should be played and for me this is everything. You can talk about wages, you can talk about ambition – but what really matters to a footballer is the feeling you get when you go out and please a crowd. There is nothing to match it. I am joining a club that has ambition. I intend to do well for the club and I hope I can repay the faith they have shown in me."

Caniggia said there was also the possibility his former team-mate Diego Maradona would be watching from the stands. He said: "As soon as I signed for Dundee I was on the phone to Diego to tell him I was back in football. Diego told me he plans to come to Scotland within the next few weeks to see me play."

Carranza, who signed a 12-month deal, was unveiled at the same press conference but was almost overlooked such was the furore surrounding Caniggia.

"I am also happy to be at Dundee," he said. "I have found a happy club. I have been made very welcome in my time here and I am pleased I have been accepted by the manager. I am also very happy about the move of Claudio Caniggia because I'm sure it will be an important one for the club."

Caniggia was introduced to his new team-mates and went out to train immediately after the press conference to ensure he would be fit to make his debut 10 days later against Aberdeen. He took part in double stints to get his fitness up to scratch and impressed his new team-mates with his dedication on the training ground.

The following day Ivano told local reporters he was just as excited as the fans to see Caniggia playing for Dundee – but urged caution. He said: "This is a player who has scored the winning goal against Brazil in the World Cup finals, a player who with

The Bird & The Feather

Diego Maradona formed the most famous forward partnership in the world. To have him here, playing for us, is a great thrill. He has been working very hard in training and should be ready for the Aberdeen match. While I have no doubt that he will do big things for us, I think that supporters should not expect too much from him in the first match as everyone needs time to adjust to the pace the game is played in this country."

However, Ivano insisted he would not risk throwing him in until he was ready and suggested Caniggia might start the match on the bench and come on in the second half.

Caniggia was even more cautious when he spoke to reporters. He said his fitness was improving and he was aware of the expectations of the Dundee fans.

"I have had a good week and am looking forward to playing at least part of the game at Aberdeen," he said. "From meeting the fans in the town, I know how much it means to them that I am involved and above all my aim as a footballer is to make supporters happy. To best do that, though, I need to be fit and I cannot yet say if I am ready to play from the start against Aberdeen. That decision will come before the game and it will come in consultation with the manager. Ivano and Dario, who I played alongside at Roma, are two men who know me very well and it is great to be working with them. It helps also that both my wife and I like what we have seen of the town so far. But the thing that has pleased me most is to see at first hand the type of football this club is playing. Other players will take time to adjust to my style as I will to theirs – that is only to be expected. I already know, though, that the way they play the game is the way I think it should be played and the way I enjoy playing it. This style of football, the passing, the intelligence, will give me the platform to achieve what I want to achieve with Dundee. As I said, I am here not just to sit about and pick up the wages but to win my place back in the Argentinian national side and I know the coach will consider me if I can play to a good level in Scotland."

Dundee midfielder, Javier Artero, having grown up playing his football in the Bernabeu for Real Madrid, was not a man you would have expected to be easily awestruck. But even he found himself asking for Caniggia's autograph when they were introduced. Caniggia fever, it appeared, wasn't simply reserved for the fans.

"I played in Argentina with San Lorenzo for over a year so I was very aware of Claudio's stature in the game," he said. "His partnership with Maradona made him legendary. Individually they both have brilliant ability and together they were unstoppable. The best defenders in the world could not handle them. To see a player of his calibre arriving at my club was a great feeling for me and I really was a bit in awe of him at our first meeting. There has been a lot made of the fact our fans are so excited that Claudio has come to join us but what has not been mentioned is that the players are very happy too."

Dundee director Jim Connor said he was just as excited as the players by Caniggia's arrival. "These are incredibly exciting times for Dundee Football Club and we feel all the work we have put in to try and build a family atmosphere here is paying off," he said. "The main thing is what Claudio can bring to the team but we are also confident that he can be a great signing for us in commercial terms. By that, I do not mean simply the number of replica tops we sell with his name on the back but several other avenues that his arrival will open up. We are working on a lot of different things at the moment and are optimistic these will pay off to the benefit of the club. Today we have been looking at the way Aston Villa marketed David Ginola when he joined them from Spurs. We will be looking to do a similar thing, not only with Claudio but with several of our other stars."

Dundee was firmly in the grip of Caniggia fever and, in just two hours, more than 1,000 season ticket-holders excitedly snapped up tickets for the game against Aberdeen at Pittodrie. The stampede prompted a club spokesman to describe the demand as "unbelievable". He said: "We had to bring in extra staff to cope. We would normally only have three people working but we ended up with eight."

The signing followed the publication of a review of the finances of Scottish football clubs by PriceWaterhouseCoopers which revealed top flight teams spent more than £70 million on salaries in season 1998-99. More than half went to Old Firm players. The figures marked a 36% rise from the previous year.

Dundee FC were one club highlighted, with a national radio station claiming they were paying Caniggia £20,000 a week while taking just £30,000 gate receipts. A club spokesman said: "It seems that certain people are simply plucking figures out of the air when it comes to Claudio Caniggia's wages. A player's salary is a private matter between club and player, regardless of who they are. But we can categorically state Claudio Caniggia's weekly wage is nowhere near £20,000, or other inflated guesstimates we have seen reported. While Dundee FC was happy to report a small profit last year, we are acutely aware of rising players wage levels in football. Our wage bill has risen significantly this year. Gate money is a considerable part of the club's income and, of course, we would like to see Dens Park filled to capacity for every home game. The team Ivano Bonetti is assembling has already increased the average attendance at Dens by almost 2,000 on last season and the arrival of Claudio Caniggia is certain to boost the crowds further. But gate money is not the sole source of revenue and we are working hard to maximise the club's commercial activity.

"Since Claudio Caniggia signed last week, Sky have mooted the possibility of covering an extra two games at Dens Park, business at the new club shop is booming and two Argentine satellite companies have expressed a desire to cover a Dundee tour of South America should such a trip take place this season. The club is receiving attention from all over the globe, from fans, the world's media and, significantly, potential sponsors and investors."

Caniggia picked 33 for his squad number to match his age. His arrival also caused a sudden surge in sales of Argentina strips in Dundee. Hair salons across the city reported that blonde wigs were in high demand. The club shop at Dens Park was also enjoying excellent sales of replica Dundee strips which were flying out the door with Caniggia's name and number 33 on the back.

Sales were only stopped momentarily when the shop ran out of the letters N and G.

The enormity of what was happening in Dundee was further emphasised when one such call for a Caniggia jersey was made by his great friend and former team-mate Diego Maradona. Dundee were only too happy to oblige. The package was sent out the next day to the man, who, along with three-time Brazilian World Cup winner Pele, was considered the greatest player of all time.

"The thought of Maradona wearing a Dundee shirt in public is one which fills us all with great pride," said Jim Connor.

It appeared that even the Hand of God was now in Dundee's corner. A leading Dundee bookmaker then began offering fans a chance to make some money, with a selection of special bets to mark Caniggia's debut – including 50/1 for a hat-trick.

"We are in good shape for this match, perhaps the best we have been in for any match since I arrived," said Ivano. "Of course there are still a couple of days training to go, so I cannot be certain that the situation will not change, but at the moment everything is going well."

Caniggia's arrival ironically came at a time when Dundee was in the grip of a tourism slump. Owners of visitor attractions said they were struggling to survive and they had just attacked the Scottish Tourist Board over its "phenomenal" advertising fees. Visitor numbers at city attractions were down 10% which wouldn't have been helped when Caniggia's debut saw an exodus of almost 3,000 Dundee fans up the A90 to see the Argentine turn out against Aberdeen on October 14, 2000.

The pandemonium surrounding Caniggia's arrival had encouraged the Dons to rethink their original plans for the Pittodrie match and make it an all-ticket affair for away fans. The remaining 200 of the 2,500 tickets allocated to the Dark Blues were snapped up quickly before the game.

Caniggia's team-mates soon found out that his pre-match routine included having a cigarette in the dressing room toilet. Many Dundee fans wore Argentina tops and blonde wigs in tribute to their new hero who – as expected – started on the bench.

His opponents were as star-struck as the Dark Blues legions. Aberdeen defender Kevin McNaughton admitted he was slightly nervous at the prospect of facing a player that he had admired since his days at primary school. "I am really looking forward to playing against him and he was a sort of boyhood hero of mine, along with Maradona, as Argentina were a top team when I was at school," he said. "It's actually quite scary when I think that I will be on the same pitch as him. But once the game gets started you don't think about who is in the opposition. It is quite overwhelming beforehand looking at players of the calibre of Caniggia, but that gives me a real buzz for when the action starts."

Caniggia looked on from the bench as Ivano opened the scoring with a brilliant chip over Aberdeen goalkeeper Ryan Easson on the half-hour mark. Ivano would later describe it as "the best goal that no one will ever remember".

The excitement reached fever pitch when Caniggia made his appearance earlier than expected when Stevie Milne got injured just before half-time.

From the off it was abundantly clear Caniggia still had pace to burn. He worked tirelessly hard but endured a frustrating time, playing as a lone striker as Dundee spent most of the second half with just 10 men after midfielder Gavin Rae was sent off for retaliation. Things were evened up eventually when Aberdeen defender Philip McGuire was sent off for a late challenge on Caniggia with time running out. But Caniggia had the last laugh with a sublime strike in the dying minutes to seal the points. The Dons had pushed too many players forward in search of an equaliser. Substitute Georgi Nemsadze broke down the right before feeding Caniggia with a perfect pass. Caniggia showed split-second precision. He took a touch with his right foot to cleverly evade his marker. Then he rolled the ball coolly past the outcoming Ryan Easson with his left, at speed, into the far corner of the net.

The goal sparked incredible scenes of celebration in the away end. Caniggia blew a kiss and raised his arms aloft before running to the Dundee fans.

He went back to the away section again at the final whistle to throw his shirt into the crowd. "I was delighted to give them my jersey, it was the very least I could do for a set of supporters who had given me such an amazing welcome," said the striker through interpreter Dario Magri. "It was more than I had expected and it makes me even more determined to do everything I can for this football club. Though I had not played for a while, I felt fit and could probably have played more than 45 minutes. As a striker you look to score in every game you play but, of course, it was a great feeling to get a goal on my debut."

Team-mate Marco de Marchi raised concerns after the match for Caniggia's long-term welfare in Scottish football following McGuire's dismissal.

"Claudio is a brilliant footballer to play alongside but I am a little bit scared for him," he said. "We lost a great player in Caballero a few weeks ago to a bad tackle which has put him out of football for three months and we don't want the same to happen to Caniggia. McGuire's challenge was a very, very dangerous one from which Claudio was lucky to escape without a problem. Something has to be done and, yes, maybe the referees can play a part in protecting him."

Ivano's star pupil had passed his first test with flying colours. But while Caniggia's Dundee adventure was just starting, across the city it was the end of an era for Jim McLean. The news that McLean's long and illustrious Dundee United career of almost 30 years was over had started to filter through to the legions of Dundee fans that were making their way back to Beach Boulevard to board their supporters' buses for the journey home. McLean was the man who had single-handedly turned an unfashionable fringe club into league champions as well as a European force in the 1980s heyday of Scottish football. He had resigned as chairman just a few minutes after he assaulted BBC sports journalist John Barnes with a single punch during a post-match interview following a 4-0 home defeat to Hearts.

Some 400 United fans had gathered at the main entrance at Tannadice to call for the heads of McLean and the board. Asked for an interview as the storm clouds gathered, McLean agreed to answer two questions. When two became three, he grew irritated. When three became four, he finally snapped. Out of shot but with the microphones of both the BBC and Sky on, McLean landed a blow on a startled Barnes.

McLean's time was up.

His football obituaries were being written in the week of Caniggia's home debut which would be the first time in living memory that a match against Motherwell had been made all-ticket. The on-the-up Dark Blues were sitting joint fifth after emerging from the first quarter of the campaign with 16 points and there was great excitement in the city. Well over 7,000 of the home allocation of 8,500 tickets were sold after Ivano told the Dark Blues faithful that Caniggia was a certain starter this time.

"At Aberdeen, I think he showed he has more than 45 minutes in his legs, so I believe this time he should be on the pitch from the beginning," he said. Ivano warned that nothing could be taken for granted, despite Motherwell currently sitting 10th in the table after picking up just eight points from 11 games. "The fans expect us to beat them, but we know we must respect them and be focused if this is to happen," he said.

Ivano also stressed the importance of doing well to keep the fans coming back. He was well aware that the packed Dundee end would contain many erstwhile supporters who hadn't been through the turnstiles for many years. He said: "It is important that we do well for the fans so as to bring more and more to the stadium. The enthusiasm and interest is very important for the players and if we do well then hopefully the supporters will keep coming back."

Dundee captain Barry Smith was full of praise for Caniggia before the game. He highlighted what he described as the "impressive professionalism" shown by the 33-year-old since his arrival at Dens Park. "I am not the sort of captain who shouts and bawls all the time at team-mates," he said. "I like to lead by example and know what to do to get my point across. But these guys are seasoned professionals and you don't have to tell them what to do, they know. There are 11 captains out there, really. We all have to do our own jobs."

Smith was keen to stress that this wasn't a prima-donna who had turned up with a big ego. He said: "While on the training pitch Caniggia, for example, is just like any other player. Obviously he has great ability and has played in World Cup finals but he works hard just like the rest of us. Had someone told me last year that all this would be happening then I would have said, 'no chance'. But it is not hard to take in now because we see each other at training every day."

The excitement ahead of Caniggia's home debut even prompted a press release to be issued by police, reminding fans to arrive in plenty of time because kick-off would not be delayed. It was the kind of safety message usually reserved for home games against city rivals Dundee United or the arrival of Celtic or Rangers. The fact that it was put out before a game against a team struggling near the foot of the table was all the more remarkable. Match commander Chief Superintendent Brian Powrie said: "At previous all-ticket games large numbers of supporters have been arriving in the 10-minute period prior to kick-off, and expecting to pass through the turnstiles before the game starts. In those circumstances we will not delay kick-off. We hope that a friendly atmosphere prevails as in previous games, and that everyone enjoys the match."

In goal for the home side, following the transfer of Robert Douglas to Celtic, was Jamie Langfield. The match had been billed in some sections of the press as "Claudio Caniggia Day".

Motherwell didn't read the script and raced into a two-goal lead. But after 22 minutes Caniggia delivered the moment the home fans had been waiting for. Accepting a pass from Patrizio Billio, Caniggia turned his marker and darted forward towards the edge of the box. He looked up, spotted home keeper Stevie Woods off his line, and beat him from 25 yards with a beautiful chip.

Caniggia's home debut was also covered as the main match on BBC Scotland's Sportscene highlights show where commentator Rob MacLean's voice rose higher and higher with excitement. "Nice touch from Caniggia away from Oueifio. Chance to pull a goal back. Superb from Caniggia! Dundee back in business. This a finish out of the top drawer. The mistake from Oueifio, who committed himself, and Caniggia had time to size up the opportunity and that was a delicate finish over the head of Stevie Woods."

It remains one of the most watched goal clips on YouTube from Dundee fans.

It was a goal that sparked jubilant scenes in the home end. Caniggia's team-mates were not surprised by the goal after watching him regularly stay behind after training with a dozen or so footballs on the halfway line. One by one he would dribble the balls up the channel before chipping for goal from around 22 yards. He was looking for the "postage stamp" top corner and would "score" 80% of the time.

However, the sprinkling of magic dust from Caniggia wasn't enough to stop the Dark Blues losing their first home game of the campaign. Afterwards, the Dundee manager said he was pleased that his "gamble" in bringing Caniggia to Scotland – certainly at what was still a very early stage – appeared to be paying off.

"The upsetting thing is that a victory today would have allowed us to stretch our lead over the teams below us. However, when you have a bad day you lose," said Ivano. "I was very happy for Claudio. He has shown already that he will be a success here. He told me afterwards that he isn't really fit at the moment – but if he plays like that when he isn't fit then I really look forward to seeing him when he is completely fit. Not only did he score a wonderful goal today, he produced some quality passes and I cannot recall him losing the ball."

Dundee midfielder Alessandro Romano said Caniggia would be fundamental to Dundee's success. "He still has quality and has shown that if we give him chances he will score," he said. "We had an exciting talent like that in Fabian Caballero and it was important he was properly replaced. Claudio has his job to do and I have mine and it is further back. If we all do our jobs we can be a successful team."

Motherwell manager Billy Davies said: "It was a fantastic performance, especially when we knew Caniggia's talents were being welcomed by the home support for the first time. We knew it would give them a lift, so we had to set the tone from the start – and getting the two goals was a bonus."

After the match, a Dundee film company released the first in a series of short videos which aimed to paint a present-day picture of the city. Inspired by black and white footage of old Dundee, filmmaker Scott Summerville began the task of filming every street from the Seagate to the Wellgate. He was recording the views of local people on their doorstep.

Dundee was also proving a popular filming choice for broadcasting giant ESPN. The cable TV company decided to show the Dark Blues next league match against Dunfermline from East End Park – live in South America.

Former Italian under-21 goalkeeper Marco Roccati was brought in on loan from Bologna to take over from Robert Douglas. Roccati was looking to get his career back on track and Ivano said he could become the club's first £1 million player if his switch to Scotland became permanent at the end of the season. "We are talking approximately £1 million," he said. "That is a lot, but in the future we are looking to become the third force in this league, and to do that you have to sign good players – they cost money. Nobody thought Caniggia would come here but he has, so many things are possible. I would point out, too, that Roccati is a very good goalkeeper, and this would be an investment. If he does well, he could be worth £2 million or even £3 million to us."

Bologna had paid £1.3 million for Roccati, where he was understudy to Italian international Gianluca Palgiuca who played in three World Cups for the national team.

Before the match, young Dundee striker Stevie Milne said he was already benefiting from Caniggia's guidance and experience on the training pitch. "To start off, I couldn't believe he was here just because of his World Cup involvement, but he has become just a team-mate like the rest of the boys," he said. "There will be a lot of hype surrounding him at Dunfermline, what with the TV coverage and all the publicity. But maybe that will help the team as a whole because it could take pressure off the rest of us. He has brought something different to the club. He has his own style and you can learn a lot just from watching him."

Dunfermline manager Jimmy Calderwood said his staff had been working hard during the week on the training ground to make sure his team kept things tight and didn't give Dundee space to play. "We'll have to be really short on them and pressurise them because they're good individually if you let them play," he said. "If you give them space, they are going to hurt you and we will have to be at our best to beat them. It says a lot for Dundee that they can be without the services of a player like Fabian Caballero and bring in someone of the calibre of Claudio Caniggia. It's tremendous what they have done for themselves and their supporters getting players of that quality."

Loan signing Marco Roccati would immediately come in and take over from Jamie Langfield in goal, while Gavin Rae returned to the midfield after suspension.

"They are more familiar with this division now and have done some good things since we last met, but we will still be looking for a result from this game," said Ivano.

"Last week we missed too many opportunities to score, and we will be doing our best to change that."

Caniggia was again handed a lone striker shift by Ivano against Dunfermline in a defensive looking line-up. The Pars ran out 1-0 winners thanks to a David Moss header in what was a fairly dismal offering for the television audience watching on the other side of the world.

Despite a lack of support alongside him, Caniggia once again displayed his class. His first-half header from a Javier Artero cross was only kept out by a terrific Marco Ruitenbeek save. Caniggia then took the game by the scruff of the neck. He left two defenders in his wake as he picked out Barry Smith with a cross which Smith should have put beyond Ruitenbeek instead of over the bar. Finally, with the Dark Blues chasing an equaliser, Caniggia cleverly chested a Beto Carranza pass into the path of the oncoming Gavin Rae, who could only put the ball wide from 20 yards.

Afterwards Ivano declared himself happy with Caniggia's contribution. But he promised Caniggia's lone striker shifts would be kept to a minimum in future. He said: "We had three great chances through Claudio Caniggia, Barry Smith and Gavin Rae. Rae shot three times, and for the last one he was in a very good position. I'm very sad – not for the performance, but the result. They had just one shot and scored one goal. I was actually never worried during the game that we might lose it because I hadn't felt much danger in our area and I think that if we replayed this type of game 10 times we wouldn't lose it again.

"But between this match and the last we have made many mistakes up front and you cannot afford to do that. I asked Claudio to play up front on his own at Dunfermline and although he is now 33, he did not complain, and played very well. He worked very hard, but that is what I expected because he a very good professional and has great pride in his performance. Most of the time I will play another striker alongside him. When Steven Milne came on at Dunfermline I thought he and Claudio did well together, and we also have Juan Sara and Willie Falconer."

Caniggia and Ivano shrugged off the disappointing defeat and were soon drinking lager in sombreros in the improbable setting of Kirkcaldy's newest Mexican restaurant. They proved they had a sense of humour as they performed the venue's official opening ceremony before going behind the bar to pour themselves pints.

Ivano jetted off to Italy the following day on a four-day trip home. Before he got to the departure lounge he was forced to laugh off newspaper reports that Caniggia was set to cut short his stay in Dundee to join Diego Maradona in Argentina. Maradona had been offered a lifeline back into football as general manager of struggling first division side Club Almagro following a spell in Cuba to undergo treatment for drug addiction.

"Caniggia has a contract here and there is more chance of Maradona coming to Dundee than Caniggia going back to Argentina," said Ivano.

One little magician already in Dundee that week was Paul Daniels. However, even his mystical powers were unable to extend the size of the city's Bonar Hall stage. Daniels and his wife Debbie McGee were eventually forced to cancel the Dundee leg of their touring ballet production due to lack of space. The problems stemmed from there being not enough room for the colourful and extensive stage designs, and a fear that the lighting rigs would be unable to take the weight of the planned effects. To add to the confusion surrounding the Dundee leg of the tour, BBC cameras were also filming the showbiz couple for a Louis Theroux documentary which has now gone down in TV history.

Dundee's own magic man needed a painkilling injection after a rib knock he picked up against Dunfermline to ensure he wouldn't have to cancel his own performance against Hibs at Dens.

Alex McLeish's Hibs side were gathering real momentum in the league. They were putting together a serious challenge to Rangers and Celtic with former French international and Champions League winner Franck Sauzee pulling the strings in midfield.

"Anything could happen this season – they could break Celtic and Rangers," said Ivano. "Hibs have quality players but more than that they have a great mentality and trust of each other. I think they believe they can get to the Champions League, and they might be right. We must do better and I think we will once we settle on a system, something I feel we are within 15 days of doing. Playing just one striker against Dunfermline we created three chances. I am searching for a system which will guarantee seven, eight, nine chances a match. You cannot of course invent or create anything new in football but you can put players in positions that they have the quality to play in and which suit the team best."

Before the match Dundee took delivery of more than £50,000-worth of their new red and blue away strip. Daily sales of the home strip had more than doubled following Caniggia's arrival and Dundee were expecting the new design to fly off the shelves.

A spokesman for Dundee said: "We are expecting them to be very, very popular and it goes without saying that the majority will have Caniggia on the back. He is the man of the moment and there is a carnival atmosphere about the club just now so we are expecting a busy time."

Caniggia's rib knock didn't stop him from lining up against Hibs in a televised clash which was shown live across the UK on Sky.

John O'Neil opened the scoring for Hibs following a defensive error, before Caniggia's clever control forced the foul which led to the Dundee equaliser. Georgi Nemsadze's delivery from the subsequent free-kick gave Steven Tweed the opportunity to head home on 33 minutes. Dundee should have gone up the tunnel ahead at half-time, but Gavin Rae and Willie Falconer both scorned gilt-edged chances which had been set up for them by Caniggia's trickery and guile.

The Dark Blues were made to pay the price when Frenchman David Zitelli's stunning overhead volley on 62 minutes wrapped up the points for the Hibees in sensational fashion.

"When you lose to a goal like Zitelli's there is nothing you can say because it was a wonderful thing, but the other goal is different," said Ivano. "We can do very much, but not if we make mistakes like this and that makes me very angry. It is about concentration and you can't take risks, but we did and lost a goal. Sometimes we have had bad luck, and we must work hard to change that because the last three games have brought us zero points and that is very bad. Now there will be a big derby on Saturday, because United are in trouble and we need a win to get back into the top six."

The SPL would split into two for the first time that season. Once the 12 teams had played 33 matches, those finishing in the top six would play each other once more. The bottom six would also fight it out amongst themselves for relegation.

After the match Dundee fans rushed to snap up tickets for Caniggia's first derby at Tannadice which again forced the club to draft in extra staff to cope with demand.

The ageing gunslinger might have left his sombrero in Kirkcaldy but city rivals United were now in his sights.

SPL Table, November 6, 2000

		Pld	Pts
1	Celtic	14	38
2	Hibernian	14	35
3	Rangers	14	28
4	Kilmarnock	14	26
5	Hearts	14	19
6	St Johnstone	14	17
7	Dundee	14	16
8	Dunfermline Ath.	14	16
9	Motherwell	14	15
10	Aberdeen	14	12
11	St Mirren	14	10
12	Dundee United	14	2

CHAPTER FOUR

Winning Derbies And Pulling Pints

These games are the same the world over. Football usually goes out the window. Victory is the only important thing.

Claudio Caniggia

IVANO'S designer jackets were certainly brightening up Dens Park. But the vision being dreamed up for the city's future would make Dundee just as fashionable.

In November, Dundee City Council unveiled radical plans to regenerate the central waterfront area which included extending the city centre into the dockland. The road bridge ramps would also be changed and buildings such as the much-maligned Tayside House, the Hilton Hotel and the Olympia Leisure Centre would be pulled down.

A vision of how the waterfront area could look in 30 years was presented at a meeting of the Dundee area branch of the Institute of Civil Engineers, the Royal Town Planning Institute and the Dundee Institute of Architects in Dundee University's Tower Block. The proposal would change the city's skyline, although trains travelling northbound across the Tay Bridge would still be offered a view of the nearest league grounds in Britain sitting side by side next to the Derby Street multis against the backdrop of Dundee Law. The two grounds are approximately 200 yards apart and only MTV and BKV Elore in Budapest are closer together in the whole of Europe, as their grounds actually back onto each other.

The Dundee derby is also distinctive in terms of its rivalry. It is probably the only derby in world football where players and management of the opposing team walk to their opponent's ground amongst the fans on the morning of the game.

United's new signing Beto Naveda – a former Boca Juniors team-mate of Caniggia – said it would be nothing like the derby games they had played in their native Argentina. "Though I love derby football, I know the most important thing is that everyone involved is safe and not in fear of their life," he said. "Derbies will produce passion wherever they are played but in Argentina things are much more dangerous.

"Robberies and guns are not uncommon and even with crowds of up to 80,000 at the games no-one who goes to the match can truly say that they are safe. I was with Boca Juniors three years ago when our fans killed two River Plate fans in the streets after a bad home defeat and it made me wonder if this was a country where I should be playing my football. Of course, a lot of fuss was made about the deaths and how the violence had to stop. In the end, though, there is not that much they can do, for it is not just the problem of football, it is the problem of the country. Argentina is a dangerous place where a lot of people die before their time. It is sad but is also true.

"I have a wife and a young child so for me the most important thing is to be safe and I am pleased to be in Dundee because I can see that things are good here. You look around the stadium and there are none of the fences you would expect. Back home you could not have that for the fans would simply run on to the pitch when something happens that they do not like. Beto Carranza and Walter del Rio are my friends from Boca and I also know the other Argentinian players at Dundee, which is definitely a help to me.

"Claudio Caniggia, of course, is one of the greatest players that our country has ever produced. There is nothing I can say about him which others have not already done. I wish them all well but they are not who I am concerned with at the moment. I am a United player and my job is to help the club win games."

Before the match it emerged that Caniggia's rib injury had flared up again. He would need an injection but would be fit enough to start against a United side that was bottom of the table. The manager was hoping Caniggia's influence would help Juan Sara get back among the goals again after failing to score since his hat-trick in the first city derby of the season.

Ivano said: "Juan is going through a difficult time just now because the goals are just not going in for him. These things happen in football and the main thing is to keep working hard and not let it affect your confidence. He would have scored a wonderful goal on Sunday night had it not been for the Hibs goalkeeper somehow managing to get a hand to the ball and push it over the crossbar. On another occasion that would have gone in for him and I have no doubt he will soon be on the mark again.

"When you play up front alongside Claudio Caniggia you are always going to get chances, for he is a top-quality player with a great ability to see a pass."

Ivano gave his team talk at Dens before the players made their way on foot down Tannadice Street with the kit hampers being wheeled behind. Dundee were going into the match in poor form themselves, having lost their last three games. But United's run was altogether worse. They had failed to win in the league all season. It had also been an incredible 11 months since United had managed to pick up all three points from a home game.

Fans in South America were able to view coverage of the Dundee derby for the first time. Cable channel ESPN International decided to screen the match. Derek Rae went back to his Scottish roots from the commentary box.

The injured Fabian Caballero flew back from his base in Italy to watch the match and was given a standing ovation by the Dark Blues support as he took his seat before kick-off. The Caniggia factor also saw the game being shown live in Australia and New Zealand, while audiences in Latin America and the West Indies were to receive delayed coverage of the fixture.

Viewers from the Southern Hemisphere and further afield were given a Caniggia masterclass as the veteran striker helped his side to a 2-0 win in front of 11,454 fans.

United started brightly despite their troubles but Dundee had a chance to take the lead on 10 minutes when Caniggia's close range shot was blocked by home goalkeeper Alan Combe. As the match progressed, it was Dundee who were looking more threatening. The Dark Blues were creating a string of chances from open play but when the first goal arrived it was with the help of a mistake in the United ranks.

Jamie Buchan misjudged a hopeful punt up the park from Barry Smith. He chested the ball into the path of Willie Falconer. The tall striker played in Caniggia, who clinically drilled the ball low past Combe and into the bottom-right corner from 16 yards.

Dundee fans sung a song for him to the tune of Culture Club's Karma Chameleon. They sang: "Can-a Can-a, Can-a Can-a, Can-a Caniggiaaaaah. He comes and scores, he comes and scores."

Georgi Nemsadze proved Dundee were still on song when he ended United's hopes on 73 minutes. The goal was started by a magical back heel from Caniggia, whose delicate flick helped lay captain Barry Smith's ball into Nemsadze's path. The Georgian skipper beat David Partridge and Hasney Aljofree before chipping Combe from 12 yards.

Dundee fans also taunted their bottom-of-the-table rivals throughout the encounter with their chants of: "Two points, you've only got two points". The singalong even merited a mention in Rob MacLean's BBC Scotland commentary.

"I feel I have scored better goals than this," said Nemsadze afterwards. "But I am very happy because it is my first goal for Dundee and it has come in a derby. As I turned towards goal, I was at an angle and the keeper was shutting down the goal completely. My only option was to put it over him. I only believed it had gone in when I saw it in the back of the net. Caniggia's goal at Aberdeen was a special one for him, and this one was just as special for me."

Dundee's fans greeted it just as loudly as debut boy Caniggia's Pittodrie roof-raiser. Ivano then dedicated the 2-0 win to the 5,000 Dundee fans who had made the short journey. He said: "We scored two wonderful goals to repay the wonderful support we received from our 5,000 fans at Tannadice.

"When our players concentrate, we are a difficult team to beat. However we don't think about being the best team in the city. We want to be among the best in Scotland. If Dundee finish in third position and United in fourth, that would be wonderful for the city."

United fans – at this stage – would have settled for a fourth from bottom finish such was their woes.

Tannadice boss Alex Smith was understandably dejected. He stood with shoulders hunched and summed up the mood in his dressing room. Smith said his team would never start winning games "until we stop shooting ourselves in the foot". He said: "We were mugged at both goals. You can't give the ball away to a world-class striker like Caniggia."

After the match Caniggia complained that his mobile phone couldn't receive a reception in Dundee. But he also said he liked the quietness of Dundee which helped him think.

Caniggia would drive his son Alexander to school before going to training. He would then spend the afternoon drinking coffee in the Italian ice cream shop Visocchis in Broughty Ferry, which was popular with Dundee FC's foreign legion. He signalled he was so happy with life that he was ready to finish his playing days at Dens Park.

"I'm committed to Dundee until the end of this season," he said. "However, I intend to have talks with the management about staying longer. The way I'm feeling just now I'd like to finish my career with Dundee. I certainly want to stay for at least one more season after this, perhaps even longer. As time goes on, the option of staying becomes more and more real. I've been made to feel so welcome in Dundee, remaining longer than intended has now become a definite possibility. I know Argentina coach Marcello Bialsi has been watching me, as Dundee's games are being shown live in Argentina at present.

"My ambition is to play in the finals of the World Cup one last time. I'm definitely confident of a recall to Argentina's side. Even more importantly, I still have the desire to succeed that I had as a 20-year-old. As long as I feel this way, I'll continue to set myself targets."

Caniggia was also asked after the match how it had compared with his previous derby experiences in Argentina and Italy. Caniggia responded to the reporters with a degree of diplomacy which wouldn't have looked out of place at the United Nations. "I've played in derby matches in Argentina, both for River Plate and Boca Juniors," he said. "I've also played in derby matches in Italy for Roma against Lazio.

"These games are the same the world over. Football usually goes out the window. Victory is the only important thing.

"However, I felt the fans were treated to some good spells of football in this derby at Tannadice. The atmosphere was good. However it was nothing compared to derby games in Buenos Aires. These games attract crowds of 80,000 and the stadium shakes to its foundation. It's quite unbelievable."

Caniggia famously served drinks in the High Corner after the match. The players gave the Dundee fans a night to remember as they celebrated together in Jimmy Marr's pub. Caniggia's popularity also helped Dundee's new online shop attract orders from across the world within its first few days of business.

Thousands of hits were logged, with orders for jerseys bearing Caniggia's name and squad number 33 received from places ranging from Brazil to Brisbane.

"There has been a great reaction to this facility," said a spokesman. "It is very pleasing because it shows just how much interest there is in what the club are doing."

The editor of the UK's oldest football publication, World Soccer Magazine's Gavin Hamilton, said the global shirt sales were proof positive that Caniggia was still one of the game's hottest properties.

Dundee were hoping for similar success on the park against St Mirren at Dens Park where they had been struggling with just nine from 21 points picked up at home.

Captain Barry Smith said: "It is so important we win our home games as that will ensure we keep the fans with us. But, just like last year, we've not done as well at Dens as we would like. I don't know why that should be and you certainly cannot point the finger at the supporters and say they are putting us under pressure because with the arrival of the Argentinian and Italian lads they've shown greater patience when games haven't been going well and been more willing to give us a chance."

Caniggia spent the week trying to shake off a groin strain picked up in the derby win to make sure he was available for selection against St Mirren.

He wasn't the only one struggling to get up to full speed in the city that week. A go-slow protest journey in the fight for a cut in fuel duty took place in the build-up to the St Mirren match before Dundee City Council eventually put the brakes on the 84-vehicle convoy. The council refused to give official permission for the procession because there was concern there would be traffic chaos on the Kingsway ring road because of ongoing works.

The procession reached the outskirts of Dundee where it was broken into groups of 10 by police. The gathering of vehicles reassembled again at Invergowrie before heading off towards Stirling.

A few days later, there was little protest from the St Mirren team at Dens Park where Dundee went full throttle and recorded what was their biggest and most emphatic SPL win of the season.

The quality of play at times was spellbinding. Caniggia – typically – was the tormentor in chief. He left players barely half his age in his wake at times. He strolled through a game which was arguably one of his best in a Dundee shirt. He hit an easy double to take his tally to five goals in just five-and-a-half games. Gavin Rae, Javier Artero and substitute Stevie Milne all got in on the act as well. Dundee had enough chances to have been five goals up by half-time. Caniggia's first goal on 22 minutes was an easy tap in. Willie Falconer's header came back off the post and Caniggia didn't wait to be asked twice.

Despite Dundee's first-half supremacy the fans had to wait until eight minutes after the break for a second goal. Caniggia again was on hand to follow up a rebound after St Mirren goalkeeper Derek Scrimgeour had saved Gavin Rae's snapshot. Rae himself got on the score sheet on 66 minutes with a tremendous shot from 20 yards. Caniggia was involved again for the fourth on 75 minutes. He looked up and combined perfectly with Javier Artero who converted the Argentine's cross with what was an easy finish from close range.

Caniggia was given a standing ovation from the Dens Park congregation when he was replaced by Stevie Milne who went on to finish the scoring. Milne poked home from just six yards after fellow substitute Juan Sara had knocked down Artero's right wing cross.

After the match, Ivano said: "When you create so many chances and show confidence, it is great, but it's never easy until you score. After the second goal by Claudio, it was wonderful for us and very entertaining for the fans."

Caniggia was asked for his early thoughts on the Scottish game afterwards. He said it was a league where there was simply no time to relax.

"It is a good league, one in which it is difficult to tell how games will turn out," he said. "We won 5-0, but we've recently lost games we should have won. Every single player in the league gives everything in every game, and it means that there can be no relaxation, or you will lose. We have to learn lessons from each game as I found that the Scottish players are very competitive. They play as if each game is their last."

While Caniggia was hoping his stint at Dundee could get him back in the Argentina fold, his team-mate Gavin Rae also spoke of an ambition to realise his own international dream. He was confident playing alongside Caniggia could help him win full honours for Scotland. "Obviously that is an ambition I have and maybe in a few years I will be good enough to play for Scotland," he said.

"We will have to wait and see, though, and I have to keep playing for Dundee every week and performing to a high level. It is good for me to be playing with the foreign players as I am learning so much from them. My game involves getting forward a lot and Claudio is brilliant at linking up with the midfield."

Caniggia's strike partner Willie Falconer said Dundee could go on improving after a result which moved the Dark Blues up to fifth place in the league. "You have to say it was a tremendous result," said Falconer.

"It takes time for all the new players that have come in to settle into the Scottish style of play. We made a good start to the season but you could tell that it would take time for the foreign lads to get used to the game here. But after hitting a dip the signs are that we are beginning to come on."

Caniggia and Dundee were now a big box office draw. They were also seemingly proving better value for money than media mogul Rupert Murdoch was when he put a value on the rival top-flight product from England's top league. Dundee Licensed Trade Association president and pub owner Jim Brownlee came out after the game and accused Sky Television of having "a gun to our heads" over the cost of screening English league football.

He was speaking after it emerged that 1,000 pubs across the UK had already removed their big screens in protest at the ever-increasing charges being demanded by Sky for the right to show live matches involving the likes of Manchester United, Liverpool and Chelsea.

"We are not forced to have Sky installed, but if we don't show the games we may end up losing even more money through the loss of business," he said. "The matches are extremely popular and if we don't screen them our customers will just go somewhere else. Sky has a gun to our heads over this and it is causing a lot of unhappiness from pub owners."

Dundee were out to prove their own worth when they finished the month with a trip to Tynecastle to face troubled Hearts. The Gorgie outfit were without a manager and had just lost six goals against Celtic.

Ivano said: "Because we scored five and they lost six last time out does not mean we must win on Saturday. Football is not like that. For a start we were playing St Mirren and they were playing at Celtic. How many goals they have lost, or because they do not have a manager right now, all this does not matter – they can still play well in a game. I think we can win on Saturday, not because of what has happened, but because of what can happen. If we concentrate and play like we can, we can win."

Ivano had been cast in the role of villain last time out against Hearts in August when he had brought down Juanjo and enabled Colin Cameron to salvage a point from the spot.

"Now we are playing Hearts again I would like to make up for my mistake by scoring a goal to help us beat them," he said.

Hearts caretaker boss Peter Houston said he would not single out Caniggia for special treatment, despite admitting he presented "a huge threat" to his team. He said: "Dundee have done well in the last couple of weeks and I think Caniggia has found his feet in Scottish football.

"He's world class and has obviously still got bags of talent and a great appetite for the game. We've got to stick to our own game plan and can't concentrate only on him. We know what we want to do against him – you've got to mark him in the right areas because he drops off to get the ball."

Caniggia's groin strain had again restricted him to light training. But he managed to start against Hearts in an exhilarating clash which showed off everything that was good about Scottish football. So good, in fact, that both sides were given a standing ovation by all sides of the ground at full-time.

Dundee deservedly took the lead. Gordan Petric was booked for taking a kick at Caniggia. But Claudio's fellow Argentine, Beto Carranza, stepped up and curled a 28-yard free-kick round the wall and past Antti Niemi.

Dundee should have been out of sight after the first goal but somehow managed to lose. Hearts got back on level terms when Grant Murray headed in a Juanjo corner from close range.

The home side then took the lead when Colin Cameron drove a low shot into the bottom of the net after he seized upon a loose ball.

Dundee threw bodies forward in search of an equaliser but found themselves pegged back. With time running out for the Dark Blues, Ivano's curse against Hearts struck again when he stupidly brought down Steve Fulton in the box deep into injury time. Cameron stepped up confidently and closed the door on any hopes Dundee had of taking something by firing home the spot-kick to clinch all three points.

Ivano left the ground in an almighty rage. He was largely critical of the referee for giving decisions against Dundee for the second and third goals.

"I am very unhappy about all three goals and cannot understand how this can happen," he said.

Perhaps he should have listened more closely to Caniggia's warning the previous week. "There can be no relaxation, or you will lose," were Caniggia's words of foreboding.

It was to prove another lesson learned the hard way.

CHAPTER FIVE

Maradona Is A Dundee Derry Boy

"To be precise, Diego suggested it and I said I'd arrange it."

Claudio Caniggia

THE Christmas Lights had just been switched on in Dundee City Square and things were also looking a little brighter at Dens Park, where Caniggia appeared to have finally put his recurring rib and groin problems behind him. He declared himself fit for the Tayside derby clash with St Johnstone. Sandy Clark's charges were on a good run of four wins and two draws from nine away games. Dens was also a place where St Johnstone had taken nine out of a possible 12 points previously, so they travelled from Perth in confident mood.

Juan Sara replaced the injured Willie Falconer who had been showing promising signs of forming a potent front pairing with Caniggia. "Willie's ankle is badly swollen and Juan Sara will come in," said Ivano. "We have other options, such as Steven Milne, but I think the time is ideal for Juan to come back in. I have been very happy with Falconer's form, particularly the way he has linked up with Claudio Caniggia. But it is a chance for Juan."

Before the match St Johnstone's Canadian international midfielder Nick Dasovic admitted he had been hugely impressed by what he had seen of Caniggia since his arrival. "There seems no doubt that Dundee have managed to do a great job with the numbers as they have brought a whole crew of exciting new players to the football club," he said. "Caniggia is a world-class talent and I am a big fan of Nemsadze, too, as he is brilliant at picking up the ball and taking on opponents. Collectively they pass the ball about really well and are a slightly different style of team than you usually come up against in Scotland in that they are comfortable being in possession for extended periods."

Following a disappointing run of results, Ivano challenged his stuttering players to show greater consistency. "To give a pattern of play to a team takes time and we have only had 17 games to do that," he said. "But I feel we could have done better results-wise. We might have had five or six more points than we actually have and now we have to take advantage of the fact we are stronger than when we started out by finding three, four, five or six results. I feel it is important we now go on such a run."

The game was again beamed back to South America.

Despite Ivano's pre-match rallying call Dundee once again threw away two points late in the game after taking an early lead.

Caniggia started the match and Dundee were in front on 14 minutes. Ivano's tantalising cross was headed home by Juan Sara from 10 yards. Two more headers from Sara flew just over as the home side began to dominate. After the break goalkeeper Alan Main blocked a close-range header from Sara. The ex-United man also saved a 10-yard drive from substitute Lee Wilkie and kept out Beto Carranza's shot with the help of the post. Ivano then fired over from 16 yards late in the game and Dundee were made to rue those missed opportunities when Wilkie put the ball through his own net in injury time. A Momo Sylla delivery into the six-yard box was chested towards goal by Wilkie and goalkeeper Marco Roccati couldn't prevent the ball from agonisingly creeping over the line.

Wilkie came in for criticism from Ivano in the dressing room afterwards where he received an angry tongue-lashing in front of his stunned team-mates. "I will not be able to sleep tonight as I will think about this game over and over," said Ivano after the match. "It is unbelievable that we dropped two points. If you cannot win matches when you are playing well, it's going to be very difficult to do so when you play badly. It's nice to hear people praise your team for playing good football, but the fact is we need points. These last two games have hurt our chances of getting into the top six."

The disappointment was nothing compared with the sense of loss when it emerged that Malcolm (Mac) Hendry, known as The Dens Park Bard, had died at the age of 88. Although born and raised in Glasgow, Mr Hendry had moved to Dundee in 1936 after accepting a job as a civil engineer and he became a fan of the club almost immediately. As The Dens Park Bard, he wrote poems for the match day programme for 18 years.

Mr Hendry made his final journey just a day before Dundee welcomed Celtic to Dens on December 10 for the first of what would be four games in 16 days ahead of the winter shutdown. St Johnstone, Dundee and Motherwell were sandwiched in between Hearts in fifth spot and Dunfermline in ninth in the race to finish in the top-six before the split.

"We don't want to talk about the league table just now, but we must try to win more matches," said Ivano. "In the last six or seven games we have done well, but obviously we need the result, too. I think we have failed because of silly mistakes or unlucky situations, but that is something we can try to rectify. The good thing is, at least we are creating five or six good chances in games. The problem is, when we score it is not because teams have given us a gift, but, when we lose a goal, normally it has been because of a mistake."

Lee Wilkie was dropped and told he would no longer be considered for the first-team following a heated exchange during a practice match which was viewed as a serious disciplinary matter.

Celtic's new £6 million midfielder Neil Lennon did play, making his debut alongside top scorer Henrik Larsson in a match shown live throughout the UK on Sky Sports.

Before the teams took to the field Dundee defender Marco de Marchi warned that Caniggia was just as dangerous a proposition as Larsson. "We have to worry about players like Lennon and Larsson for they are real talents, but make no mistake, Celtic have to worry about Claudio," he said. "He might not be as lightning quick as he was when he was young but he is still very, very fast. Add that to his great technique and his brain for the game and you have someone who can be a real threat to any team. When I was in Italy I always used to enjoy the big games more than others. To play against the best players in front of the biggest crowds – that was what I enjoyed more than anything. I had to mark Diego Maradona in matches, which I still consider to be a privilege. He was most certainly the best player I have ever seen in my life."

Dundee were looking to overturn a 12-year winless streak against Celtic and Ivano told reporters before the match the away side were expected to win. But he insisted "anything can happen" and predicted "a beautiful game". He said: "Celtic have many good players and are very entertaining to watch. We too have some top class players in guys like Georgi Nemsadze, Carranza and Javier Artero and it is my belief that they will be inspired by the occasion."

Caniggia did indeed shine on the big stage but it was a familiar story. Dundee failed to hang on until the final whistle, losing another late goal for what was now the third week running. It was becoming a recurring plotline for Ivano's men.

The visitors took an early lead through Stiliyan Petrov but they were pegged back for most of the encounter by a Dundee side which was inspired by Caniggia. The Argentine's quick feet, speed and trickiness caused Celtic problems throughout. A few of his tricks included coming to a dead stop at full stride with the ball at his feet and a magical back-heel which put Barry Smith in at the by-line.

Caniggia's skills were bringing the Dundee fans to their feet with deafening approval. He then broke free and dribbled the ball around Celtic's former Dundee goalkeeper Robert Douglas but defender Joos Valgaeren managed to get his head in the way of Caniggia's goalbound effort to ensure Celtic stayed in front.

Dundee kept knocking at the door. They finally got the reward their persistence deserved when intelligent play from Beto Carranza gave Caniggia space to run into, wide on the left-hand side. Caniggia broke free and sent in a dangerous cross towards Sara which was diverted into his own net by a diving Tom Boyd header on 55 minutes.

Dundee were now looking the more likely of the two sides to take the lead. Another quick move involving Georgi Nemsadze and Gavin Rae put Caniggia in on goal once again but he could only hit the side netting. The play was end to end. Both sides left nothing in the dressing room and went all out for the three points.

But Dundee were once again left to pay the price for being unable to defend a late corner. Defender Chris Coyne's clearance thundered off team-mate Steven Tweed and rebounded round the Dundee box like a pinball before breaking to Didier Agathe. The Celtic wing-back was perfectly placed to head home his side's winner.

"I don't know what I can say – that was unbelievable," said Ivano afterwards. "We played some wonderful football but once again we have failed to take the points and we need to be taking points. It probably says it all that at half-time for probably the first time in my life I was not concerned to be losing a game. I told my players to go out and carry on doing what they were doing and they would get their reward. They did just that, got the goal we deserved but then we go and lose it all in the last minute. It is so hard to take."

Celtic manager Martin O'Neill was courteous in victory. He said afterwards that a draw would probably have been a fair result. "Dundee have some top quality players and they did really well, with Caniggia in particular absolutely excellent throughout," he said. "To my mind it could have gone either way in the last 10 minutes. We kept plugging away and got the break. Some people will say we were fortunate but sometimes you have to make your own luck."

Swedish sensation Henrik Larsson was already being lauded as the greatest player to have ever graced Scottish football and Rangers had just completed the record £12 million signing of Tore Andre Flo from Chelsea – but Ivano declared he wouldn't swap his own prize asset for either of them.

"There are many good strikers in Scotland and I think Larsson is a fantastic footballer, but if you asked me to swap Claudio for any of them, I'd say no," Ivano told local reporters at his daily press briefing the morning after the Celtic defeat. "He is a quality person and a quality player and he has shown that in every game since he came here. Against Celtic I thought he was wonderful and, like my other players, did not deserve to finish on the losing team. When people saw Claudio coming to Dundee, many said he was on the way down. He knew that was not so and I knew that was not so. Last night the whole world was watching the game on television and now everyone knows this as well. For the second time in eight days we were very unlucky at the end and I am going now to look for some luck. I was very happy with my team's play, but we know as well as playing good football, we must get points."

Caniggia flew home to Argentina after the match for a civil court case in connection with money he alleged he was due from Boca Juniors following his second spell with them. The timing of the case had been agreed several months before and it was predicted that it would last just a day or two. But – as often happens with such cases – complex legal issues cropped up and Dundee were anxiously left hoping that Caniggia would make it back in time for the visit to Kilmarnock.

Ivano said: "Claudio is booked on a flight and we are keeping our fingers crossed that he will make it in time. We obviously want him to play but we will have to see how he is feeling before making a final decision."

Defender Marcello Marrocco watched Caniggia at his peak playing in the 1990 World Cup and said he thought his team-mate was actually getting better with age. He also afforded his team-mate the ultimate compliment and said they would need him if they were to get back to winning ways against Kilmarnock at Rugby Park.

"He is our number one, a footballer who when he is playing gives us a chance of winning any game," he said. "I have played alongside many great players in my years with Genoa, Napoli, Modena and now Dundee and, for me, Claudio is the best. I went to watch him when he played in the World Cup in Italy in 1990 and was greatly impressed by what I saw for he was clearly a man blessed with great technique and pace. Since then I believe he has improved into an even better performer for he has more experience, which he uses to hurt opposition teams."

Caniggia eventually arrived back in Edinburgh on the afternoon of the game after a 16-hour flight but Ivano decided that he couldn't risk throwing him in.

"We couldn't take a chance on Claudio," said Ivano. "He had a long flight and he has been carrying an injury."

However, Caniggia was with his team-mates in spirit. He phoned Ivano straight after the final whistle to tell him that he had been asking for divine intervention as he sat listening to the radio commentary of the match in his hotel room. The power of prayer worked as Dundee got back to winning ways with a 3-2 win despite the absence of their talisman. Dundee hauled themselves back from 2-0 down to win with two-goal Stevie Milne and Gavin Rae giving Caniggia plenty to cheer about.

Dundee fans made up for the disappointment of Caniggia's absence with a bit of humour. Out of the murky stand behind one of the goals came the chant: "He's blue, he's white, he must have missed his flight – Caniggia."

Goal-hero Stevie Milne accepted his reward would almost certainly be to return to the bench when Caniggia was back in the squad for the visit of Aberdeen at Dens. "I know Claudio is back now and I'd expect the manager to pick him," he said. "I don't mind that – I'm just glad I helped us get a result."

Midfielder Gavin Rae said: "Even when we were on the bus travelling through to the game we still thought he could make it. But, to be fair, I think the boys handled it very well without him."

After the match it emerged that the man with the rock star looks would soon be joined in Dundee by another global superstar.

Canadian rock legend Bryan Adams was used to playing in front of huge crowds and – just like Caniggia – was coming to the city to perform in a smaller and more intimate venue. It was announced that Adams would be Waking Up The Neighbours at Dundee's Caird Hall the following month as part of a long weekend of Scottish shows. It was good news for Dundee and the Caird Hall, which had only just started to become a popular venue once again since the glory days of the 1950s, 1960s and 1970s when acts like Frank Sinatra, the Beatles, the Rolling Stones, Elton John and Queen performed regularly.

Dundee's own headline act returned from Edinburgh and joined Javier Artero at Downfield Golf Club where he presented the junior section awards to the star-struck youngsters. Caniggia would be back in the starting line-up to replace Stevie Milne against Aberdeen two days before Christmas where festive cheer was in short supply. Ivano said: "Claudio is a special player and so will play, but I am happy with Steven. He is young, but we know he can do a job for us now and perhaps one day soon he and Claudio will play together."

Morgan Academy's 10-strong samba band were there to welcome Dundee's Latin players on to the pitch and whipped the crowd up into an all-singing, all-dancing frenzy. The idea behind the band's appearance came from Dundee fan John MacDonald, who saw them play at a charity concert and immediately set the wheels in motion for their big break at Dens against The Dons. Principal music teacher Carol Sim Sayce said: "He set about organising it for them to play because he wanted to make sure that Claudio Caniggia and the other Latin American players felt at home. He reckoned the samba band were the best people to do that."

Steven Tweed struck a bum note when he made a mistake inside the box and Aberdeen took the lead when Alex di Rocco pounced and fired a low-angled drive beneath Marco Roccati. Dundee might have gone level when Caniggia appeared to have been barged in the penalty area by Thomas Solberg. Referee Alan Freeland – who actually lived in Aberdeen – waved play on and Caniggia received a yellow card after vehemently arguing against the decision.

Dundee did manage to level things up on the hour mark.

Beto Carranza collected a pass from countryman Sara and fired home an exquisite low shot from the edge of the area.

The Dark Blues then went ahead 11 minutes later. Caniggia scrapped hard to gain possession on the left. He looked up and switched the play to Carranza who left Jamie McAllister in his wake before crossing for Sara to head home. However, Aberdeen left with a share of the spoils following another contentious refereeing decision just three minutes later. Alan Freeland this time did point to the penalty spot. He judged that Barry Smith had fouled di Rocco inside the box. Aberdeen striker Arild Stavrum stepped up to blast his kick home from 12 yards.

A red mist then descended over Caniggia. He continued to complain to Freeland after the game. He lost his rag and was shown a second yellow card by the match official.

"It is not a matter of opinion – it was a penalty," said Caniggia afterwards. "We have been playing well but haven't always reaped the fruits we should have. If one day we can start to take 50-60% of the chances we are creating then we will go a lot further than we have and surprise a few people."

Ivano declined to comment on Caniggia's red-card for "administrative reasons". But he admitted he was surprised that an Aberdeen-based referee had been put in charge of a game involving his home-town club. "I thought it was a bit strange that the referee comes from Aberdeen when we are playing against Aberdeen," he said. "In Italy that would never happen, although I am not saying it was a problem. But when supporters told me before the game that is where he came from, I thought they were joking. I didn't see the penalty incident and would have to wait to see it on video before I could comment. All the players were very angry and didn't understand what had happened, but the reason we didn't win is because we missed chances to score."

Dundee City Council was also forced to defend itself afterwards when motorists claimed not enough had been done to keep the roads free of ice during Christmas. Many roads in Dundee froze over to create hazardous conditions for drivers, and police reported dozens of minor incidents across the city, although there were no serious injuries.

Things were just as frosty at Dens Park where Patrizio Billio looked to be heading for the exit. He decided to go public over Christmas on what he described as the Scrooge-like and unfair way he was being treated by Ivano. Signed on a free transfer from Ancona in October 1999, the Italian had been a permanent fixture in the team the previous season. But he had now fallen completely out of favour. Gavin Rae and Georgi Nemsadze had made the central midfield berths their own.

"What happened was that about a month ago I spoke with the gaffer, the last time I have spoken personally with him," said Billio. "He told me he does not like my reaction when I do not play and that it is better that I find another team. My personal opinion is that I never see one player who is happy when he is not playing but I do not say anything because for me what happens on the pitch is all that decides who plays."

Peace at Christmas and goodwill to all men was in equally short supply on the other side of the world when injured striker Fabian Caballero's recovery suffered a setback. He was left with a broken nose and facial injuries following a vicious street attack. The Argentinian star, who was still recuperating from major knee surgery, was beaten up outside a Paraguayan nightclub in the early hours of Christmas Day. A group of troublemakers targeted him because he used to play for one of their city rivals. The incident was described as particularly nasty according to news reports in South America where it was alleged the attack was only broken up when a security guard fired a gun in the air.

"Fabian has been through a bad experience but the important thing is that he is okay now," said Ivano. "Though he was taken to a local hospital for treatment, he told me he was not badly hurt and he has not only been able to get back to Argentina, but also resume training. Fabian is very happy with the progress he has been making in terms of his recuperation and said the attack will not set him back in any way. Fabian was taking the chance to use his holiday time to visit with friends which is certainly not a problem with us. He is a teetotaller so there is no question of him misbehaving as a result of having taken drink and I know that he is a firm believer in taking care of his body. Unfortunately, when you are a professional footballer and well known, there is always the danger that troublemakers will single you out and that is what has happened to our player. It is very sad that such things take place but at least on this occasion there has been no real damage done."

Caniggia's mobile phone was still struggling to get a reception and phones were causing nothing but headaches elsewhere in the city. Approximately five million more mobile phones hit the market to meet the Christmas demand, creating a huge backlog for networks as people tried to get their new sim cards connected. In Dundee, frustrated customers descended on retailers in the hope that the shops themselves would be able to help only to be told they would have no option but to be patient.

Dundee's star man would also have to be tolerant for his return to first-team action. Caniggia missed the impressive 3-0 Boxing Day away win at Motherwell following his sending off against Aberdeen. The Dark Blues, missing Caniggia, Marco de Marchi and Chris Coyne, also had to contend with freezing fog, icy patches on the pitch and the sending off of Marcello Marrocco. Juan Sara struck early and late and his double sandwiched a fine single from Gavin Rae.

It transpired Caniggia would have to wait until the new year to return to action. Dundee's next match against Dunfermline was called off 90 minutes before kick-off. The Dark Blues were unfortunately left counting the cost of the late postponement. An army of ground staff and volunteers were called in to clear snow from the pitch while the club also hired tractors and diggers to make sure the streets around Dens Park were safe. Unfortunately, despite battling for three days to keep the match on, referee Tom Brown eventually decided it couldn't go ahead because the pitch was still solid and icy in patches.

The new year started with the news that the leading explorers of land and space – including Sir Ranulph Fiennes and the director of space agency NASA – would gather in Dundee to celebrate the centenary of the ship which had started the age of scientific exploration – the RRS Discovery. A whole year of events had been organised, under the banner of 'Discovery 100', including a plan for the space shuttle Discovery to carry a piece of wood from its historic namesake into orbit.

There was just as much excitement among the Dark Blues faithful when Dundee's own rocket man, Caniggia, returned to lead the line against Hibs at Easter Road on January 2. Strike partner Juan Sara admitted before the encounter that he was playing for his first-team place with the injured Fabian Caballero scheduled to return after the winter break.

He said: "Hibs are a very strong team indeed and similar to ourselves in that they like to pass the ball about. I admire the ability of players such as (Russell) Latapy but I am sure they will also be respectful of Claudio (Caniggia) and Georgi (Nemsadze). We know what we can do and know also that this is a very important match for the club. We are going to be very strong when we get Fabian back as he is a top player and I know he will relish the chance to play alongside Caniggia. I believe they can do great things together but I am not downhearted about my own prospects as I feel I can offer different qualities to the team. You need competition at a football club and that is what we will have because in addition to the three of us, there are also the likes of Willie Falconer, Steven Milne and Beto Carranza."

He admitted it was "like a dream to play in the same team as Claudio".

"It is also very good for the team and the fans, because he is a great player who can do great things on the park," he said. "He has come here and helped all the other players become better."

The Dark Blues had lost 5-1 and 2-1 to Hibs earlier in the season. That dismal record didn't look like improving when Dundee went behind on six minutes. Steven Tweed misjudged Ulrik Laursen's high cross and Finnish striker Mixu Paatelainen was left with a free header which he dispatched without fuss.

Caniggia was Dundee's main threat throughout. He almost conjured an immediate equaliser with a fine effort from the edge of the area that goalkeeper Nick Colgan could only deflect back into play. Juan Sara followed up the loose ball but lost his footing on the slippery surface and allowed the tailing Paul Fenwick to blast the ball clear.

Dundee fell further behind on 41 minutes just as they were gaining a foothold in the game. Russell Latapy's corner found its way to David Zitelli who drove a shot towards goal. The ball hit Paul Fenwick's shin and deflected into the bottom corner.

Dundee looked impressive after the break despite being two goals down. Caniggia had Colgan scurrying across his box with a glancing header from a Beto Carranza cross before Sara had the near 2,000 travelling support up on their feet with a clever run that only just failed to beat the offside trap.

As was becoming a running theme, Dundee again failed to turn their impressive build up play into goals. They were made to pay for the third time on 69 minutes with the help of another deflection. John O'Neil made it 3-0 when his shot from 20 yards struck the legs of Barry Smith, wrong-footed Dundee goalkeeper Marco Roccati and trundled into the net.

Things got worse when Roccati twisted his knee and had to go off. He was replaced by Jamie Langfield. The Scotland under-21 international managed to impress in his short time on the park. He pulled off a great save to touch a ferocious effort from Hibs' substitute Dirk Lehmann on to the Dundee crossbar.

If one player deserved a goal it was Caniggia who never gave up. He flew past a couple of Hibs defenders on 83 minutes only to be denied again by the impressive Colgan. Hibs held on for a clean sheet and a 3-0 win in the race for a Champions League place.

"I thought we played quite well overall but paid heavily for not shutting down our opponents," said Ivano afterwards. "Hibs are a very strong side and you can't afford to give them anything at all. They only really had three chances yet have scored on each occasion."

Ivano decided to take the squad to his native Italy for a training camp during the winter break. He turned down global invitations to instead head for the likes of Saudi Arabia, Argentina and Paraguay to play glamour friendlies.

"I'm happy because I believe we have produced some high-quality football and I am happy because of the warmth of the welcome with which we have been received," Ivano said before jetting off. "Yet as I look back over the few months we have been here I must admit to feeling a little disappointed we have not achieved the standard of results I feel we are capable of. I look at the league table and I think that we should be up there with Kilmarnock, because to my mind we should have taken eight more points than we have picked up so far. We have drawn games we should have won and, in others, we have handed our opponents their victories by making silly mistakes. Of course things are not always going to go your way but the number of errors we have made is not what I consider acceptable.

"There have been some difficulties for myself and my brother Dario to deal with but that is only to be expected – it is what managers do. All along I have stressed that our aim for Dundee is not a short one. You need time to let strategies develop and, inevitably, you are going to have some setbacks to deal with. Hibernian are a great example of what I am speaking about. They have a side which has been carefully built up over a three-year period and it shows. Perhaps they have a little fortune when it comes to avoiding injuries but they deserve the success they are enjoying.

"I hope to achieve similar with our club. The squad is a good one but it can get stronger and that is what we will work towards. Some people may move on, but if they do then replacements will be brought in – players who we believe can help us get nearer our aim of becoming a third force in Scottish football."

Ivano said Caballero's impending return from injury would hopefully trigger a change of fortune. He said: "Obviously Fabian's return will be a real boost for us. Like our supporters, I am very much looking forward to seeing him link up with Claudio."

Ivano said he also wanted to get more out of the players that were currently in his team. "Beto Carranza is getting better all the time," he said. "I feel he can be a strong player for us in the year 2001. As can Gavin Rae, who is a young man with a fantastic attitude to the game. And then of course there is Claudio. He is a wonderful talent and one who should continue to bring joy to all who watch him."

Ivano suggested the 11-day-long training camp in Riccione would provide Dundee with the perfect platform for the challenge to clinch a top-six place come the SPL split in April.

Just before they got to the departure gate it emerged that Caniggia had decided he would finish his playing days at Dens Park.

Caniggia signed a new deal after the Dark Blues rejected a lucrative bid for the striker from Club America in Mexico who were prepared to pay what chief executive Peter Marr described as "serious money" for his services. However, instead of taking the immediate return on offer for a player they picked up on a short-term contract for wages only, Dundee instead decided to offer him a new extension on even better terms than the £10,000 a week he was presently being paid. Caniggia agreed a two-and-a-half year extended deal which was worth £1.5 million.

Marr said Caniggia had breathed fresh life into the Scottish Premier League. He said: "I am delighted that Claudio has chosen to extend his stay at Dundee. There is no doubt he has set the Premier League alight since his arrival and has proven that he is an undoubted world-class talent. His commitment to the club over the last three months has been outstanding, both on and off the field. This extended contract not only shows the tremendous faith we have in him but I believe it shows the faith he has in us as a club and what we are trying to achieve.

"He is happy here and, for the foreseeable future at least, here to stay. This is a massive deal for us – I am told it is easily the largest amount of money this club have ever invested in a single player. It is an undertaking we are absolutely delighted to be embarking on, though, for Claudio is a world-class talent who has done fantastically well since joining us. I am sure he would excel in any league he was playing in, whether it was Serie A or the English Premiership, and having him here has done wonders for the club's profile. Who could have imagined a few years ago that we would have the style magazine GQ coming all the way up here to do a big feature on the club? The higher profile has already generated a significant amount of revenue for us, what with the ESPN television coverage in South America and the hundreds of extra replica shirts sold.

"We believe there are some extremely exciting commercial opportunities open to us over the remainder of Claudio's time with us, opportunities we will certainly be looking to maximise. Our current shirt sponsorship deal, for example, is up in the summer and we have been holding off on agreeing a new deal, hoping to get his signature tied up, because we knew it would make a difference to the amount of money we could expect to take in."

Marr said the marketing drive would be with the blessing of Caniggia himself. "You hear a lot of things about superstars but Claudio is a genuinely nice guy who has been a pleasure to deal with from the word go," he said.

"The contract he has signed contains no get-out clause and he signed it without even involving his agent. He knows that there is a demand for anything connected with his name and has no problem with it."

Marr was able to justify the financial investment because he was aware of the risk of losing Caniggia for nothing if a bigger club did make a move for him in the summer.

Ivano was just as happy. He described Caniggia as a "wonderful talent" and immediately predicted he would perform even better for Dundee in the future when his family got settled in Scotland.

"It is not only about what he does himself, it is about the way he makes others around him perform," said Ivano. "Young Scottish players such as Steven Milne are learning so much from him and that is only to the benefit of the future of this club. I am pleased for Claudio, the club, Dundee's fans and myself that he will be staying with us. I think Claudio has shown that he still has the qualities that make him an exceptional player, but just as important he still has a big appetite for the game and for success. There is no doubt that his quality and mentality have had a positive effect on the squad. His attitude and manner make him as popular with his team-mates as he is with the fans and we are all delighted that he will be with us for a longer time. My thanks go to Peter and Jimmy Marr for making this possibility a reality."

Director Jim Connor declared it was good news not just for the team but also for the city. "We're putting our money where our mouth is," he said.

Caniggia said he still had enough gas in the tank to continue playing until he was 36. He said he was just as focused on helping to bring through the club's young talent.

"When you have played football for a long time, you learn to ignore the past and only look at what is ahead," he said. "I like the Bonetti brothers, I like the friendly atmosphere and the owner (Peter Marr) has shown himself to be a nice guy. I also like the project at Dundee, and I am sure it is one that is going to bring international recognition for this club. I had looked at all these things carefully, and it was not a spur-of-the-moment decision. I am committed to being in Scotland for the next couple of years. I don't pretend Dundee is as glamorous as some clubs I have played for and the league in Scotland is not as big as others. But for me it isn't a comfort zone. Because people will say it is a lesser league, I know they will expect me to play well every week and I want to show I still can. I am proud of my name as a footballer, and the only way I know how to keep it is by helping Dundee do good things.

"That puts me under pressure, but I have played with pressure all my career and I would not want that to change. There are areas where there is a need for improvement, but when you look at the talent you can see what we are capable of, and I want to be part of it. We will continue to get better – we can win something for the club."

Caniggia said he was getting more space to play in Scotland than in Italy which was "a very committed game in which the philosophy is never to spare yourself".

He said: "When I get to the end of my contract with Dundee I'll be 36. If I've still got enough petrol in the tank to play at this level, God knows what I'll do. If not, I'll maybe look for a quieter and less demanding league, such as the United States."

Kit man Willie Dryden was among those delighted Caniggia was staying at the club but he also warned there might not be a shirt for him when he returned to action. Caniggia tossed the one he wore on his scoring debut at Aberdeen to the crowd after the final whistle but since then he'd been obliging requests from all quarters for his tops. Despite the best efforts of kit manufacturers Xara, demand was in danger of exceeding supply and Willie was forced to step in.

"Claudio is an obliging boy and he's happy to help people when they ask for his shirts," he said. "There's just too many people wanting them, though. Xara keep them coming, but it has reached the stage where I've had to say to the club we'll have to stop or he'll not have a shirt to wear on a Saturday."

Meanwhile, Caniggia topped a festive poll held by scotsprem.com – the official Scottish Premier website – to find the player who had made the biggest impact on the SPL so far. The Argentinian pulled in more than half the votes cast and was some way ahead of Hibernian's Trinidad and Tobago international midfielder Russell Latapy, who was second.

Beto Carranza wasn't to be left in the shadow of his fellow countryman however and was awarded the accolade of scoring the best goal of 2000 in South America. The former Boca Juniors and Racing Club player collected the silver salver from representatives of the TV channel Fox Sports Network in a ceremony in Buenos Aires. Carranza ran the length of the field, beating several defenders, before driving the ball past Lincoln Mosquera, while playing for Universitario Deportes of Peru at Union Minas.

The new year also brought sensational rumours that Diego Maradona would arrive in the city to line up alongside Caniggia in a Dundee shirt in a glamour friendly. It was already well known that Maradona had been following the progress of Dundee since his friend and former team-mate arrived at Dens in October. There were reports that during their regular telephone conversations the pair had hit on the idea of the partnership that had steered Argentina to the final of the 1990 World Cup being reawakened in Scotland for one game only against one of Maradona's former clubs, Italian giants Napoli.

A club spokesman said: "I can confirm there was written correspondence between Diego Maradona, his representatives and Dundee Football Club which outline both parties' desire for Diego to play in a one-off glamour friendly for Dundee. We hope to settle upon other details such as date and time of game within the next few days, but it's increasingly likely that any match involving Maradona

will take place at Dens Park. That is obviously great news for Dundee fans."
He said the terms agreed between Maradona and Dundee FC would remain "a
confidential matter between both parties" although reports suggested he would be
paid a quarter of a million to play.

"To be precise, Diego suggested it and I said I'd arrange it," said Caniggia.
"He's now looking after himself – in Cuba most of the time – and I was pleased to
find him in good shape. I know Diego like no one else does and he's a very nice
guy."

Peter Marr said he was excited at the prospect of seeing Maradona pull on a
Dark Blue jersey but stressed the long-term aims would still take priority at Dens.

"Ivano's ambition is to be challenging for a place in the top three, and we
now believe that is something we can achieve," he said. "Already we've got
the fans coming to Dens expecting to see something spectacular every time we
play and, as well as getting back to the kind of good football that Dundee were
always known for, I think we can have a winning team as well. What Jimmy and I
are doing is taking a gamble. It is not one we expect to make a profit from, but we
do believe that in the long term we can get our money back – I think the interest
that we have generated this season shows that. Against Aberdeen just before
Christmas we had 7,000 Dundee fans inside Dens Park, and crowds like that are
very encouraging. I don't for a minute believe we can get back to the kind of
crowds the club was getting in the sixties, but I do believe we can get even more
coming through the turnstiles."

The prospect of Maradona arriving from Havana to turn out at Dens
unsurprisingly made headlines around the world.

"This will give the city the profile we've been striving for," said Colin Smith,
the chief executive of Dundee's tourist board. "It's pretty gobsmacking. Dundee is
always known as the city with the two football clubs on the same street, but this is
incredible."

Former Lord Provost and Stobswell councillor Mervyn Rolfe said the friendly
match would be "a morale-booster for the city". He said: "The eyes of the world
will be on us and the attention can only be good."

But just a day later the Dark Blues were brought crashing back down to earth.
Maradona stepped off a plane in Italy and straight into the middle of a tax fraud
scandal. Police were waiting at Fiumicino airport in Rome where they informed
him that he was being investigated for an alleged tax fraud of around £16.6m.

"It is always the same story when I come back to Italy," Maradona told
Radio Mitre of Buenos Aires. "I have not got the money on me at the moment.
I am fine and I want to reassure my mother, my daughters and the people of
Argentina. Of course people are trying to make this into a big deal but it is just
a storm in a teacup."

Maradona had travelled to Italy to appear on television shows. He was also there to unveil a limited-edition coin engraved with his image and continue his negotiations with Napoli about a potential return in a management role.

A Dundee spokesman later admitted he was just as surprised and shocked as everyone else at the welcoming party Maradona received on his arrival in Rome. He said the conclusion of the fraud probe being carried out by the Italian authorities was just one of a number of "significant factors" that might derail the showcase match. He continued: "Dundee FC has said all along that the proposed friendly between ourselves and Napoli at Dens Park, with Maradona taking part, is not set in stone. That said, we do have an arrangement with him that he will turn out in a Dundee FC shirt at some point and we still expect that to take place."

However, Ivano suggested that the chances of Maradona turning out in a Dundee shirt before the end of the season had been blown out of the water.

"What has happened is that we have spoken to Diego and he has said he will play, but a game with him would have to be special, with quality opposition," he said. "We have not been able to arrange something with a big-name team so I do not see a game being played this season, and it is important for now we say it is finished. If it happens it will be in the future, and once it is arranged, we should talk about it then. We should not keep speaking about it now, as we must concentrate on what is to come in the league and cup because that is most important. We have big games coming up, and we must be ready for them and not be distracted by anything."

Maradona's chances of turning out for Dundee might have been looking slim but a sensational bid to bring another global superstar to the city was now creating just as many headlines. Dundee University students Benni Esposito and Graham Phillips were behind the bid to "put the city on the map" by bringing the world's most watched television star to Dundee.

Benni and Graham – of Edinburgh Fringe comedy fame, you'll recall – had been heavily criticised the previous summer for talking down Dundee. Now the two were attempting to make amends by launching the seemingly unlikely bid to get Knight Rider and Baywatch star David Hasselhoff to become the university's rector. They spoke of their dream of Hasselhoff giving surfing lessons on Broughty Ferry beach and his low-budget made-for-TV movies like Gridlock and Avalanche being shown in Dundee cinemas.

"David Hasselhoff is a legend," said Graham. "He is seen on TV by 1.1 billion people in 244 countries round the world. We know Diego Maradona may play a football match in Dundee and that Claudio Caniggia is here already. David Hasselhoff being the rector of Dundee University would be the best thing of all."

Within weeks Hoff Fever had taken off. There was a Knight Rider comedy show taking place in a city pub and Benni even decided to audition on TV show Stars in their Eyes as Hasselhoff...singing in German. They somehow managed to get enough nominations at the university. Hasselhoff ended up on the ballot paper alongside Fred MacAulay, Richard Whiteley, MSP Nick Johnston and Islamic academic Dr Abd-al-Fattah El-Awaisi. There was speculation the whole thing was a hoax until Hasselhoff described the nomination as "a great personal honour" but one he eventually turned down due to his work schedule.

Dundee were proving just as popular whilst staying in Riccione during their training camp with local journalists and Italian TV crews in attendance throughout the visit. The Dark Blues were boosted by the news that midfielder Gavin Rae wanted to sign an extended deal despite being watched by scouts from the English top flight before Christmas.

"The Premiership is one of the best leagues around and, like a lot of players, I'd love to play in it – but there are not many teams who have players like Georgi Nemsadze and Claudio Caniggia playing for them," he said. "I am enjoying playing with them and the team as a whole has gelled well. I'd say this is my most enjoyable season so far. If I sign a new deal it would take me until I was 26 and, if I was doing well enough, I'd still have time to move to England when I was reaching my peak."

At their training camp in Italy, Ivano said he was delighted with the way his players had adapted to his training methods which were used to great effect by Juventus.

"When my brother Dario and myself took over we intended making many changes, but we realised we could not put them all in place immediately," he said. "Now we have made some and in the future we will be making more, because it is important that we go with what we are comfortable with and with the things we know have worked for us. We must be pleased with our progress so far, because we said this season we believed sixth would be success, and we are sixth.

"Still, when I look at some games, I think we could have had many more points than we have now. I do not get annoyed, though, as I know we are a new team and there would be times we made mistakes. However, the quality is there and we are improving, so I feel happy when I look to the future. People do need time to get familiar with a new country and a new league. Scottish football is certainly very different from most other leagues my players have played in. However, they need time to become used to each other. That has been happening, and having everyone together in Riccione this week has helped. We have great talent like Caniggia, Nemsadze and Carranza in our group, and players now know when they like the ball, how they like the ball and the things they do when they have it."

Ivano predicted Beto Carranza would emerge as a key figure over the next few months and the Argentine said he was enjoying playing alongside his former Boca Juniors team-mate. Carranza said the publicity Caniggia had received since arriving in the SPL was nothing compared to the hype each time he goes back to Argentina.

"In Argentina there has only ever been one footballer who has been loved more than Claudio and that is Maradona," said Carranza. "Great players like Batistuta are very popular, but Claudio and Maradona are loved. Myself and the other Argentinian players know this and it is a very big thing for us to play in the same team. Claudio is a nice guy, but in Buenos Aires I did not spend much time with him away from training.

"In Dundee we see each other a lot and get on very well. Most of Dundee's games are shown in Argentina and it has been very easy for my family and friends to follow what has been happening. I would think the national coach watches, too, but I am not thinking about that. All I want to do is make sure I play for Dundee each week. I think in some games so far I have played well, but I know I can do even better and would like to show that in the coming months."

The only match Dundee played during their break was a 5-1 win against local conference side AC Riccione which saw everyone with the exclusion of the manager, goalkeeper Marco Roccati and injured pair Juan Sara and Marco de Marchi, given a run out.

Dundee opened the scoring on 14 minutes when Javier Artero made use of space on the right. Artero's low cross was turned in by Stevie Milne. Three minutes later a Gavin Rae cross was prodded home by Caniggia for number two. Steven Tweed, Beto Carranza and Artero were all then denied by terrific stops from teenage goalkeeper Simone Santolini. Eight minutes into the second half Milne rounded the keeper for the third goal. Dundee moved further clear when a Georgi Nemsadze pass released teenager Marco Russo who rounded Santolini to score. The Dundee scoring was completed on 70 minutes. Australian defender Chris Coyne ran fully 70 yards before setting up Willie Falconer, who lashed the ball home from 14 yards. Dario Merendino grabbed a deserved consolation with two minutes left to ensure the home players did not go completely unrewarded for their efforts.

Caniggia said he was enjoying getting away from the weather in Dundee but admitted he was a big fan of the Scottish game and the mentality of the players in it. "In big leagues like Italy and Spain, there is more quality and the football is very technical and more complicated tactically," he said. "However, there is not much space for you to move into where you can hurt teams and very often games are played in midfield.

"In Scottish and English football it is different. Teams want to attack and that means there can be more space, so the football is much more entertaining. I am sure that is good for the fans and it is good to play in. Also, I like the way the teams approach the game. In other countries many games are over when a team scores the first goal. In Scotland you can be 2-0 up or 2-0 down with just minutes left, but you know the game is not over until the 90 minutes are up.

"That is a good thing. I myself only know one way to play-that is by giving 100% in every game. I like playing in a league where I know most players are that way too."

Caniggia said he was enjoying being one of the elder statesmen of the Dundee team. He said: "When I was young I liked playing with experienced players and learning good things from them. Now I am one of those experienced players I enjoy passing on these things and being able to guide the young players. I know I am an older player now, but I feel good and fit and I believe in my ability. It was relatively easy to sign my contract, but I thought everything through before signing and I am committed to being here. The only thing I do not like much about Scotland is the weather, but that is not something that will make me turn round in several months and say I cannot cope."

The Dark Blues then flew back to Scotland from Bologna. Their first game after the three-week interval was what appeared to be a favourable home tie against First Division Falkirk in the third-round of the Scottish Cup.

Before the match Ivano spoke of his desire to ensure that his first appearance in the national cup competition was as successful as his English FA Cup debut had been in 1996. The mercurial Italian was already wowing the fans at Grimsby with his silky wing play when he became the first Italian to score in the competition as the Mariners ran out 7-1 winners against Luton Town. Ivano said his painful experience of giant-killings would also ensure there was no complacency.

"When I was a player with Juventus we lost in the Italian Cup to Cagliari, who were then only a Serie B side," he said. "It was not something I enjoyed and I have already told the players we want to do as well as possible in the Scottish Cup."

He said he was also aware cup football was held in higher regard in Scotland than in Italy. "Now it is bigger in Italy than it was, but it is not as important as in Scotland," he said. "If a team is doing well in Serie A, they may not pay much attention to their cup-tie. I know the team has lost to teams from lower divisions in the last two seasons, so it would be nice to go far in the competition this time.

"To do that, we must play to our potential because I know Falkirk have good players and a cup tradition. They have been to quarter-finals, semi-finals and even the final in recent years, so they have the quality to beat bigger sides.

"They also have the advantage of playing games in recent weeks while we have been on the break, so this is a hard match for us, but one we can win."

Kevin McAllister – the man Falkirk boss Alex Totten had dubbed the First Division's Claudio Caniggia – predicted before the match that the Argentine superstar would only improve with age having turned 34 on January 9.

The 38-year-old McAllister also described Caniggia as "an international class" player. McAllister went on: "He's been an exceptional signing for Dundee. At 34 he is playing fantastic football and I see no reason why he can't get even better still in the months and years to come. As you get older you have to adapt your game a little – my own days of picking up the ball wide and beating nine players on a mazy run are long gone. That doesn't mean you can't be just as effective by using your brain and your experience. In the end I think it is all down to the individual – whether he has the necessary appetite and desire to keep on trying to improve.

"From what I have seen of him, Caniggia possesses both in abundance. He looks to be in great physical shape and is still very quick over short distances. In addition, he has excellent awareness of everything that is going on around him."

Ivano confirmed Caniggia would be a definite starter against Falkirk. The choice of second striker went to 20-year-old Stevie Milne who was emerging as an exciting prospect following a year spent on loan at Forfar.

But things didn't quite go to plan at Dens as the Bairns proved to be rather a tough nut to crack.

On 16 minutes Caniggia worked a clever one-two with Stevie Milne. His attempt from just eight yards looked like giving Dundee the lead until Falkirk goalkeeper Myles Hogarth got a hand to it.

After the break, Dundee's quality began to tell. They dominated proceedings and should have gone ahead when a Shaun McSkimming pull-back found Caniggia, but the resultant effort was blocked. Falkirk hung on in the face of intense second-half pressure being dished out by Dundee. The home team continued to push forward in search of a winner but Hogarth made sure the tie finished goalless with a string of stunning saves.

Delighted Falkirk boss Alex Totten heaped praise on his young central defender, Steve Rennie, following the match. "Although ours was a very good performance all round, young Steven's display was exceptional, in that it was against a player of the quality of Claudio Caniggia," he said. "As far as the tie is concerned we have now got Dundee back at Brockville, where we get the opportunity to finish them off."

Falkirk goalkeeper Myles Hogarth said afterwards that he was looking forward to welcoming Caniggia to Brockville for the replay. Having housed Falkirk since 1885 – and posted a record attendance of 23,100 for a match against Celtic in 1953 – the ground had fallen into a state of some disrepair. Brockville was crumbling and looked like something from the dark ages.

"It should be fun to see his face when he sees the ground," said Hogarth. "He is a very, very good player who is used to performing in the world's great stadia. No matter how generous you want to be I don't think you could describe Brockville in those terms. I am not just speaking about Caniggia either – a few of the Dundee players could be in for a bit of a shock because it is not the most modern of grounds."

Caniggia then came in for harsh criticism when he went looking for a home in Edinburgh. Caniggia started house hunting in Edinburgh because he wanted his children – two boys and a girl – to be educated at a school which specialised in either Italian or Spanish, the two languages his family used. As well as searching for a property in the capital, he was also looking for a flat in Dundee where he would stay several nights a week.

Maggie Lennon, of the Chamber of Commerce and Industry in Dundee, said: "I think that it's outrageous. If people are making their living in a city then they should consider putting as much of their wealth back into the area as possible."

Dundee City Council's economic development convener, Councillor Mervyn Rolfe, said: "I think that whoever has made the decision to live in Edinburgh – whether it is Caniggia or his wife – hasn't given Dundee a chance. It's a wonderful city without having all of the troubles of a big centre. It's close to the Highlands, it has six flights to London every day, it has a strong arts community and, of course, there is the beautiful Tay."

Ivano was disappointed to learn there was criticism of Caniggia's decision and explained the striker was also looking for a flat in the City of Discovery.

"Like any parent, Claudio has to do what is best for his children and their education," he said. "That is why he will buy a house in Edinburgh, but he also wants a place here where he will spend part of the week."

He pointed out that Caniggia's decision to have two homes in Scotland was his own because club rules would have allowed him to live in Edinburgh.

"My captain (Barry Smith) lives in Glasgow and drives here," he said. "No-one would question his commitment. Also, in Italy it is normal for players to stay outside of the town where they play. Brescia is the town of my birth, but when I played for them I lived in Milan."

Caniggia did find a home in the pages of The Beano. His legendary status was immortalised when he was given the alter-ego of a posing mummy's boy character in the longest-running British children's comic magazine. The comic's newest superstar's appearance was described as being a tribute to the Caniggia fever which had raged through Dundee since he signed for the club in October.

"Claudio Poserello" had signed up for Beanotown United, with a storyline suggesting he didn't care for Scotland's waterlogged pitches: "Poserello no want to get ze tootsies wet".

When a hot air dryer blasted his flowing locks revealing he was actually bald, the striker suffered a Latin hot flush "and wants to go home to his mama". Beano editor and Dundee United fan Euan Kerr said: "Everyone knows how there has been Caniggia fever in Dundee and the fans are wearing the wigs, and although we don't name him, it is all very tongue in cheek. It's inspired by Caniggia's presence in Dundee and all of the publicity surrounding him which we can't ignore."

Euan said he was sure no offence would be taken within Dens Park, although he conceded it was doubtful if the great man himself bought The Beano.

A spokesman for Dundee FC said: "A spot in The Beano is better than a waxwork at Madame Tussauds. Claudio's superstar status is assured. As a club, we do suspect the hand of a Dundee United fan in all this, but Claudio and everyone else at Dens is having a good laugh and enjoying reading the comic this week."

The city's own transformation into a vibrant shopping and commercial centre over the past decade was also being recognised that week at an awards ceremony in London. Dundee beat off stiff competition from 19 other urban regeneration projects from throughout the UK to win the Royal Town Planning Institute's prestigious Urban Renaissance award. The judges were impressed by the way Dundee planners had "taken the view that change could not happen overnight" whilst recognising that the "planning process takes time".

Dundee United were hoping to transform their own stuttering fortunes when they made the trip across the road for a Dundee derby to be played out under the floodlights at Dens.

The Dark Blues had lost Fabian Caballero to a long-term knee injury following a bad tackle when the sides last met at Dens in September and relations were slightly strained. The tackle was an incident which provoked Ivano into labelling United as the dirtiest team he had ever faced in his long professional career.

Before the match Ivano was guilty of whipping up further ill-feeling by calling on referee Willie Young to afford more protection for his players after "what has happened in the past".

"This is an important issue for us because we like to play good football and have a few players of real skill, with Caniggia the obvious example," he said. "I was worried for Fabian before he got injured and I have similar concerns for Claudio, who puts himself at some risk because of the way he runs with the ball at pace.

"There were three or four tackles in the Falkirk match that I felt merited at least a yellow card. If a player is injured as a result of an accident there is nothing you can do, but if it is something else…

"Provided the referee is strong and shows personality there should not be a problem."

It was perhaps not surprising that the man who was the victim of arguably the World Cup's worst ever tackle backed his manager's call for more protection. Caniggia said he believed he could come in for some "special attention" against United. Dundee fans were quick to remind their opponents of what had happened the last time they came to Dens. Before the match they taunted the United fans with a chorus of: "Juan Sara, Sara, whatever will be, will be, he gave United three, Juan Sara, Sara".

As it turned out, United pulled off a win against the odds. They ended a run of three straight defeats against Dundee with what was their first away win in the SPL since the previous April to move off the foot of the table.

United started brightly and had the best of the early chances. They had a penalty claim denied when Charlie Miller claimed he had been clipped in the box by Steven Tweed but referee Willie Young waved play on. Hugh Davidson put United ahead after 34 minutes before Dundee levelled things up. Javier Artero's perfect delivery on the stroke of half-time was met by Caniggia who fired home from two yards.

With the second period just a minute old, United crept back in front. A Jamie Buchan through ball found Craig Easton racing into the area and he fired high past Marco Roccati for his fourth goal of the campaign. With 78 minutes gone the visitors wrapped up the points. Jim Lauchlan was on hand to score his third goal in two games. Willie Falconer pulled one back for Dundee two minutes from time when he finished off a terrific cross from Caniggia with a looping header. However, it was to prove too little too late for the Dark Blues.

After the match, battle lines were drawn when United boss Alex Smith took a pop at Ivano. The wily old fox couldn't resist making mention of Ivano's claim after the stormy first meeting of the clubs earlier in the season that United were the dirtiest team he had come across.

"We won convincingly with a performance which from the first minute to the last was almost complete," said Smith. "Things were said about us earlier in the season which were unjust and unfair but there was no sign of any malice or need to be physical tonight. We proved that we can play – every dog has his day."

United's Beto Naveda played the closing minutes of the 3-2 success as a substitute. He said that what he had seen from the bench from Caniggia had left him impressed.

"It was a quality performance and as an Argentinian I know that it is not often a team with two players as good as Claudio Caniggia and Beto Carranza are as well beaten as this," he said. "But for the special things Claudio did, I think we would have won without losing a goal."

Dens number two Dario Bonetti had to speak to reporters after the match after Ivano had to hop his way back to the dressing room at full-time. Ivano's appearance as a second-half substitute was over after just seven minutes when a calf injury developed into a full tear which would likely rule him out for the rest of the season.

Dario praised the United players' attitude but criticised his own team.

"We have been unfortunate recently with injuries but that had nothing to do with this result," he said. "We lost because we played badly and had the wrong mental attitude and lacked ideas."

The winter chill was showing no signs of abating.

CHAPTER SIX

No Tears Before Bedtime
At Brockville

*This is the mark of the man. No one at the club put
any pressure on Claudio. He made the decision
entirely off his own back.*

Peter Marr

A PLAYER sent off for spreading the word of God; a £1 million gamble on a
Scottish Cup third-round replay against Falkirk; and fire crews rushing to the
stadium as an electrical fault risked a power failure.

Life was certainly never dull playing for Dundee in those days.

Things went from bad to worse following the derby defeat when Juan Sara was
sent packing just 34 minutes into the Dark Blues match against St Mirren at the start
of February. With Claudio Caniggia in menacing form, Dundee were immediately
in control and creating chances with regularity from the first whistle. Sara missed an
open goal on nine minutes but made amends for his error in spectacular style when
he sent an overhead kick into the net on 23 minutes.

The Argentinian, as he had done numerous times since signing for Dundee, ran
away to celebrate and pulled up his top to reveal a T-shirt bearing the message: "I can
do everything through Christ."

Messages on the T-shirts were part of Sara's life but the FIFA rules stopped
players from taking off their tops when celebrating a goal. The referee duly booked
him. Sara's misery was compounded 10 minutes later. The referee judged he had
deliberately handled the ball when attempting to challenge Tommy Turner and he
was shown a second yellow card and ordered off.

The Dark Blues, who had looked well on their way to a fairly relaxed victory,
ended up losing 2-1 after going down in personnel. The Buddies, who had rarely
troubled Marco Roccati's goal until that point, were transformed following the
sending off and came surging back into the game. Iain Nicholson saw his shot from
eight yards deflected on to the post and behind by Roccati. Chris Kerr curled the
resultant corner deep into the box. The ball came off Georgi Nemsadze and fell into
the path of Paul Rudden who stabbed home a leveller after 41 minutes. Dundee came
close to reclaiming the lead in the second half when Nemsadze found Caniggia. The
Argentine flicked a delightful back-heel to Javier Artero whose shot flew inches over

the crossbar. Deep into the second half, St Mirren made Dundee pay. A ferocious drive from Chris Kerr was deflected on to the bar by Roccati's outstretched arm. The ball came back into the path of St Mirren's French trialist Moussa Dagnogo, who fired home the second after 84 minutes.

"I am not happy with Sara but the problem is that he never killed anybody, he just showed the shirt," said Ivano afterwards. "What is the problem with the shirt? If we can't celebrate when we score then we ought everybody to stay at home."

That was the public stance. Privately, however, Ivano and Dario both had a few choice words for Sara afterwards. They told him to immediately stop doing it as it was no good to him or the club.

Team-mate Gavin Rae had a degree of sympathy for Sara, despite the red card heavily contributing to what was Dundee's third consecutive Paisley defeat. "St Mirren were not really in the game until then and it all seemed to turn on the sending-off," said Rae. "He believes in God – that's what he follows. It was not a gesture to their fans but the ref has chosen to book him for going to the opposition support. I tried to explain to him (the referee) that there was nothing sinister on the T-shirt – it's just his beliefs. He tries to spread the word. He did it before and didn't get booked. He went to the Rangers end after scoring against them and the referee just waved him back and told him to behave himself. He is not the sort of person who would do anything to upset opposing fans but this time he was booked and it ended up costing us dearly."

When he emerged from the dressing room afterwards to speak to the press, it was clear that the incident had deeply affected Sara.

"I didn't understand why I got a yellow for showing the T-shirt," he said. "It may have been (aimed) at St Mirren fans but it's my message for everybody. I (will) do it again. Yes, I forgive (the referee) but still I will continue to wear the T-shirt. The manager was upset but it's normal because we finished with only 10 players. The first 30 minutes we did very well but were not very good with just 10. I want to put it behind me now and play on Tuesday because we have a very important game versus Falkirk."

But with Brockville under two inches of snow, the replay was postponed until the following Monday. The freeze also affected Dundee's training schedule, with all work being done in the gym.

Tayside was among the worst hit areas as wintry weather battered much of Britain. The cold snap brought chaos to the roads, school closures and power cuts as the weather damaged power cables and knocked out the electricity to 410 homes in the city. Ice and snow drifts of up to 20 feet closed a number of major roads with police advising drivers only to make essential journeys. An army of gritters, snowploughs and snow cutters were out in force across Dundee.

A TV crew from TV's Football Italia show arrived in the area while Dundee was six inches deep in snow. Dundee's Italian connections ensured both the club and the city were put under the media microscope. Fans were sought out in the chilly conditions to give their opinions of the goings-on at Dens. Ivano and Caniggia were interviewed for the popular Channel 4 programme by the show's Benito Montorio.

"Our interest was sparked by the fact that Ivano and his brother Dario are former Serie A stars, and of course there is Caniggia," said Montorio.

Dundee's next home league match against Hearts was eventually postponed after the Dens Park inflatable dome failed to make any impression on the snow-covered surface. "Now we are thinking about the cup match," said Ivano. "It is always a disappointment when a game is called off but we will be training instead and preparing for Monday."

The Dark Blues had to pick themselves up for the replay against Falkirk.

Caniggia took a £1 million gamble to make sure he could play by insisting a court case in his native Argentina be deferred. The striker was battling to win £500,000 in unpaid wages but would also be accountable for a further six-figure fee in legal costs if he lost. Dundee had lost his services for the match at Kilmarnock and the latest hearing had been held back in the expectation of Dundee not having a midweek game. The replay put a spanner in the works and Caniggia got in touch with his legal team in Argentina to get the date put back further in order to play against Falkirk.

"As soon as I realised it clashed with the Falkirk replay, I demanded my legal team get the date altered," Caniggia said. "I know how much the cup means to Dundee and our fans. I was determined not to miss the game, especially as we have so many players injured."

Dundee chief executive Peter Marr said: "This is the mark of the man. No one at the club put any pressure on Claudio. He made the decision entirely off his own back."

Before the match Javier Artero said the ability to fight together as a unit would be given priority over individual brilliance as the Dark Blues aimed to halt their losing streak.

"The important thing is to play as a team and then we can maybe think about Claudio, Beto, Juan, myself or another doing something special," said Artero. "We must all fight for one another because this is a very important match for the club. We are aiming to get into the top six in the league but the cup is also important. I think it will be a very difficult match as they had one or two chances during the first game at Dens and overall are a very strong team. However, we are the Premier League side and we must win."

Caniggia's big-money gamble ultimately paid off. Dundee finally returned to winning ways with a 2-0 victory with Caniggia scoring the second.

However, it later emerged the replay at Brockville was under threat of being abandoned not long after getting under way because of a fault related to the electricity supply. The fault appeared around 15 minutes after the game started. An emergency electrician from Scottish Power and fire crews rushed to the scene. Unknown to the 6,000 fans packed into the stadium, both were placed on standby and remained outside the ground for a full two hours.

Luckily the power kept flowing but if there had been any danger the electrician would have immediately cut the main fuse which supplied the power for the ground's floodlights. The lights stayed on throughout but when the match started it was abundantly clear that some parts of the pitch were noticeably darker than others. San Siro in the sun on the opening day of the 1990 World Cup this wasn't.

But Caniggia and his Dundee team-mates played through the eerie conditions to earn a fourth round trip to Tynecastle five days later despite leaving it late. Both defences remained in the ascendency during a sluggish first half before Dundee almost grabbed the opener three minutes after the restart. A Beto Carranza cross found Caniggia in the area but he was thwarted by Steven Rennie who cleared the danger.

Sara made amends for his sending off at St Mirren with his 12th goal of the season. He forced home convincingly from four yards from a deflected Caniggia corner on 72 minutes although, unsurprisingly, his goal celebrations this time involved keeping his shirt on.

Six minutes from the end, Caniggia made certain the scoreline gave a fairer reflection of Dundee's supremacy. He converted a chance that was all down to magic from Javier Artero. Showing his electric pace and intelligence, the Spanish ace ran 60 yards, bouncing past two tackles in the process, to set up Caniggia who ensured his young son went to bed happy. Alexander was watching on from the directors' box alongside Dario who was on babysitting duties and he took to his feet after watching dad score number two with a classy finish. Caniggia left the pitch after his goal to a standing ovation to be replaced by Stevie Milne.

Dundee defender Chris Coyne admitted afterwards that the Brockville lights had made things difficult at a dilapidated venue which continued to deny Falkirk any prospect of promotion. "I've played in places like that down south, so Brockville wasn't a problem for me," he said. "In my time at West Ham I turned out in the Combination League at the likes of Dagenham, Woking and Sutton and although the lights at Falkirk were difficult, in that it was pretty dark in the corners, you adjusted."

Ivano then confirmed his club's interest in signing Bradford City's out-of-favour Italian striker Benito Carbone on loan until the end of the season. "I have spoken to Benito, who I know from when I was playing against him in Italy seven years ago, and I would like to bring him here," he said. "But being realistic there is only a 20% chance of this happening because there is big finance involved. If we can find a way of doing it we will, if not it is just a dream. At this stage it is just an idea. It is very early to speak about it. But we will see."

Dundee would have had to pay a huge slice of Carbone's £32,000-a-week wages to get him to move north and team up with Caniggia.

The club then won the backing of the SPL when they applied to play in the Intertoto Cup. The much-maligned tournament was a summer football competition for European clubs that had not qualified for one of the major UEFA competitions.

"We welcome wholeheartedly the news that Dundee Football Club has applied for entry to the Intertoto," said an SPL spokesperson. "It is important that as many of our clubs reach the European stage as possible and we wish them all the best. The Intertoto Cup is a great opportunity for Dundee as in the past we have seen successful clubs progress to the latter stages of the UEFA Cup and even the Champions League."

Although the Intertoto offered three places in the UEFA Cup proper, it was usually shunned by teams in Scotland because it forced them to cut their summer short in order to take part. The Dark Blues had not been involved in a European campaign since 1974 and Ivano stressed the sacrifice of time on the beach would be worthwhile.

"This is a great opportunity for players and fans to see other European teams come and play at Dens Park," he said.

European football was coming to Dundee. But in the same week it was announced that Hollywood movies would no longer be shown at the city's Odeon multiplex in Lochee. The Odeon at the struggling Stack Leisure Park was closing due to a lack of trade which wasn't being helped by the opening of a new cinema complex at Camperdown. The cinema had opened in 1993 and was part of an urban regeneration programme. The leisure park replaced a part of Lochee which was previously dominated by the former Camperdown Works jute mill which at one time was the largest in the world. The jute mill was turned into housing and Cox's Stack – one of the remaining relics of Dundee's once buoyant jute industry – was the landmark feature of the complex. The chimney stalk could, and still can, be seen from almost any point in the city.

Dundee travelled to Tynecastle for the fourth round Scottish Cup encounter in confident mood that they wouldn't produce their own video nasty against Hearts.

There was a minor doubt over the involvement of Caniggia who had picked up a knock against Falkirk but he started despite making little impact on proceedings. The Dark Blues were also boosted before the match by the news that Argentine pair Juan Sara and Fabian Caballero had agreed in principle to extend their stay at the club.

Things started well when Juan Sara's first-half strike put Dundee ahead. Steven Tweed and Caniggia had combined in the air to direct a Beto Carranza free-kick into Sara's path and he beat Antti Niemi with a fierce shot from just eight yards. Hearts went straight up the park and were rewarded when Italian defender Marcello Marrocco pulled down former Dundee player Steven Boyack. The referee pointed to the spot but Marco Roccati brilliantly saved Colin Cameron's spot kick and Stephane Adam's rebound.

Suddenly it looked like luck might finally be on Dundee's side.

Dundee survived most of a second-half onslaught from the home side. But just when it looked like they might escape with the win they eventually came unstuck when former Barcelona winger Juanjo equalised with just nine minutes remaining. Juanjo miskicked completely with his first effort but he managed to regain control and hammer in a shot that left Roccati with no chance. A draw meant they would have to do it all again at Dens Park.

"I was very happy with our lead at half-time and the fact we had created some chances against a strong team shows we are heading in the right direction," said Ivano afterwards. "In the second half, Hearts did come back strongly, but this is a special competition and you would expect this. It is good that we have another game and it can also be a very special one for the fans."

Goalkeeper Roccati revealed after the match that his Tynecastle heroics were just the latest in a string of spot-kick saves.

He told reporters that in one season alone in Italy's top flight he had stopped five penalties. "My first-ever game in Serie A was for Empoli and, that day, I saved a penalty taken by the Italian international Beppe Signori," he said. "Before that, he had never missed in 36 kicks as a professional. I have saved from other big stars in Italy and when there is a penalty against me, I believe I have a good chance to save it."

For the second time in a fortnight, Caniggia risked a fortune by refusing to miss a game to continue his protracted legal battle for unpaid wages with Boca Juniors in Argentina. Caniggia successfully attained another court adjournment. He managed to get the next round of his legal fight held back until the week of Scotland's World Cup qualifier against Belgium when no club games were scheduled. The postponement also allowed Caniggia to play in the midweek SPL clash with Dunfermline at Dens, which had been rescheduled from December 30.

The news was a huge boost to Ivano whose lack of available bodies had given him a major selection headache. Juan Sara, Steven Tweed and Georgi Nemsadze were all suspended. Shaun McSkimming was injured, Alessandro Romano was a doubt and Beto Carranza and Marcello Marrocco would both have to undergo fitness checks before the match.

Bodies were also dropping that week among the city's feline population. Cat owners in Dundee were on red alert following the poisoning of a cat in the Craigie area, two years after the owners of the pet lost four cats at the hands of a callous poisoner.

There was also an investigation at Dens into the fitness of defender Marco de Marchi which ended Dundee's interest in Bradford's Italian striker Benito Carbone. The move to bring Carbone to the club went up in smoke after de Marchi – who had played just once since early December – declared himself unavailable for selection against Dunfermline. "Our physio says Marco is okay and he has worked with us for the last two days, but he says he is not ready and I have to believe him," said Ivano.

Relations between the pair were somewhat frosty. Ivano was already on record stating that if de Marchi was still injured he would be forced to sign another central defender. De Marchi's withdrawal from the Dunfermline match prompted Ivano to intensify his search for a new defensive face at the expense of any slight chance of Carbone ending up at Dens.

"The Carbone idea is finished for now," said Ivano. "We cannot go through with it at the moment. I need to look for other players and at the back is the area that it is most important we strengthen."

Caniggia wasn't fully fit but played through the pain barrier once again. He took his place as part of a front three alongside Stevie Milne and Willie Falconer.

Dunfermline had the best of the early pressure and opened the scoring on 12 minutes. Dundee's run of misfortune in the league was summed up by Barry Nicholson's goal. Scott Thomson laid the ball into the path of Nicholson at the edge of the Dundee box. The midfielder's snap shot deflected off the legs of Marrocco and beyond Roccati in goal. Dundee had gone into the match missing eight first-team players through injury and suspension. They suffered a further dose of bad luck during the match when Beto Carranza, Stevie Milne and Marcello Marrocco all had to come off. There was also a further injury when referee Tom Brown had to retire. The whistler sprained his wrist after being struck by a fiercely hit shot from a Dunfermline player and his place was taken by fourth official Colin Hardie. Carranza and Milne, both clearly struggling, had gone off just before the interval, to be replaced by Lee Wilkie and Michael Yates, which made for an unfamiliar-looking Dundee midfield.

But stop-gap midfielder Wilkie almost rescued a point. He headed over from a Javier Artero cross before going even closer after hitting the side netting when a fine through ball from Caniggia put him in on goal.

With Lady Luck clearly absent, Ivano was struggling to stay upbeat. He said: "So many injuries, so much bad luck, it is hard for me to know what to say to my players. The situation was bad enough anyway and then we go and lose two players early on and have a third get to the stage where he is only able to play at a fraction of his capabilities. There was some skill from my players but for me there was very little quality in the game and it was disappointing. Steven Milne will definitely miss the Rangers game, as will Alessandro Romano, who has had to return to Italy with a recurrence of his problem (pancreatitis). That is obviously a big blow for us because it is a serious condition but I will carry on giving the young players the chance to show what they can do. People ask me why I have not recalled Patrizio Billio and there are many reasons for this, some which I cannot say because it would not be fair to the player. The fact is Patrizio is on the transfer list and, even in the situation we are in just now, there are other players I wish to play ahead of him. This result obviously makes it harder for us to finish in the top six but we can still do it and are not looking at failure as a possibility."

The busy treatment table was not the best preparation for the visit of Rangers. The desperate situation in terms of boots on the ground was underlined by the signing of well-travelled free agent Beto Garrido on a short-term contract. A former team-mate of Caniggia, Beto Carranza and Walter del Rio at Boca Juniors, the 26-year-old midfielder had found his way to Dundee from Argentina following spells in France, Italy and Spain.

"The chance to come and play football alongside Claudio Caniggia and the others was a big draw for me and I hope to be able to win myself the offer of a longer contract," he said. "Thanks to ESPN I have seen quite a lot of Scottish football and Dundee in particular and am confident that my style will suit the game in this country."

Before the match Dundee chief executive Peter Marr gave Ivano a dreaded vote of confidence with the Dark Blues hopes of reaching the top six appearing to be fading fast. He also issued a controversial call for SPL fixtures to be handled by referees from the English top flight, or even further afield, in response to the increasing influx of foreign talent in Scotland. He said: "Take out the start of the season and I think we are as good as anybody on the discipline side – and it was disappointing to see us fall back on old habits just after the winter break because our players should have learned by now. But it is difficult when you have a different culture coming into play with a different type of referee. We all watch Spanish and Italian football and see things happen that are normal to the culture of the players we've brought here but with the culture in Scotland they will end up getting booked or sent off."

Rangers winger Neil McCann was returning to Dens Park to face his former club. The Scotland international told reporters before the match that he could well remember watching Caniggia on television during the 1990 World Cup in Italy.

"If anyone had suggested I would be playing against him at Dundee in a few years I would have asked them if they were okay," he said. "It's great for Scottish football and great for Dundee. They have paid a lot of money to get into the top six and they are not going to give up getting there without a fight."

The game was shown live to a remarkable 132 countries, including customers paying £8 on pay-per-view in the UK, much of Europe and the whole of South America.

Ivano said it was a match that Dundee simply needed to win. He said: "Rangers will be a very difficult game, but everyone must make sure that they think only about doing their best to win the points. "Because we have lost some games it will be difficult for us to get to the top six, but it is not impossible and we must do all we can."

But the run of bad luck continued as an estimated 50 million viewers worldwide watched striker Juan Sara amazingly miss two penalties. Sara didn't even hit the target with either attempt and it was little wonder the team left the park afterwards to the strains of 'Don't Cry For Me Argentina' from the Evita musical.

Former Dundee striker Billy Dodds also missed from the 12-yard spot for Rangers in a topsy-turvy game that the visitors eventually won 1-0. Dundee held the upper hand for long spells and in Caniggia and Georgi Nemsadze had the two best players on the pitch. Caniggia almost broke the deadlock when he headed past the post with Stefan Klos stranded. He picked himself up and produced a sparkling run shortly afterwards. He cut through the heart of the Rangers defence with explosive pace, skipping past defenders one by one, to set up Sara, whose shot was superbly saved from just eight yards out.

On half-time, Rangers defender Scott Wilson brought down Sara just outside the box and referee Hugh Dallas controversially pointed to the spot on the advice of the assistant referee. Was Dundee's bad luck about to finally change? It didn't as Sara inexplicably blasted his spot kick wildly over the bar.

The home side started the second half in similarly positive mood. They were pinning Rangers back inside their own half and creating chances. Sara was then offered the chance to atone for his previous mistake when Lorenzo Amoruso fouled Caniggia in the box. Sara stepped up again and this time sent his right-foot shot well wide of Klos's left-hand post. To rub further salt into Dundee's wounds, just a minute later Rangers scored the winner. Bert Konterman's goal summed up Dundee's run of misfortune. The Dutchman struck a low shot that found a way into the net after going directly under Sara's feet as he jumped up in the defensive wall. Rangers held on to take all three points.

A match of three wasted penalties had actually happened before in the league. Back in 1973, Bobby Murdoch, Harry Hood and Kenny Dalglish all missed from the spot for Celtic when they played out a 2-2 draw against East Fife at Bayview.

Ivano revealed he told Sara to forget about his penalty miss at half-time but he didn't say who should take the next one because he wasn't expecting a second. "When we did, there was no time to stop Juan," he said. "Claudio Caniggia and Georgi Nemsadze are both accomplished penalty takers. However, Claudio was still recovering from the tackle which led to the second award, and Juan had already spotted the ball before Georgi could intervene. We'll tackle the problem of who takes our next penalty long before our next game."

Sara said: "I still believe in God, and I'll have no worries about taking the next penalty Dundee are awarded. If we get one next Saturday against St Johnstone, I'll volunteer to take it. I've never missed a penalty in my life, and have already scored twice from the spot for Dundee this season. If I'd scored with either, I'm certain Dundee would have won.

"However, this is football – this is life. I also have four stitches in a wound just above my right eye, so obviously this wasn't my day."

Dundee might well have been going through their worst run of the season but the individual performances of Caniggia were recognised when he was named the Bank of Scotland SPL Player of the Month for February – which was also his first since arriving in Scotland in October.

Already, in some quarters, Caniggia was being tipped as the only serious challenger to Celtic's Henrik Larsson for the Player of the Year prize, which would be handed out in May. Fergus Duncan, the Bank of Scotland's director of sponsorship, said: "It is very pleasing that someone of Claudio Caniggia's pedigree is gracing the Scottish Premier League. Dundee FC are to be congratulated for bringing this world star to Scotland."

Caniggia was presented with his prize at the team's temporary HQ at Seamill on the west coast. The squad had travelled to the seaside to escape the snow in Dundee but their luck was out again. The mercury dropped almost as quickly as the players arrived and they were forced to train in freezing conditions.

Ivano was in slightly sunnier climes, though, as he spoke to transfer targets in Italy. After picking up his award, Caniggia voiced his confidence in the direction the Bonetti revolution was taking Dundee. He also likened the team's problems to those experienced in Europe by Sir Alex Ferguson's Manchester United side of the early 1990s.

He said: "When you have eight or nine individuals in the team who are new to the Scottish game it is always going to be difficult to gel in the short term. The fact that so many times we have played really well only to end up with nothing shows the quality is there. Of course I am disappointed about recent results, but I believe in the work that is being done at Dundee and am sure that, when this team has been together longer, we can do far better. I am not the only one here who believes this to be the case.

"We are not happy to be in the bottom half of the league but we have belief that things will improve with time. Provided we can sort things out our quality should allow us to compete for much higher targets than those we are currently pursuing. We are just babies in terms of knowing one another as players and the past has shown even teams like Manchester United can take time before they start winning at all levels. As a young side they managed to win the English league, but they had to grow together before they were able to also deliver success in Europe. That also applies to us because, as I said, we can grow stronger and stronger in future.

"More immediately, what we have to focus on is making sure we finish in the top six when the league separates. It won't be easy but we are determined to succeed, and that means putting together a sequence of wins beginning with the weekend's match against St Johnstone."

Bonetti's Babes were finally about to enjoy a change of fortune – for now.

CHAPTER SEVEN

Govan Goals Before
The Goodbye

We want to reassure the fans that Claudio is going to stay a
Dundee player for a long time yet.

Dundee Football Club spokesman

JAVIER ARTERO hailed Dundee's seaside expedition a big success. The break had brought the squad closer together and determined to finish the season strongly. Artero insisted they could turn the tide when they returned to league action to face St Johnstone after a run of five successive SPL defeats had seen the Dark Blues seemingly slip out of contention for a top six finish.

"The accommodation and facilities were unbelievable – really, really nice – and there was no snow or ice," said Artero. "It was great to get away even though we worked hard and we are now looking forward to the St Johnstone match. It will be difficult, of course. I have found that in Scotland teams are often evenly matched. It is a very important game and we need to get back to winning again. I feel, though, that although we lost to Rangers last Saturday we were unlucky. It wasn't just that we missed two penalties, I believe we played good football in the game and deserved something from it. I am hopeful we can turn good play into a victory this time."

After missing two penalties against Rangers, Juan Sara kept his place in the team. He returned to partner Caniggia in the Tayside derby and helped revive Dundee's season at McDiarmid Park as they edged out St Johnstone 3-2 in a close-fought encounter. A first-half free-kick from Gary Bollan gave the home side the advantage. The former United defender's 25-yard drive flew past Marco Roccati into the corner of the net. Dundee were poor in the first-half and reduced to working off scraps.

What they lacked in creativity in the opening exchanges they more than made up for when they returned after the break. Looking a completely different side, Dundee were rewarded for moving through the gears with a 57th minute equaliser when a ferocious left-foot shot from Gavin Rae squared things up. Dundee then went in front when Javier Artero's cross was deflected into the path of Juan Sara, who kept his composure and swept the ball home on the half-volley from 12 yards.

Saints pulled themselves level with 12 minutes left. Marco de Marchi pulled down Paul Hartley as he sprinted on to Paul Kane's through ball and the former Hibernian and Aberdeen man levelled from the spot. Caniggia was guilty of being too casual just seven minutes from time when he tried to roll the ball past goalkeeper Alan Main from eight yards rather than putting his laces through it. The goalkeeper saved Caniggia's nonchalant effort and the derby seemed to be fizzling out towards a draw when Gary Bollan floundered and lost possession to Javier Artero 20 yards out. The Spanish midfielder strode confidently into the Saints box and planted a low, right-foot shot past Main to send the away fans behind the goal into delirium. Bollan's topsy-turvy afternoon was completed when he was sent off in the final minute for arguing with Caniggia having earlier picked up a first-half booking.

Ivano said afterwards: "In recent weeks, I have been happy with our performances, especially against Rangers, but the difference is, today we took our chances. We can still chase the top six position. We have a lot of quality in our team, like Gavin Rae, who scored a wonderful goal. He worked very hard and helped us a lot overall as did all of our players. And Artero did very well for us up front. I told the team to be more aggressive in the second half and, overall, I believe we were wonderful to watch. We have always believed in ourselves, and after this win we can now look to the future."

The delight was tempered by a sense of foreboding when reports surfaced after the game suggesting Rangers manager Dick Advocaat was weighing up an audacious bid for Caniggia. However, while recognising there would unquestionably be speculation over his star player, Ivano insisted that Caniggia's future at Dens was long-term. He said: "Claudio is not on the transfer list. We are keeping our good players. I am not surprised if big clubs are looking at him – that only shows that our decision in bringing him here was a good one. But there is no point in their being interested because there is no chance we will let him go. It doesn't shock me that Claudio is attracting interest. He is doing very well and is a top-class player. However, Dundee will build a good team for next season and he is very important for us. There is no chance he will be allowed to leave the club – absolutely not. We are building for the future so why would we sell Claudio? And although I expect he will be flattered that big clubs are looking at him, I know he is happy here and wants to remain with us."

A club spokesman later affirmed the manager's hands-off warning. "Claudio Caniggia is not for sale," he said. "We want to reassure the fans that Claudio is going to stay a Dundee player for a long time yet. He believes in what the manager and the club are trying to do. He is happy in Dundee and the way the club is progressing, and sees himself very much as a large part of those plans."

Dundee were looking to improve on what they had. Talks with £5m-rated Georgian defender Zura Khizanishvili were also progressing well and his signature was imminent. Khizanishvili was available at a knock-down price despite his international pedigree because his club Lokomotiv Tblisi had gone bust and had started a fire sale.

Georgi Nemsadze tipped Zura to become the new Rio Ferdinand.

"He is three or four years younger, but he is very good and in two or three years can match what Ferdinand can do," said Nemsadze. "I have known him since he was a boy and every year when he was growing up he was well ahead of his age in talent. He has something special and is the best young player in Georgia. Already he is a regular for our country, and he has done very well in the last 10 or 11 games."

Caniggia might not have been for sale but there was panic buying across Dundee. Food retailers were swamped by customers buying up stocks in response to the foot-and-mouth crisis after the virus had started to spread across Britain. Businesses in the city reported increased levels of trade with some twice as busy as normal, as consumers reacted to reports of possible shortages and imminent price rises.

Back at Dens Park, there was no such panic. Weekend hero Javier Artero was in relaxed mood and confidently predicting a Dundee victory before the visit of Hearts for the Scottish Cup replay.

"In my time in Scotland it has always been a very difficult game when we have faced Hearts," he said. "This season we have been one goal up in three games, but we have lost once and drawn the other two. They have always been very close, and I don't think this will be any different. However, I believe it is now our chance. I hope someone like Claudio Caniggia, Georgi Nemsadze or myself can do something to make sure this time we win."

Meanwhile, the importance of football was put into perspective when Dundee were left shattered by the news that beloved kit man Willie Dryden had died suddenly. The popular 54-year-old worked with Dark Blues directors Peter Marr and Jim Connor during their spell in charge of junior outfit St Joseph's before following them to Dens.

"Willie will be missed enormously by everyone at Dens Park," said Connor. "He was the type of person who was always there for everyone. Nothing was too much trouble. The players, management and staff at the club all respected him dearly as a human being and our thoughts are with Willie's family at this sad time."

Ivano echoed those sentiments as he fought back tears. "I am deeply saddened by the untimely death of a wonderful person – our ever willing Willie Dryden, who will be incredibly missed in our changing room," he said. "I can genuinely say that Dens Park will not be the same without Willie. Neither I nor the lads will ever forget you Willie. Every victory will be dedicated to you."

As a mark of respect, the club cancelled a press conference, at which new signings Zura Khizanishvili and Australian midfielder Mark Robertson were to be paraded. A closed-doors game was also called off. Khizanishvili and Robertson had signed on three-year deals and it was decided they would instead be introduced to the crowd before kick-off in the cup tie against Hearts. However, as a player with Atalanta and Grimsby, Ivano had seen new signings unveiled on the pitch amid huge fanfare and the matches that followed had ended in defeat. He put the brakes on the presentation.

But Dundee still couldn't avoid bad luck.

The Dark Blues were forced to play most of a closely-fought encounter with 10 men. Marco de Marchi got himself sent off after 34 minutes when he retaliated and aimed a kick at Hearts midfielder Lee Makel right in front of referee John Underhill.

De Marchi hit out after Makel had downed his team-mate Gavin Rae. The sending off was a blow because Dundee had started brightly and almost went ahead.

It was a gripping cup tie with Caniggia in the thick of things as usual. Straight from the whistle he went on a terrific run from inside his own half. He finished off the dash with a neat cross for Barry Smith whose knock-down was well saved by Antti Niemi. Caniggia was then put clean through by Juan Sara but was denied by a brave Niemi diving save. The ball rebounded to Rae, whose follow-up header from the edge of the area was knocked off the line by Thomas Flogel. The Finnish goalkeeper also had to rush from his box to clear the danger when Caniggia almost got there first following a fine through ball from Georgi Nemsadze.

The winning goal followed the substitution of former Dark Blues midfielder Steven Boyack. The midfielder's every touch had been met with booing from the Dundee fans and he actually looked relieved when he was replaced by Robbie Neilson on 59 minutes. It was to prove a crucial switch. On 71 minutes Neilson's inch-perfect cross from the right found the unmarked Robert Tomaschek. The Slovak beat Roccati at his near post with a downward header from 10 yards.

Ivano was furious at full-time and left the media in no doubt as to who was the fall guy. "I have seen the incident on TV and the referee was right," said Ivano, when asked about de Marchi's dismissal. "It was a stupid thing for such an experienced player to do. All the hard work we had done on the training ground in preparation was left counting for nothing and I am very, very angry. Marco will be fined for sure, but let me sleep on this before I say any more. What happens on the pitch does not lie and what I saw tonight tells me there is something wrong within my group. I must do something about that. Someone is going to pay."

De Marchi was firmly in the doghouse and would eventually be put on the transfer list. But the rest of Ivano's charges earned nothing but praise from their manager.

The day after Dundee were brought back down to earth, the Space Shuttle Discovery was launched from the Kennedy Space Centre in Florida. It carried a piece of Captain Scott's Discovery exploration ship. Once the space shuttle returned to earth the piece of its historic namesake would be returned to Dundee to go on permanent display at Discovery Point.

The Dark Blues touched down at Ibrox just days later when they returned to midweek league business to square up against an injury-hit Rangers in front of 45,000 fans. The squad was boosted by the return to normal training of Fabian Caballero after nearly six months out, although he wouldn't play any part in proceedings in Glasgow.

"I feel good now, 90% as far as fitness goes," he said. "But as far as playing is concerned I need a little more time for at the moment 10-15 minutes is as much as I could manage."

Striker Juan Sara was desperate to continue his partnership with Caniggia and said Caballero's return would only serve to motivate him to keep improving. "I am very happy that Fabian is now back because like Claudio he is a wonderful player," he said.

"But I have big confidence in myself. I am the second-top scorer in Scotland and think I have had a good season and having another good player available to the manager will only give me greater motivation to do better every day."

The evening before the match at Ibrox a spectacular blaze destroyed the former Logie School in Dundee's Blackness Road. Around 50 firefighters from Tayside and Fife had fought to control 100-foot high flames which could be seen from as far afield as Wormit and Broughty Ferry. Within 30 minutes of the fire being discovered at 9pm, around 50% of the roof was ablaze, although it looked as though the flames would be contained to the east and north of the building. Firefighters in breathing apparatus were sent to tackle the fire from inside but it became apparent that flames were racing through the roof space to all parts of the building. The firefighters were ordered back out of the school as the night sky lit up once more. At 11pm a poignant reminder of the historical significance of the school – the clock tower with the hands showing the time at 8 o'clock – disappeared into the inferno.

At Ibrox it was looking increasingly likely the clock was ticking on Caniggia's Dundee career. If the Argentine wasn't already high on Rangers manager Dick Advocaat's shopping list, he would have been afterwards, following a quite outstanding performance.

It was a night that remains part of Dundee folklore. Caniggia and Stevie Milne's goals secured only Dundee's fourth victory at Ibrox since the inception of the Premier League in 1975. More importantly, though, it moved the stuttering Dark Blues into seventh place in the table. Caniggia's goal when it arrived was magnificently created. Georgi Nemsadze fed Barry Smith just inside the Rangers half. Smith played a neat one-two with Javier Artero before sprinting towards the box. He played in Caniggia before taking the brunt of a heavy Lorenzo Amoruso challenge. It could have been a penalty but Caniggia didn't hang around to debate the matter. The Argentine had already slipped his marker and made easy work of what appeared to be a difficult angle to score past Rangers goalkeeper Stefan Klos at his near post.

Dundee should have been even further in front at the break. Gavin Rae wasted a clear-cut opening when he side-footed wide from five yards. It would have been just as good a goal as the opener. Rae's poor finish marked the end of a terrific move involving Marco Roccati, Barry Smith, Javier Artero and Caniggia, whose final ball should have been dispatched.

Dundee remained on top in the second half against a threadbare Rangers rearguard. As Rangers committed more resources to squaring things up, Dundee came close to scoring on numerous occasions as they continually surged up the field.

With time running out a perfect through ball from Rae freed Caniggia. He went through one-on-one against Klos but the German goalkeeper managed to keep out his effort despite falling backwards as Caniggia pulled the trigger.

Deep into second-half stoppage time, Dundee substitutes Stevie Milne and Walter del Rio joined forces to finally put the match beyond doubt. Del Rio fired in a deep cross and Milne completed a night of misery for Rangers when he managed to squeeze home a header at the back post which Klos should have kept out. The rows of empty seats told their own story. Rangers had gone out of Europe before Christmas and their title hopes were all but gone.

After the match Milne said he was still in awe of Caniggia even after five months of training and playing with the former World Cup star. "You cannot fail to learn from Claudio even just through watching him in training and games, never mind playing with him," said Milne. "The thing which strikes you most is his attitude. He does things you cannot believe he can still do at his age and the way he puts himself about you'd think he was a 21-year-old."

Ivano dedicated the momentous win to Willie Dryden whose death – along with that of former Rangers chairman John Paton – had been marked by a minute's silence before kick-off.

"This victory and every victory is for Willie," said Ivano. "Everyone at the club is missing him, although in a way it felt like he was here with us tonight. It was a good result and one we were worthy of because I felt we produced a little bit more than Rangers. Last time we played Rangers we had two penalties and five or six clear chances and did not score. This time we create three or four and score two goals and that is easily good enough for me. It is a good win for us because it is the first time we have beaten Rangers this season and my players have done very well in this match."

Caniggia might have been the player attracting interest from elsewhere but Ivano also spoke of his admiration for midfielder Gavin Rae following his midfield masterclass. He said that it would take a substantial offer from any suitor looking to take him away from Dens.

"Gavin could go and play in Serie A now because he has everything but he is going to get even stronger," he said. "At this moment if any club offered six or seven million for him I would not take it. Peter and Jim (club owners Peter and Jimmy Marr) might want to but I would tell them to hold off because we will get £10 million later."

Dick Advocaat – who saw Lorenzo Amoruso stretchered off with a knee injury and Craig Moore shown a red card – was polite enough to concede the Dark Blues fully deserved the three points.

The Ibrox win would go down in Dundee folklore. For years afterwards the fans would sing: "Were you there at the Ibrox fiasco? Were you there when the Dundee boys won? Were you there when Claudio Caniggia silenced every single one? Were you there when young Stevie Milne scored the second of the fabulous goals? Were you standing in the Dens Park choir singing 'Who is Michael Mols?'"

Dundee's poor home form continued with a goalless draw against Hearts in the league. The fleet-footed Caniggia again pulled the strings and was a constant menace. Dundee had the two best chances of what was an end-to-end, if ultimately unproductive, first-half. The Dark Blues' first chance came when Caniggia cleverly flicked an outside of the foot pass from Georgi Nemsadze into the path of Juan Sara.

He elected for power but his fierce drive was thwarted by the advancing Antti Niemi. The second chance was just as clear-cut when Caniggia pulled the ball back for Nemsadze but the Georgian international could only slice his effort high and wide from 10 yards.

Hearts should have found the back of the net themselves following an uncharacteristic error from captain Barry Smith who lost his footing 25 yards out. Smith's slip left Gary Kirk with a free run on goal but he fired wide. There was another close shave when Smith struggled to deal with a careless throw-out by goalkeeper Marco Roccati and the ball rebounded to Thomas Flogel, who was sent through on goal. Marcello Marrocco managed to hastily clear for a throw in.

Dundee went on to dominate the second-half proceedings but couldn't find a finish despite creating the majority of chances. Sara headed a Nemsadze free-kick over the bar from six yards. Niemi was then forced to beat out a well-struck shot from Sara from a Javier Artero delivery. Artero also fired wide of the far post from a tricky angle after being released by Caniggia. That was as close as Dundee came to scoring but they almost lost the game when Colin Cameron's attempted finish hit the diving Roccati and shaved the crossbar on its way behind for a corner.

After the match Ivano spoke of the need to be more clinical in front of goal and admitted his side's failure to notch up results at Dens was something he would have to address. "My players made two or three mistakes I was not happy with, but apart from that I cannot be angry," he said. "They made four or five chances to score, but did not take them. If you do not score you do not win, but many of the things they did were good and I can be happy about that. I know it is a better result for Hearts than for Dundee, but we still have a chance of getting to the top six."

Javier Artero said he was puzzled by Dundee's inability to win their home matches. Despite the talent at Ivano's disposal, the team had gone four months and nine league and cup games without a win on their own turf. Artero said he was struggling for a reason why.

"Always when we play at home we seem to play well and create many chances, and it is important the fans enjoy the football they are watching," he said. "But it is an incredible run we are having of not being able to win. I don't think there is any more we can do to change things because we are already working very hard. But perhaps if we could score in the first half it would make a difference because then our opponents would have to open up."

He acknowledged that Dundee's struggles at Dens were beginning to affect the team mentally in the same way that it was damaging their pursuit of a top-six place. "Maybe it is bad luck but the truth is we can't score here and that is very frustrating," he said. "Perhaps the return of Fabian Caballero will bring a change of fortune for he is a wonderful player. But then Claudio Caniggia is a wonderful player and Juan Sara is very good and still we cannot get the results we want. This is not a new situation at Dundee – when I arrived at the club I think we did not win any of our last 10 home games that season. But it is one we must sort out. I hope that will happen before this season is over but if not it must happen next year.

"I don't know how it is that we can play an unbelievable game at Ibrox then only draw at home to Hearts a few days later. But I hope this changes soon - for the sake of the fans as well as the players."

Caniggia rushed from the ground to begin his voyage back to Argentina. He would spend the week chasing his court battle with former employers Boca.

The centenary of a much longer journey was marked when members of the public joined descendants of the men behind RRS Discovery's 1901-1904 Antarctic expedition to salute the famous ship on its 100th birthday in Dundee. Raising a glass with them on Discovery Day was the greatest living explorer, Sir Ranulph Fiennes, and NASA astronaut, Dr Bonnie Dunbar.

RRS Discovery was launched from Dundee on March 21, 1901, which was the beginning of an epic voyage to Antarctica by one of the finest ships ever to put to sea. At 3.20pm, Sir Ranulph, patron of the Discovery 100 fundraising appeal, marked the exact time that Discovery launched and toasted the ship. Falcon Scott, the grandson of Captain Robert Scott, uncorked the champagne.

Celebration would soon turn to despair however just a few hours later. The city was soon mourning the 133-year-old Morgan Academy. One of Dundee's biggest ever fires reduced the historic school to a shell. Visible from miles away, the building was gutted by 100-foot flames. Firefighters fought a losing battle to control the blaze, which quickly spread across the roof and throughout the building. More than 1,000 people, including rector Alan Constable, watched the horror unfold from the street. The roof caught fire shortly before 5.15pm and high winds helped fan the flames quickly throughout the building, with thick clouds of smoke engulfing neighbouring Forfar Road. At 7.45pm the clock tower disappeared into the centre of the flames. At the height of the blaze, more than 70 firefighters were engaged in the battle. They had to ask the council to increase the water supply to allow them to tackle the fire.

The following day it emerged the Dark Blues were considering manufacturing a third strip that would be identical to the Argentina kit in tribute to the Argentinian contingent at Dens Park. "It's one of the designs on the drawing board," said a club spokesman. "Given the large contingent we have from Argentina and Claudio's popularity we are sure it's a strip that would draw an encouraging response from fans."

Meanwhile, along with neighbours United, Dundee joined the race to sign Newcastle midfielder Stephen Glass who was told by Magpies boss Bobby Robson that he was free to leave. Negotiations with the Dundonian's representatives were ongoing, although there was plenty of competition for his signature including Blackburn, Bolton and Hibs.

Reports later broke during the week that Dundee had decided to turn down an offer to join forces with Chesterfield who were currently top of Nationwide League Division Three. A syndicate with business links to Monaco, which was headed up by

Rotherham businessman Andrew Cooke, was understood to be close to taking over at Chesterfield. Cooke had taken in Dundee's clash with Hearts as a guest of the Dens Park board and put forward an offer which would have seen the two clubs create a formal co-operation arrangement. However, Dundee eventually decided against taking the matter further.

There was also speculation the group had wanted to buy out Jimmy and Peter Marr's controlling interest but that was wide of the mark. "Any suggestion that a business consortium is about to buy this football club is pure nonsense," said a spokesman. "Mr Cooke was a guest of the board on Sunday and he gave us a general outline of the business plans he is formulating. His business affairs are a matter for him to comment on and not us, as these plans will not involve Dundee Football Club. We have our own very distinct project here and we will not be diverted from it."

Chief executive Peter Marr had also just leapt to the defence of his manager over his alleged treatment of three players who appeared to be heading for the exit door. Under-21 international goalkeeper Jamie Langfield had grumbled about the dearth of first-team opportunities and wanted a transfer, while seemingly unwanted Italians Patrizio Billio and Marco de Marchi had already protested to the SPL over the way Ivano had dealt with them.

Marr was further annoyed that Langfield had decided to go public and talk to a tabloid newspaper. "I am a bit disappointed in Jamie because he did speak to me about his situation and we agreed I would speak to Ivano, so I don't understand why he has come out with this," said Marr. "Jamie has seen young boys do well at Aberdeen and Dundee United and probably feels he should have had a chance by now and I understand that.

"However, he has to respect the manager's decision, and Ivano's view is that he does not yet have enough experience. We rate him very highly and that is why we have been trying to fix him up with a loan. We've even been talking to people in Italy about going to a club there next season to bring him on. Jamie should look at the likes of Robert Douglas and realise it took him until he was 28 to get where he wanted to be. Jamie is a goalkeeper, he has plenty of time on his side and can do very well if he concentrates on working hard. But, at the minute, I would say that if he is ready for the Premier League, why haven't any other clubs come in for him?"

Ivano had apparently still to forgive Billio and de Marchi for indiscipline that had played a major part in Dundee's exit from both cup competitions.

Marr didn't pull any punches and he made it clear that neither had a future at the club. Billio had been sent packing in the 3-0 League Cup defeat at St Mirren in September, while the manager had publicly held de Marchi to blame for the Scottish Cup exit against Hearts.

"They got sent off in cup ties we lost and that cost the club a lot of potential income," said Marr. "In de Marchi's case if he had not done what he did against Hearts, we could have had a Scottish Cup quarter-final at Celtic to look forward to.

Everyone saw what he did. It was the kind of thing you would expect from a kid, not an experienced professional who has played at the very top level. As for Billio's situation, Ivano has not attacked the guy, he has simply said he does not need him and that, again, is any manager's right. And seeing as he was sent off twice in the first four weeks of the season, it is easy to understand why Ivano feels that way. We have tried to help him and there was an English First Division club interested in taking him on loan, but Patrizio was not even prepared to speak to them. To both of them I would say that if things are so bad here they are free to leave. We are not keeping them here and if they want out we will be happy to cancel their contracts."

While de Marchi and Billio were being cast adrift, Broughty Ferry's new lifeboat, Elizabeth of Glamis, arrived home, following the culmination of a year of fundraising by the local community, which raised more than £1 million to pay for the lifeboat. The arrival of the vessel would ensure what was traditionally one of the busiest lifeboat stations in Scotland would now be equipped with the latest technology.

Meanwhile, rumours linking Rangers with a move for Caniggia just wouldn't go away. They cropped up again on back pages in Scotland just before the transfer deadline but were again dismissed by the club ahead of the crucial Dens clash with Kilmarnock.

Caniggia was then linked with a move to Celtic, who were so infuriated at the reports that a phone call was made at director level from Parkhead to Dens Park to categorically deny all knowledge. The speculation also prompted Celtic manager Martin O'Neill to pull the plug on a trip to watch Dundee's game against Kilmarnock for fear of adding further fuel to the fire.

In a peculiar twist, Caniggia's agent, Pablo Cosentino, later claimed Caniggia and O'Neill had been at Celtic Park the day before the Kilmarnock clash to discuss a potential move. However, it emerged that Caniggia didn't leave Dundee on the day in question. Dundee were putting the story down to a case of Caniggia's agent attempting to whip up what was described as "unwanted business".

The Killie game was the latest to be broadcast around the globe by satellite channel ESPN International and included a special report on the impact Caniggia was having in Dundee. After the talking had stopped, the match itself finished 2-2. Dundee remarkably failed to kill off Kilmarnock while they were completely on top and had been playing against 10 men for the last 30 minutes. In the end, Dundee paid the price for their inability to press home their advantage. Despite the visitors being there for the taking, Dundee conceded a fairly feeble equaliser at a time when the game should already have been put well beyond Kilmarnock.

The visitors started well and sprinted into an early lead when Jesus Sanjuan threaded a defence-splitting pass to Craig Dargo who drew the keeper before scoring. Marco Roccati kept Dundee in the game minutes later when he saved a net-bound Dargo shot. Dundee had rarely threatened before drawing level on 28 minutes. Beto Carranza strung a tremendous pass through to Juan Sara who slotted the ball into the net for his 15th goal of the campaign. Dundee then took the lead just after the break with Caniggia involved in the build-up. Javier Artero played the ball into Caniggia's path and from his lay-off, captain Barry Smith swung in a fine cross which Gavin Rae glanced in at the far post. The impressive Rae was being watched by Scotland manager Craig Brown with a view to starting a friendly against Poland later in the month.

The equaliser for the Dark Blues came shortly after Craig Dargo had been sent off for lifting his hands to defender Steven Tweed on 61 minutes. Tweed reacted to Dargo first by grabbing him by the shoulders and wagging a finger in his face. Dargo responded by catching Tweed in the face with a stray hand then throwing out an arm which failed to find its intended target.

Despite being 2-1 down and reduced to 10 men, Kilmarnock kept two up front and went man-for-man at the back in an effort to put pressure on Dundee and it paid off. Caniggia was largely kept quiet in the latter stages as Dundee threw away their advantage. Goalkeeper Marco Roccati and left-back Marcello Marrocco failed to clear their lines on 74 minutes and Kilmarnock captain Gus MacPherson got a header on target. Alan Mahood then managed to bundle the ball into the net from a couple of feet.

The only bright spot of the afternoon was the late appearance as a substitute of Fabian Caballero who was returning to the first team for the first time since being injured in September. After the match Cabellero pledged to shed the pounds and get back to his best. "I have got bigger legs than before due to the hard work I have done building up the muscles following my operation," Caballero said. "But I also have a spare tyre which I have got to get rid of. And I will be looking to lose the weight over the next week or so. The manager has told me I have to lose three kilos (almost half a stone) and I know that if I do I will get my strength, agility and pace back. The doctor told me I would have to work hard to get everything back the way it was before the injury and that it could be the start of next season before I am at my best again. But I plan to work very hard now so that I am back in shape sooner than that."

Dundee's chances of making the top-six were now hanging in the balance and the Kilmarnock draw also killed off any possibility of qualifying for the UEFA Cup. Until then it was still mathematically possible to qualify for the UEFA Cup which would have led to Dundee scrapping plans to contest the Intertoto Cup in the summer. However, UEFA made it clear that a withdrawal would result in a heavy fine.

Director Jim Connor said: "If results had gone for us, we could still have been in contention for a UEFA Cup place. Incredibly, UEFA wanted us to decide on Saturday which competition we wanted to play in. If our UEFA Cup hopes were still alive, they said we'd be fined 300,000 Swiss Francs by pulling out of the Intertoto Cup. To say we're angry is an understatement. We were disgusted at the prospect of being penalised by UEFA for being successful."

Dundee later confirmed their application for admission ahead of the deadline.

The Dark Blues were given a lift, however, when the Scottish signing deadline closed without any effort being made to grab Caniggia despite reports from Argentina that his agent Pablo Cosentino had been involved in talks with Celtic and four unnamed English top flight clubs.

Ivano said: "The transfer deadline for this season has passed and, of course, we don't want to sell Caniggia. He has two years on his contract and these are just rumours at the moment. If Celtic or other clubs are interested, they have to go through the official channels and approach the club. Nobody has done that. A club would be in serious trouble if they have approached any player without our permission. It would be very dangerous for them. However, as far as I am aware, that has not happened and I don't want to waste energy thinking about it. Caniggia is the best striker in Scotland, along with Henrik Larsson, but he will play for Dundee against Celtic on Wednesday, that's for sure."

Just after the Dark Blues had been at pains to stress no official approach had been made by Celtic, Rangers chairman David Murray entered the fray when he revealed his club were considering making a bid for the 34-year-old striker during the summer.

"We showed some interest in Caniggia a month ago, but nothing materialised at that stage," said Murray. "He remains under contract at Dundee, but we will be making changes in the summer and could do something then. Nothing will happen at the moment, but we will review the situation in the next few months."

Ivano called for the talking to stop until a concrete bid was made. He said: "It's normal for good players to attract attention. That doesn't bother me. But, we have said all along that we do not want to sell the player, he is under contract here and we have had no official approach from any club – so the speculation should finish."

There was similar interest being shown in Dundee author Pat Kelly. He was negotiating with television executives to produce a controversial documentary on the assassination of American president John F. Kennedy. Mr Kelly had gathered new evidence having recently travelled to America to interview influential figures involved in the murder investigation to finally uncover the truth. He submitted a synopsis of his evidence to executives from Channel 4 and Channel Five who immediately declared interest in screening the project and was hopeful of striking a deal. The documentary, 'Guns of Dallas – The Cover-up Which Proves the Conspiracy', aimed to show rogue elements in the CIA were responsible for the murder. Mr Kelly also claimed to have uncovered evidence proving there were "two Oswalds" involved in the conspiracy to allow government officials to cover their tracks.

There might, or might not, have been two Oswalds but there was only one Caniggia and the conspiracy theories surrounding the striker were becoming just as far-fetched. Dundee travelled to Parkhead to face Celtic, who were just six points away from the title. Celtic manager Martin O'Neill again stressed before the match that any suggestion he had made a bid for Caniggia was a lie.

"It is not true," he said. "I have not spoken to anyone, including Dundee. I wouldn't even know who his agent is. He is a very fine player and I admire him but I can deny categorically that there has been any contact made."

The Bird & The Feather

O'Neill paid tribute to Dundee's cosmopolitan squad before the match got started and insisted that the Dark Blues were well capable of picking up all three points.

"I think Dundee have been incredibly entertaining, but they have been inconsistent, too," he said. "They have a lot of really decent players. On their day, they are capable of beating any one of us. But they haven't had enough of those days."

Things started desperately for Dundee when goalkeeper Marco Roccati was stretchered off. The Italian was injured before the match had even started after falling heavily during the warm-up. The injury finally gave the recently outspoken Jamie Langfield his first-team chance.

It was a baptism of fire for Langfield at Celtic Park. After just five minutes he was picking the ball out of the net. Alan Thompson's cunning ball down the left played Henrik Larsson in behind the Dundee defence. Larsson sent a dangerous cross in to the near post and Tommy Johnson was first to fire it into the corner of the net.

A few minutes later Dundee broke up the park and forced consecutive corners on the left which allowed Caniggia to test Celtic goalkeeper Robert Douglas. Dundee's renewed vigour lifted the band of travelling fans in the corner. They showed they had not lost their sense of humour, despite being behind so early, when they hailed a wild free-kick from Larsson with the chant: "You're not very good. You're not very good. You're not very, you're not very, you're not very good..."

Larsson's ears might have been ringing but things could have got worse for the Parkhead side when another Dundee corner saw Beto Garrido head just wide. Dundee were now taking the game to Celtic and Javier Artero's dangerous cross just moments later was kicked to safety by Celtic defender Ramon Vega. The Dark Blues returned for the second half without talisman Caniggia who was forced off. The disappointment of his departure was tempered when he was replaced by Fabian Caballero following his 11-minute run out in Saturday's 2-2 draw with Kilmarnock. The Argentine striker showed he had lost none of his ability despite clearly being far from 100% fit. The fans chanted: "He's got black hair and navy boots and he wears Armani suits, He was sent down from Heaven to wear number seven, He's Fabian Caballero."

Caballero linked up well with Beto Garrido in a passage of play which saw the latter force a late save from Douglas before Dundee's desire was rewarded on 68 minutes when they got the equaliser. Georgi Nemsadze collected the ball in midfield. He glided out left and drifted a stunning chip over the Celtic defence which Juan Sara judged perfectly and he squeezed in to prod the ball past Douglas from close range. It set up a grandstand finish.

Celtic threw everyone forward in search of the three points they needed if they were to keep alive their hopes of wrapping up the title the following Saturday. Those hopes of maximum points were significantly enhanced eight minutes from time. Barry Smith was sent off for pulling Johan Mjallby back as he attempted to sprint into the box. The Swedish defender took advantage of the extra man five minutes before the end when he knocked in Alan Thompson's corner at the back post and Celtic held on to win. Ivano admitted the late goal was scant reward for the efforts of Langfield and his team-mates.

The defeat left the Dark Blues trailing Dunfermline by three points in the top-six race. The mathematics were simple. They had to win at Aberdeen, whilst hoping that Kilmarnock did them a favour by beating Dunfermline, but their ultimate destiny was now out of their own hands.

"We still have hope because Kilmarnock are a very strong team," said Ivano afterwards. "Also, I believe that if we play some of the football which we managed tonight then we can go and pick up all three points in Aberdeen. I have said all along that the important thing this season was to change things, to show that Dundee can challenge at grounds like this. Even if we don't make the top six I think we will have achieved that. Of course, we want to win more often than we have but the quality of our football has pleased me."

Ivano also congratulated Celtic on the title they would go on to clinch against St Mirren at Paisley.

"They have done so well and I think the difference is their mentality," he said. "I would like to see my players adopt some of that attitude and perhaps have more trust in themselves. This is perhaps not the night to speak of this because they have put so much effort in, and from a personal point I thought it was wonderful to see Fabian (Caballero), who has been out for seven months, play 45 minutes. He is a great player, someone who people will all be talking about once he is fit again."

Ivano also had a special message of thanks to the travelling support. "What can I say? They were magnificent once again," he said. "Celtic had almost 60,000 supporters in the ground and I still heard our fans cheering the team on. They have been the largest travelling support outside the Old Firm all season. We are very proud of them."

Celtic manager Martin O'Neill was full of praise for Dundee afterwards. He predicted they could be future title contenders if they could find a degree of consistency. "Dundee played exceptionally well in the second half and it's my view that if they can become more consistent they could challenge because they have some fantastic talent in their squad," he said.

It emerged afterwards that Caniggia had picked up a leg strain and was substituted at half-time as a precaution to make sure he would make the starting line-up against Aberdeen. But the extent of injured Roccati's problem was still not clear.

The Dark Blues needed a victory at Pittodrie to be in with any chance of securing a place in the top six but Caniggia's participation was looking increasing doubtful as the week progressed. It was looking likely they would have to do it without their star man. Roccati was having a scan to determine the extent of his damage, while Artero was having a damaged toe X-rayed. Caniggia was heading for a chiropractor to relieve a hamstring problem.

Ivano said: "Artero's toe may be broken but if it is not I would expect him to make it. With Caniggia, I don't know and it is the same with Roccati. However, in Jamie

Langfield we have a ready-made replacement for Roccati. I thought Jamie did very well against Celtic. It was a big test for him but he showed personality."

The build-up to the Aberdeen game started with Dundee again being forced to publicly deny speculation over an employee's future. But for once it wasn't Caniggia's name that was in the spotlight. Reports in a national newspaper suggested Dundee had targeted former Atletico Madrid player Pedro Braojos as the man to take over the reins from Ivano. Braojos – who was in charge of Spanish La Liga 2 outfit Real Jaen – had made claims that he had been approached by the Dens board with a view to taking over as manager.

A Dundee spokesman insisted Ivano was staying put. He described the newspaper article as a "work of fiction" which was in "very poor taste".

He said: "If, as the report suggests, Ivano Bonetti is under fire then it is from snipers from outwith Dens Park with their own agenda. We will go on record yet again to say that we have been delighted with the progress made both on and off the field since the managerial appointment of Ivano and Dario Bonetti. This latest work of fiction is an absolute joke but one that is in very poor taste. With no disrespect to Senor Braojos, we hadn't heard of him until we saw this back page story, so it goes without saying that no approach has or will be made by Dundee Football Club for him. In fact, Ivano Bonetti and chief executive Peter Marr were in Italy just last week to learn from the set-up at Juventus. Our other directors will fly out with Ivano to Italy after the split as preparations for next season continue. Dundee Football Club has ambitious plans for the future that can and will only be driven forward by the current board and management team."

Before the match Dundee's annual accounts were published which showed the club had lost just under £760,000 the previous season. Chairman Jimmy Marr noted in his official statement that the stated aim of the club for the current season remained a top-six finish in the SPL and European football within three years. The report added that since the end of the year the club had acquired the player registrations of Javier Artero, Georgi Nemsadze and Caniggia for a total of £992,000. The registrations of Juan Sara and Fabian Caballero had been acquired on loan until June 2001 for a total of £185,000.

Marr said season ticket sales had continued to rise with more than 2,500 holders now occupying the Bobby Cox stand. Marr continued: "The new season has started with great excitement following the appointment of Ivano Bonetti and his brother Dario as team manager and assistant manager respectively. They in turn have brought new and exciting players to the club, culminating in the arrival of the World Cup Argentinian star Claudio Caniggia. I hope this major investment will prove worthwhile."

It did prove worthwhile as Dundee managed to deliver the desired place in the top six.

The Dark Blues triumphed in the face of adversity with star man Caniggia forced to watch from the sidelines after being ruled out with a hamstring strain. Dundee were worthy winners at Pittodrie and took the points thanks to excellent individual goals from Georgi Nemsadze and the newly-returned Caballero. The impressive 2-0 win over Aberdeen was also Dundee's fifth victory in a row in the Granite City which was proving to be a happy hunting ground. The 2,000 away supporters celebrated in the sunshine at the final whistle as news filtered through of Dunfermline's defeat to Kilmarnock at Rugby Park which cemented Dundee's spot.

Ivano and his men then danced for joy in front of their enthusiastic fans, knowing that the likes of Celtic and Rangers would await them in the few remaining weeks. Ivano rated the success as equal to anything he had achieved in his illustrious playing career, which had included Sampdoria's Serie A triumph in 1991.

"This was an important target for us," he said. "We might not have won the league or one of the cups but we have achieved something here that can set the foundation for future successes. All along I have believed that our rightful place was in the top six because of the quality of player we have here and the quality of football we produce. The errors we have made along the way have meant that we have only clinched our place in the last day but it has turned out well and for this we are all very happy. It was fantastic to see our fans enjoy themselves so much and I would like to dedicate the success to the memory of our late kit man Willie [Dryden] who I know would have been thrilled."

The mood was slightly dampened following the match with more unwanted headlines. Rangers chairman David Murray appeared to give weight to the persistent speculation that the toppled champions now wanted Caniggia in their ranks next season. He said his club were "80% along the way" to securing four or five new faces.

Reports from Italy also suggested Caniggia's agent Pablo Cosentino was due to meet Murray to discuss a two-year contract which would be worth around £2 million. Dundee again maintained – not for the first time – that they had received no contact from any club. A club spokesman said: "We are aware of the reports but our position remains the same. We have received no contact on the subject of Caniggia from any Scottish club or any other club for that matter. Claudio is a Dundee player who is under contract with us for another two years and if anyone is interested in buying him they will have to speak to us."

He also dismissed a further report that former Dens Park stars Billy Dodds and Dariusz Adamczuk would be moving in the opposite direction. "We have had no contact from any club regarding Claudio and, given that, any suggestion of player exchanges would be news to us," he said.

Dundee chief executive Peter Marr later broke his silence and said the club would not stand in Caniggia's way if he wanted to move on. Marr believed Caniggia's agent had been working to try to sell the Argentine behind their back. He warned that any suitors would need to stump up to land a player he described as "irreplaceable".

"I've no doubt this is where it is all coming from and it could be that Claudio's agent has agreed a deal with another club," said Marr. "With Claudio's ambition to play in Japan in the World Cup and possibly the chance to play in the Champions League to show he is worth a place with Argentina, I think that's what's behind this.

"If a player is determined to go, it doesn't do the club or the player any good to hang on to him. Claudio has been very good for the club and he's worked very hard, but we will be seeking proper compensation for the loss of his services and the enormous marketing potential he offers Dundee. The fact remains, though that we have received no bids for him and we'd rather none came in, as we hope he stays. You can't replace a player like Claudio, so we want him here. Financially, selling him would seem a great deal, but his marketing value is immense. Any big club looking at him knows that and that whatever they had to pay for him they'd get back. That, and the fact he is such a great player, is why we want to keep him – and the only way he will be leaving is if he feels that moving to a club that was involved in the Champions League would improve his chances of getting back in Argentina's side."

Marr also poured cold water on speculation that Dundee wouldn't receive a transfer fee. There were rumours circulating that Caniggia's wages were actually being paid by a group of South American companies who were the real owners of his contract.

"I've heard these stories," said Marr. "Once again they are coming from the west coast media, and once again they are absolutely nonsense. Claudio has a straightforward contract, he is our player and if he was sold, then the money would be coming to us and no-one else."

There was then a bigger leak than anything produced by Cosentino across the city when a massive storm water tank that took a week to fill emptied in an hour. A leak during pressure testing at the King George V wharf saw over four million gallons of water cascade from the concrete structure, which was part of the £100 million Tay Wastewater Project, flooding the surrounding dock area to a depth of about two feet. The flooding would have been more severe had much of the water not been swallowed up by holes which were dug around the work site. The tank leak reached a height of about two feet, flooding some portable office accommodation, before draining into the nearby wharf and the excavations.

In a bid to keep further leaks and unrest to a minimum, Peter Marr and fellow director Jim Connor held clear-the-air talks with Cosentino to sort the Caniggia situation out. They were becoming increasingly angry by a sequence of reports casting doubt over their bond with the player.

A Dundee spokesman said: "There will be talks later today, but it is not a summit meeting. Members of the board, including owner Peter Marr, will be having discussions with Claudio Caniggia's agent. It is a matter of fact that no bids have been received for Claudio Caniggia. However, there has been a lot of speculation surrounding this player over the last couple of weeks. This is an opportunity to discuss some of the rumours that have been making headline news and, perhaps, what, if any, substance there is to them."

Ironically, Dundee's next game was against Rangers.

Strike partner Juan Sara spoke before the game of his hope that Caniggia would still be playing alongside him when the following season got under way. "Myself, I want Claudio to stay because he is a great player and very good for our team," he said. "It is his problem, though, and I do not know his situation with the club, so all I will be thinking about is the game against Rangers and trying to win. Sometimes in Scotland I think people believe that Rangers and Celtic cannot be beaten, and sometimes they go into these games expecting to lose. They should be more positive and look at them as good games where you can show your quality by winning. In Argentina, a team like Boca is very big, but the players in the smaller team do not think they cannot be beaten and it should be the same here."

At the weekly pre-match press conference at Dens, Peter Marr confirmed he had left Caniggia's agent in "absolutely no doubt" that if the player was to leave Dundee the club would have to be properly compensated.

He said: "Players like Gary McAllister and Richard Gough were playing in the Merseyside derby, and Claudio is younger than them. So, while it would be stupid for us to name a price, we would want suitable compensation for a player who is easily good enough to still play at the highest level. I do not believe Claudio is at loggerheads with Dundee, I think it's a case of an agent who has seen an opportunity. I'd also like to point out that because Claudio is close friends with Ivano and Dario we felt it was better for all of them if the board dealt with this."

Ivano then told them to put up or shut up in a slightly bizarre clothes-themed rant. "If you want to buy the shirt you have to go to the shop and buy it," he said. "I can say I'm interested in the shirt but, unless I go to the shop, I can't have it."

Despite the constant transfer speculation, Ivano said his most pressing concern was finishing the campaign strongly. "We have made the top six and we want to do well," he said. "We are behind Hearts and Kilmarnock, but so long as it is possible to catch them we will keep trying to finish in fourth place."

Before the match, Rangers manager Dick Advocaat dismissed any suggestion that Dundee were a one-man team. "I totally disagree," said Advocaat. "They have an excellent midfield with Gavin Rae and Georgi Nemsadze. They have a strong defence, a good side and improved a lot when Ivano Bonetti took over in the summer. They like to play football, like Rangers want to do as well, so I'm looking forward to the game."

Rangers' Dutch international defender Fernando Ricksen echoed his manager's thoughts.

"Dundee have got a very good squad and very good players," said Ricksen. "They play in a very clever, technical fashion, almost like a Serie A side. They've some really good players and are really underestimated in my opinion. Their results over the season have not really reflected the high standard of players that they have got at the club. They have under-performed to some extent. Yes, they have got Claudio Caniggia, but he can't play on his own. He needs good players around him and that's what is happening at Dundee. We'll need to watch every one of them carefully if we're to get the right result. They are by no means a one-man team."

Dundee had high hopes of recording successive league wins over Rangers for the first time since 1985. However, serious errors at both ends cost them the opportunity.

Caniggia didn't play any part because of a hamstring injury. He watched from the Dens Park main stand where the Rangers fans left no-one in any doubt that they wanted Caniggia wearing their colours next season. The visiting fans chanted Caniggia's name incessantly during Rangers' 3-0 victory at Dens.

Dundee fell behind after just four minutes. Steven Tweed made a hash of dealing with a punt into the box from Bert Konterman and Rod Wallace hooked the ball over Jamie Langfield.

Chris Coyne's blunder on 15 minutes allowed Tore Andre Flo to stretch the visitors' advantage. The Dark Blues might have quickly responded, but Juan Sara missed a sitter when, left with only Klos to beat from eight yards, he shot straight at the keeper. There was further misery when Jorg Albertz got the third to leave Dundee dead and buried. Rangers were 3-0 up after just 27 minutes, although if the Dark Blues had shown some composure in front of goal it could have been an entirely different story.

Ivano refused to discuss Caniggia's situation after the game. However, he confirmed the Argentine was in the dressing room with his Dundee team-mates pre-match and would also be attending a supporters' club function in the city later that evening.

Another Dundee veteran was similarly hampered by injury the same weekend. Jenny Wood Allen pulled out of the London Marathon after nine miles when her legs seized up. The 89-year-old, the oldest woman in the race, had been determined to finish the course after a fall affected her effort in the millennium event, but unfortunately she again had to give up early. She received a massage from a paramedic on the race route and tried to get going again, but after experiencing further difficulties she retired from the race.

It was now looking unlikely that Caniggia's new contract would go the distance either. "Claudio has been unsettled by the continuing speculation about his future and by his agent's apparent determination to find him another club but he is not unhappy at Dens Park and has nothing but the highest regard and affection for the club and its supporters," said a club spokesman.

Cracks soon began to emerge in the wake of the Rangers defeat. There was the first sign that Ivano was losing patience with Caniggia when he missed training because of the latest in a string of meetings with Dens directors to discuss his future. Ivano said he understood the need for Caniggia to be absent from the training ground for these talks but made it abundantly clear that his policy was that the striker wouldn't be picked if he didn't train.

"I don't know how Claudio is because I haven't see him today as he was having a meeting with the club," said Ivano. "But if he does not train he won't be playing because it is the same for all players. I will speak to him about this. We have to be clear on the matter."

The latest round of talks was thrashed out between the player, his agent, chairman Jimmy Marr and director Jim Connor, and club co-ordinator Dario Magri. The Argentine declared during the closed-door meetings that he would be tempted by a move to a bigger club. Caniggia was understood to have said he was attracted by the greater challenges and more lucrative financial rewards such a change would bring. He was aware that going to Rangers would increase his wages, but it would also offer Champions League football which he believed could provide the perfect stage to reclaim his international place ahead of the World Cup.

"Ongoing dialogue is continuing between the player, his agent and the board of Dundee FC with a view to resolving the situation in the best interests of all parties involved," said a Dundee spokesman.

The following day Caniggia was again notable by his absence when the squad joined up for their daily training session at Caird Park in Dundee. Ivano, though, wasn't struggling for strikers for the next match against Hibs. The ranks had been filled out by the return from injury of Fabian Caballero. But the manager declared himself far from happy at the distracting sideshow.

"I am not happy about this whole thing," said Ivano. "I can't have a situation where Claudio Caniggia is not coming to training. I know Claudio has had talks (with another club) and I need to find out from our directors how things stand and where we go from here. There is no personal problem between myself and Claudio because this is a business thing, though one in which we all have to be clear about what is going on. He has his own views but, as manager of this club, I need to know if he is training and if he is fit to play."

Rangers were now understood to have struck a deal in principle with the player and his agent although they still had to make Dundee an offer. It was proving to be a protracted transfer saga.

Caniggia's stock was rising in Dundee and so was the price of the humble fish supper. Dundee fans were apparently turning their backs on the delicacy after matches because depleted haddock stocks were forcing fish and chip shops to raise their prices. The going rate for a fish supper was now £3.30. Fish shop owners were having to contend with the rocketing price of fresh fish and in some cases were being forced to buy their haddock from Ireland. The foot and mouth outbreak had also taken its toll on fish shops with many lorries unable to enter farms to collect potatoes which meant there was less choice available.

The Dark Blues by this stage were grudgingly prepared to let their own meal ticket go. However, they wanted substantially more than £1 million in return for a player who still had more than two years of his contract outstanding. The truth was that Rangers simply weren't prepared to pay that much. They hadn't given up hope of signing him but for now the transfer was in limbo.

"For the sake of everyone concerned, especially the fans, we need to have this situation resolved as soon as possible," said Dark Blues director Jim Connor.

After missing work for three days due to meetings and an apparent reluctance to train, Caniggia finally returned to join in with the squad at Caird Park ahead of the game with Hibs.

"It is a difficult situation, and I will have to speak to Claudio and look closely at him before I make my decision," said Ivano. "He has missed some of our work and has also had the problem of the injury with his hamstring, so right now it cannot be certain he will play."

Caniggia's son, Alexander, raised a giggle when he showed no signs of following in his dad's anticipated footsteps, when he was spotted at Caird Park wearing a Celtic strip.

Ivano had become so disappointed at his side's poor home form that he took the unusual decision of taking over the away dugout for himself and his coaching team for the game against Hibs. He was hoping that a change of environment would also trigger a change of fortune.

"We have not won at Dens in 2001, and I find this incredible," he said.

"The only thing I can think of is that we should be sitting in the other dugout because they have had success there. So on Sunday I am moving, and I will be sitting in that dugout to see if it brings us luck. If it doesn't, for the next game we will move to the other side of the pitch."

Sixteen-goal Juan Sara was struggling to overcome a groin problem and Ivano decided not to risk him. Ivano said: "Juan's problem is not serious, but I think it is better to leave him out for this game and give him a chance to recover. He has played in most of our games so the break will not harm him, but Fabian has been out for a long time this season so we want him to play in as many of the remaining games as he can manage, which will help his fitness for next season.

"With Claudio, his injury situation has improved and he done some work with the ball. He may be able to play for some of the game, but we do not know for sure yet."

Before the match, Fabian Caballero said he would realise a boyhood dream by lining up alongside Caniggia for what would be the first, and possibly also the last time.

"Claudio is a great player and of course I look forward to lining up alongside him if the manager picks us both," he said. "But the most important thing for me is that Dundee FC get 11 determined players on the pitch every match. If that happens we should do well because we have so much skill in our squad. I know myself that next season I am going to be stronger and I feel the same also applies to the club. We were still in our infancy as a group this year but that will no longer be the case after the summer when, I am sure, we can do ourselves justice."

Caballero also had a score to settle with Alex McLeish's team following a red card at Easter Road earlier in the season when Dundee were beaten 5-2.

Superstitious Ivano did, as promised, watch on from the opposite dugout. But it would prove to be a short-lived vantage point for Ivano as Hibs moved to within eight points of second-placed Rangers with a resounding victory. The Easter Road side still had a slight chance of surpassing Rangers and taking the second Champions League place from them, following a terrific season.

There had been considerable excitement among the Dundee fans when Caniggia and Caballero finally started a game together. It turned out to be a major disappointment. Caniggia and Caballero were kept quiet throughout by the Hibs back three.

Dundee produced the first chance when Steven Tweed jumped highest in the box to head Georgi Nemsadze's corner towards goal, only to see his effort cleared off the line. Chances were scarce but Dundee went close again on 33 minutes. Caniggia forced his way through a resolute Hibs defence but his shot went just wide. Both teams created chances before the break. The highlight was Jamie Langfield's save from Marc Libbra's header on 37 minutes.

Hibs started after the break in confident mood and they were rewarded with the opening goal when Frederic Arpinon cut an accurate pass over the top to the feet of Libbra. The striker crashed the ball into the corner from 12 yards on 55 minutes.

Dundee escaped further punishment two minutes later. Hibs should have been awarded a spot-kick. Walter del Rio's clearance bounced off the arm of Steven Tweed but referee David Somers waved play on.

Hibs then grabbed the second goal on 66 minutes. Matthias Jack played a ball down the middle which fell to the feet of Dundee captain Barry Smith, who failed to deal with it, letting in David Zitelli who took full advantage of the mistake. He drilled an assured finish under goalkeeper Jamie Langfield.

The result meant it was now mathematically impossible for Dundee to leapfrog Kilmarnock and Hearts and take fourth place in the SPL.

Dundee were uninspired, uninventive and missing a spark. The prolonged "will-he-won't-he" Caniggia saga appeared to be affecting things on the pitch. The only positive for the Dundee faithful had been the partnership of Caniggia and Caballero getting another chance to gel. However, it was looking increasingly unlikely that they would be teaming up again next season.

It now appeared very likely that Caniggia's road to the World Cup in Japan and Korea would go via Glasgow.

CHAPTER EIGHT

Show Me A Hero And I'll Write You A Tragedy

"I don't want to lose him, but what can you do if bigger clubs make very good offers?

Ivano Bonetti

THE end was nigh. Dundee were finally ready to admit defeat in their battle to hold on to Caniggia. Rangers manager Dick Advocaat had identified the Argentinian as his top target.

It wasn't difficult to see why. Advocaat's £12m striker Tore Andre Flo was still battling to win over his critics. Despite scoring goals he hadn't made the expected impact to justify his price tag. Injuries were continuing to hamper the chances of Michael Mols rekindling his Champions League glory days, while short-term signing Marcus Gayle had been nothing short of woeful.

"As stated before, talks between the board, Claudio Caniggia and his agent are continuing with a view to having this matter resolved swiftly, amicably and in the best interests of all concerned," said a Dundee FC spokesman. "We can confirm that, despite the repeated efforts of the directors to persuade him otherwise, Claudio Caniggia has intimated through these ongoing discussions that he feels his future lies away from Dens Park. While disappointed with this decision we have reluctantly agreed to allow him to leave if another club makes an official offer of appropriate compensation to Dundee FC. To date, we have had no official offer from any club for Claudio Caniggia.

"Dundee FC has notified agents throughout the game advising them to make it absolutely clear to clubs interested in securing Claudio's services that he will only leave Dens if the offer made matches our valuation of the player. If there is any deal to be done, matters will be conducted with respect for all concerned and most importantly in the best interests of Dundee Football Club."

Dundee remained resolute. The club said they would hold out for between £1.5 million and £2 million. Rangers were still interested.

They desperately wanted Caniggia, but not at the price put forward. Dundee were understood to have suggested to Caniggia that if he wanted to join Rangers that he might bridge the monetary gap by coming up with a six-figure sum to make it happen.

Ivano told reporters at the daily press briefing that he did not feel betrayed. He shrugged off Caniggia's intent to leave as part and parcel of modern day football.

"This is the way the professional game works these days," Ivano said. "If you play well, then bigger clubs will want you. I don't want to lose him, but what can you do if bigger clubs make very good offers? He cannot go for free, so we must get a good offer. But that has not happened yet, and I would be delighted if Claudio stayed here next season and the one after."

Ivano said he hoped the matter could be resolved quickly because "everyone is bored with it".

One striker was definitely leaving Dens Park, however. Willie Falconer – whose contract was due to expire in the summer – was allowed to go. The 34-year-old had struck up a promising partnership with Caniggia earlier in the season before he became a bit-part player when he became hampered by injuries.

"We have an agreement with Willie that he will be going," said Ivano. "I want to thank him and wish him all the best because as a person as well as a player, he has done very well for us."

Falconer was one of four free transfer signings from Motherwell which were made by former manager Jocky Scott in the summer of 1998. Falconer said: "I think I've a had a good rapport with the supporters during my spell at the club. I'd like to thank them. I've had a few enquiries, and I hope that I'll be playing regularly next season."

There were then claims that Dundee were also pushing Caniggia towards the exit door. Rangers chairman David Murray said Caniggia had been offered to his club through a third party and alleged that Peter Marr had been trying to sell off his prize asset. Murray said: "As far as Caniggia goes, there is no denying we have shown some interest. Peter Marr at Dundee is openly making the player available, and last week a third party approached us to see if we were interested."

Dundee however had no further news to report although it was known Caniggia's representatives had been continuing talks with Rangers in the background. Ivano said "the show would go on" if Caniggia did leave but he ruled out signing moves for Italian megastars Roberto Baggio and Dino Baggio. The unrelated Serie A pair were amongst numerous star names – Lazio's fast and diminutive forward Beppe Signori was another – who had been linked with Dundee.

That week the much talked about album, It's My Dundee, went on sale just in time for the club's last home game of the season against Kilmarnock. The CD featured contributions from local musicians, Dundee FC players and staff and the Dens Park Choir recorded live at a number of home games during the season. Dundee's top scorer Juan Sara was honoured with his own theme, Sara's Song (I Thank God), contributing a reading of The Serenity Prayer to a thunderous dance track.

The sessions were taken to the Seagate Studio, where the likes of Danny Wilson, Billy Mackenzie and Jah Wobble previously worked, and then the recording began in earnest. Life-long Dundee supporter, singer/songwriter Joe Lamb joined up with fellow Dark Blue, producer/programmer Mike Brown to lay down the foundations of the album. Songs included a new rendition of 'Johnnie Scobie', a reworking of 'Bonnie Dundee' and 'Road and the Miles Tae Dundee' which was dedicated to the memory of Willie Dryden.

The creators of the album, LBC Productions in Dundee, kept costs down to ensure a large donation from sales could be made to the Dundee FC Youth Development Fund. The initial run sold out in two days.

The Dark Blues were similarly on song. They beat Kilmarnock 2-1 to finally get a win at Dens. The club confirmed before the match that Fabian Caballero had signed a new three-year contract and negotiations were continuing with several other players.

Dundee took the lead 10 minutes before the break, when Georgi Nemsadze released Javier Artero on the right and he found Juan Sara, who netted from close range. Dundee got a second after the restart when Kevin McGowne climbed all over Sara following a harmless-looking corner from Beto Carranza and the referee pointed to the spot. Sara went to take the kick, but, after his two misses against Rangers in February, his team-mates forced him to hand the ball to Carranza, who sent goalkeeper Colin Meldrum the wrong way.

Caniggia was dropped by the manager despite arriving at the ground before kick-off. "Claudio was available, but I chose to use my three other strikers," said Ivano. "Caballero needs games after recovering from a serious injury and Juan Sara is my top scorer. On top of that, young striker Steven Milne was chosen for a place on the bench."

Ivano called on all his diplomatic skills after the match when he insisted Caniggia had not played his last game for Dundee despite his transfer to Rangers set to be finalised.

"We still have a couple more games to play this season and he is signed for this club for two more seasons," he said. "I repeat, we do not want to sell him. I admit that a little contact has been made concerning his future, but nothing serious. Claudio was not upset at my decision to leave him out of the side for the game."

Brother Dario took an altogether difference stance. He said afterwards he would be "happy" for Caniggia if he signed for Rangers. "When we talked to Caniggia six months ago we knew this could happen in the future," said Dario. "It is normal for him to play in a big team. I would be happy for him if he signs for Rangers. I think he will be there next season."

Caniggia's agent Pablo Cosentino then said there was verbal agreement with Rangers. "We are all celebrating," Cosentino said. "Claudio is a Rangers player. We have verbally agreed it. If everything goes through in the way we expect he will be signing a two-year contract with Rangers."

Dundee chief executive Peter Marr later confirmed Caniggia was joining Rangers. But he also insisted that the deal would not be rushed through. Marr said: "I am not disputing that Claudio is going. But it won't be happening over the weekend. The ball is in Rangers' court now.

"I can confirm, however, that we are closer to an agreement. A deal has to suit everyone, and that means a bit of coming and going from all parties. Claudio has spoken with Rangers, but there are other matters, like a medical, to be completed before any business is concluded.

"I have to say that I am happy for Claudio. He stated he wanted to play in the Champions League and, as far as we are concerned, that is fair enough. A deal might have been done before now had the transfer deadline not passed. That tended to unsettle things at Dens Park. The most important fact remains that, until things are finalised, Claudio Caniggia remains a Dundee player."

Caniggia was still being troubled by a niggling hamstring problem and was struggling to make Dundee's next match which was another trip to Glasgow to face Celtic.

Arthur Lynch was making a similar journey before the match. The Dundee disabled rights campaigner became the first man in Scotland to travel by rail on an electric scooter. He travelled to Glasgow to attend a tenants' participation meeting and was asked by rail officials to be a 'guinea pig' for the day after a booking bungle looked to have curtailed his journey. ScotRail admitted there had been a mix-up with his earlier booking and revealed that strict national regulations prevented them from taking electric scooters on passenger trains. However, in a dramatic U-turn, they then decided to honour the booking. They also asked him to present a review of his experience to officials in a move which could allow scooters aboard services in future. Mr Lynch, who had been fighting a six-year battle against the ban, said he enjoyed "a wonderful journey" which proved electric scooters should be allowed aboard passenger trains.

Dundee fans enjoyed a similar happy journey to Glasgow, as two goals from Fabian Caballero delivered Dundee's first victory over Celtic in 13 years. Caballero scored in the 29th minute before Zura Khizanishvili was dismissed-for a last man foul on Henrik Larsson in the 34th minute. Ivano was incensed and showed his disapproval by throwing his jacket into the crowd – breaking his mobile phone in the process – and storming up the tunnel.

Dundee went further ahead, despite the numbers handicap, when Caballero converted a Javier Artero cross on 42 minutes.

"I was delighted to get the goals today because it helped the team to a big win and also made all the hard work I had to put in when injured this season worthwhile," said Caballero. "If, as looks likely, Claudio goes he will belong in the past as far as the other players here are concerned because we have a job to do with or without him. I will stay because I am happy here and will continue to do my very best for the club."

The performance gave the fans hope that life without Caniggia wouldn't be the end of the world. He was left out of the squad for the surprise 2-0 win and Ivano admitted afterwards it did look likely that Caniggia had already played his last game for Dundee. Ivano said Caniggia's departure was almost done, with the outstanding details anticipated to be taken care of imminently.

"You can never say for certain because football can be strange but it is now 98% that Claudio will be gone soon," he said. "Claudio is a fantastic player and he has been wonderful for us but we have Fabian Caballero back now and other good players here and we will continue to grow. Fabian's goals were excellent at Celtic and you must remember he's still not fully fit because of six months out."

The Dark Blues finished the season with a 2-0 defeat against Hearts at Tynecastle but the Dundee fans left the board in no doubt as to who they wanted to lead the team next season. The fans chanted: "Ivano and Dario" for 20 minutes without stopping despite being two goals down which even earned applause from the Hearts fans when it finally ended with a crescendo.

A transfer fee was finally agreed with Rangers to bring Caniggia's time at Dundee to an end. When the completed deal was announced, Dundee were quick to pay tribute to Caniggia's "outstanding" contribution to the club since he arrived in October.

"Dundee Football Club can confirm that a transfer fee has been agreed with Glasgow Rangers Football Club in respect of Claudio Caniggia," said a club spokesman. "During his time here Claudio Caniggia has made an outstanding contribution to the team and helped raise the profile of the club to new heights.

"We wish him well for the future but we have also proved this season that Dundee Football Club are bigger than any one individual – even a player of Claudio Caniggia's world-class ability."

Rangers manager Dick Advocaat said Caniggia had agreed in principle to sign. He said: "Let's put it this way – he is the only player that we have bought and all the other players are still Rangers players, despite all the rumours. The good thing about Caniggia is that he is desperate to come to Rangers to try to get a place in the Argentina squad for the World Cup. So I think we can expect a lot of him."

Caniggia had certainly left his mark during his brief stay on Tayside.

He scored a total of eight goals in 25 league and cup games. But that was only half the story. Caniggia was box office. His time in Dundee didn't just lift the football team but the city itself. He was idolised every step of the way and had left Dundee supporters with many fond memories.

The 34-year-old's future looked secure when Caniggia passed a medical and agreed personal terms after Rangers and Dundee had agreed a package worth just over £1 million. However, while they announced he was to become their player, Rangers revealed Caniggia would not actually be signing a contract with them until he reported for pre-season training in June.

Caniggia then turned up at the Dark Blues' training ground to collect his boots.

He said a final goodbye to his former team-mates and the staff at Dens Park. Afterwards he jetted off to Italy to put the trials and tribulations of the previous weeks behind him for a 25-day holiday.

The fact he had not actually signed his new contract before leaving for Italy left the door slightly ajar for other interested clubs to make a move. It emerged that both Tottenham and Middlesbrough were interested in hijacking the move. Both clubs were said to have had the Dundee striker on their radar with reports suggesting there was a slight chance Caniggia could turn his back on Ibrox and move to England.

Reports from Japan and his homeland Argentina then speculated that the striker was also considering an offer from Avispa Fukuoka and had also been training with Cerezo Osaka. However, the reports appeared to be unfounded and Dundee stated that as far as they were concerned Caniggia was still heading for Ibrox.

"We have had no further contact with his agent since reaching an agreement with Rangers on the player's transfer," said a club spokesman.

Dundee fans still struggling to come to terms with Caniggia's departure were soon preparing themselves for losing Dens Park.

It emerged that the city's two professional clubs could share a new 30,000-seat stadium. The SFA confirmed they were seriously considering making a bid for the European Championships in 2008 which was the planet's second-biggest football tournament. Six stadia, each with a capacity of 30,000 or more, was the minimum requirement for a host country and Scotland boasted only four grounds – Hampden, Parkhead, Ibrox and Murrayfield. Two more would have to be found but Dens Park and Tannadice weren't big enough. That left the option of building a new stadium in the city to be used for the tournament which would thereafter be reduced in size and shared by United and Dundee.

Several times in the past, plans for such an arena had been mooted, but the failure of the clubs to reach agreement and worries over funding had seen them go up in smoke. The Margaret Thatcher Government even wanted Dundee and Dundee United to consider sharing a stadium in the wake of the Hillsborough disaster. Tory ministers discussed the ground merger to advance the phasing out of terraces following the Taylor Report into the tragedy, in which 96 fans died. Aberdeen FC was the only top flight club to boast an all-seater stadium at the time, while Rangers were in the process of redeveloping Ibrox.

Dundee chief executive Peter Marr believed his club would be better off at a new ground. He said: "We are Scotland's fourth city so we should be involved if there was anything like this taking place. The central belt is well covered for stadiums and, if another two were needed, they should be in Dundee and Aberdeen. Everyone knows we would prefer to move to a new ground, and in meetings with the council they have indicated to us that if both clubs were willing, they would find land for one. It would just be a matter of sorting the thing out with Dundee United and taking things from there."

One man definitely moving to a new home was Claudio Caniggia.

He finally joined up with his new Ibrox team-mates for pre-season alongside fellow new signing Christian Nerlinger who had signed from Borussia Dortmund but had also had an illustrious career with Bayern Munich. Manager Dick Advocaat said: "Caniggia showed last season at Dundee that he still has the pace and the tricks and I think he can do the job."

Caniggia insisted the fight from everyone in the squad to win a place in the Rangers first team would be the key to a successful campaign.

He said: "It is important for every player to understand that it is not possible to play all the time. I hope to play all the time in the team but there is no guarantee and that is good. It is good for every player – it makes players better because there is more competition. It's important that the players understand that it is those who play the best who get in the team. The only way for a team to reach the best level is to have so many players to choose from and for them to compete against each other to get in the first team.

"I feel very good to be at Glasgow Rangers because I know they are great club, with a great history and they have good players. Celtic and Rangers are the two best teams in Scotland and, for me, Rangers are the best team in Scotland. The opportunity for me, having already played so many years, to come to a club this size and have this opportunity is fantastic.

"Everyone in Argentina is very happy for me. They are pleased to see an Argentinian play for such a big club."

Caniggia had been heavily linked with Celtic towards the end of his time with Dundee but he denied that Martin O'Neill had made an approach. He said: "I think that, last season, Rangers had a superior level of players than Celtic but, with teams the size of Rangers and Celtic when they are playing against each other, you can have two bad months and the other team can surpass where you are. This can go on but, in general, Rangers are the better team."

Caniggia said it was just bad luck that stopped Diego Maradona watching him play at Dens and he insisted he would be inviting him to watch his first game for Rangers. "I haven't spoken to Diego since I joined Rangers," he said. "I simply haven't had the time. It's been a matter of coming straight back from a family holiday in Italy, and straight into pre-season training with my new club.

"I will, however, be getting in touch with Diego soon, to invite him over for our opening game against Aberdeen. He promised to fly over to see me when I played with Dundee. But I'd moved from Dens Park before his trip could be organised. Maybe we'll have better luck this time. I hope so.

"Diego is a very, very good friend of mine, and I'd like him to see me in my first game for Rangers."

Caniggia also said his debut season in the SPL with Dundee had made him rate the Scottish game as more entertaining than Italy's Serie A.

"In the last two or three years I've seen a lot of Italian football and I'm not sorry to be away from it," he said. "There is too much in the way of tactics, too many bad games. As soon as a team scored to make it 1-0 it was game over. That made the matches boring. The thing I've found about football here in Scotland is that it is much more fun. Of course, everyone wants to win."

Unfortunately for Dundee fans, his Scottish football adventure was continuing elsewhere.

But the Dundee leg of that journey was one that will never be forgotten in the City of Discovery.

SPL Final Table, 2000-2001

		Pld	Pts	
1	Celtic	38	97	Champions League
2	Rangers	38	82	Champions League
3	Hibernian	38	66	UEFA Cup
4	Kilmarnock	38	54	UEFA Cup
5	Hearts	38	52	
6	Dundee	38	47	Intertoto Cup
7	Aberdeen	38	45	
8	Motherwell	38	43	
9	Dunfermline Ath.	38	42	
10	St Johnstone	38	40	
11	Dundee United	38	35	
12	St Mirren	38	30	

CHAPTER NINE

The End Of The Italian Honeymoon

"Jimmy Marr has received criticism but, in my opinion, the guy deserves a knighthood.

Giovanni di Stefano

GIOVANNI DI STEFANO'S investment offer might have been consigned to the vaults of history but the ghost of Serbian warlord Arkan returned to haunt Dundee Football Club.

A return to European competition for the first time in 27 years in June 2001 had all the exotic appeal of an all-inclusive break in Aleppo. Life without Caniggia started in June with a goalless draw at home in the Intertoto Cup against FK Sartid from Serbia, following a summer break of just three weeks.

The away leg in Smederevo would give the squad a glimpse of a darker world. The city had been pounded by NATO air strikes during the Balkan conflict which ripped Yugoslavia apart in the 1990s. The town's only bridge across the Danube was bombed, its petrol storage depot was destroyed, causing an ecological disaster, and the local steelworks was twice hit by coalition planes.

Sartid vice-president Dragan Sormaz said he was disappointed they would not be facing Claudio Caniggia who was joining Rangers.

"We would have liked to have seen him play at our stadium, because he is a great player and our fans would have been happy to have watched him play," he said. "If he was there it would have been more difficult for us, but if he had scored I am sure we would have scored twice."

Sartid were previously managed by former Dundee United boss Ivan Golac during a largely forgettable six-month spell in 1999 when he almost got them relegated. The club was nicknamed the Steel Knights in reference to their links with the steelworks which were owned by a political colleague of disgraced former Yugoslav leader Slobodan Milosevic.

Ivano arrived in Belgrade similarly looking to shake off the ghosts of the past after a gang of gun-toting thugs from the Serbian capital once chased him through the streets.

"It happened back in 1992 while I was with Sampdoria," said Ivano. "We had drawn Red Star in the quarter-finals of the European Cup and the authorities moved the tie to Sofia in Bulgaria because of the war in the Balkans. Feelings were high as myself and some of my team-mates discovered when we went out for a walk before the match. We heard some people shouting and realised that we had been recognised as being Sampdoria players. Some punches were thrown and we started to run away. It was a very frightening experience because they chased after us and a few of them took out guns.

"Luckily we managed to get away and from that incident on we just stayed locked up in our hotel, coming out only for the match. The trouble was only with a small minority of the supporters and it came at a time when there was a lot of tension in their country.

"There is peace in Yugoslavia now so I really don't see there being a problem this weekend. Of course the Sartid supporters will give their team a lot of backing but that is to be expected anywhere in the world."

The team were staying in the Intercontinental Hotel in Belgrade and were given a real-life history lesson on the horrors of the past before the match.

Defender Lee Wilkie stumbled upon a table and chairs in the foyer which had bullet holes in them. Wilkie said: "There were a few in the reception desk as well and the staff told us it was where this guy Arkan and his bodyguard had been shot. He'd had his own private army and was a scary guy. He'd gone too far, though, and someone had just walked into the hotel while he was having a drink there and shot him and his guard in the head. It was not the kind of thing you wanted to hear about when you were trying to prepare for an important game. I'm maybe getting side-tracked, but it makes me laugh when people over here complain about hooliganism. Over there you were talking private armies roaming the streets."

According to witnesses, Arkan was drinking with colleagues in the lobby when a group of masked men burst in and opened fire, hitting the Serbian Tigers paramilitary group leader in the left eye. Arkan was widely implicated in the slaughter of hundreds of thousands of Croatians and Bosnian Muslims during the Balkans wars. He was indicted by the War Crimes Tribunal at The Hague on a number of charges, including personally ordering the massacre of 2,500 Muslims in 1991 and the rape of Muslim women in front of their own children.

Giovanni di Stefano previously made a bid to buy Dundee in 1999 but a deal fell through after his links with the paramilitary chief were made public.

Dundee's European adventure collapsed just as quickly in Serbia.

The Dark Blues lost 5-2 with a dubious refereeing performance proving to be their undoing. Bulgarian official Sevet Lozar Marinov awarded two suspect penalties early on and killed off Dundee's chances by sending off striker Fabian Caballero with 15 minutes to go. It was a sad end to a European escapade.

Football was then put into perspective when midfielder Javier Artero was struck down by illness. Artero had been taking part in pre-season training with the rest of the squad before he began to feel ill after going to the dentist to get a tooth pulled out. Artero complained of double vision, numbness in the arms, headaches and nausea following the dental trip and failed to respond to antibiotics prescribed by the club doctor. He was then admitted to the neurosurgery department at Ninewells Hospital where doctors began carrying out tests to see whether it was multiple sclerosis, a disease which attacks the body's nervous system. Artero and his new wife Debora had just got married and had postponed their honeymoon so he would be available to play for Dundee in the Intertoto ties against Sartid.

A spokesman for Dundee FC said: "While Javier's condition is giving cause for concern, it must be stressed that doctors have made no diagnosis of his condition at this early stage and it will be a number of days until test results are available. Javier is comfortable, in good spirits and is grateful for the many goodwill messages that the club has already received on his behalf from Dundee fans and other members of the public. Understandably, this is an uncertain time for Javier and his family. Dundee Football Club requests that people, including members of the press, respect the family's privacy. Javier is a popular and important member of our family at Dundee Football Club. All our thoughts are with Javier, his wife Debora and their family at this time."

Artero flew home to his family in Spain expressing his gratitude to medical staff and well-wishers, who included former Dundee United chairman Jim McLean.

"I really would like to say thank you to the people who cared for me, the supporters and the people who have sent messages of good will to me," said Artero. "And, of course, I would like to thank all my friends at Dundee Football Club for their support – they are like a family to me. Now I am heading home to Spain to be with my family but I am determined to return to Dundee fit and well once more."

The results of tests were unlikely to be known for some time but things didn't look good.

There was more positive news on the pitch, where a decent start to the league season prompted chief executive Peter Marr to express his delight at the club's progress under Ivano. Marr had also started discussions to look at extending his existing three-year contract until 2006.

Dundee and Dundee United's plans to move to a new shared stadium at Caird Park were proving less harmonious, with objectors already drawing battle lines against the multi-million-pound proposals.

The plan had emerged the previous season from a meeting between the clubs and the local enterprise company to discuss how the city could play a role in Scotland's bid to host Euro 2008.

Dundee chairman Jimmy Marr said: "This is a convincing proposal that we are putting forward to the SFA, in partnership with our footballing neighbours, Dundee City Council and Scottish Enterprise Tayside. We believe that Dundee as a city must be involved, should the SFA achieve their aim of hosting the European Championships in 2008.

"Of paramount importance are the interests of both clubs and their supporters but, mindful of this, Dundee Football Club will continue to play an enthusiastic part in this joint bid to ensure its success."

Scotland required at least six stadia of 30,000-plus capacity in order to be able to put together a bid for the prestigious tournament. Other bids were expected from Austria and Switzerland; Sweden, Denmark, Norway, and Finland; Greece and Turkey; Bosnia and Croatia; and solo bids from Hungary and Russia. Caird Park was chosen from a potential 25 sites in the city and the stadium would take over ground currently occupied by four holes of the golf course and two rugby pitches.

A joint statement issued by the clubs read: "The boards of Dundee FC and Dundee United FC believe that sharing a stadium would not present any major problems to either club. However, it is important that any rumours that a joint stadium would be a precursor to amalgamation are quashed. Neither Dundee FC or Dundee United FC have any interest in a merger. Both have their own distinct and separate identities of which they are extremely proud."

One of the main hurdles was the legally-binding conditions attached to the original purchase of the 270-acre site in 1913 from money gifted to the city by mill owner Sir James Caird. The legal document concerning the purchase made it clear that the land was to be used only as a public park and for recreational purposes for "all time coming".

As a jute manufacturer, entrepreneur and philanthropist, Dundonian Sir James was one of the wealthiest men in Britain during the 19th and 20th centuries. Harnessing the latest mechanical improvements, he expanded the business aggressively and extensively, and profits grew more and more rapidly. In 1910, James Kerr, who had a bootmaker's business in the old Wellgate, and whose hobby was said to be "scheming", began a crusade to secure a municipal park near the city's northern boundary. Through his efforts, Mr Kerr managed to obtain promises from owners to sell their lands, but needed someone to fund the grand scheme which is where Sir James stepped in. He said he was prepared to purchase the ground for £25,000 to be provided "for the use and benefit of the inhabitants of Dundee". Objectors were pinning some of their hopes on the fact that the conditions would carry sufficient force to stop the stadium project in its tracks.

Javier Artero was just as determined after pledging to get the better of multiple sclerosis. The popular midfielder conveyed his aspiration to return to the game at the highest level after confirming he was suffering from the disease in a letter sent to the club from Spain.

He wrote: "It is hard to write a letter like this – a letter to include everyone, saying all the things I must say. I will try anyway. As you all know, I have been recovering in Spain for a month now and, to be honest, it feels like a year. I have been diagnosed with multiple sclerosis. But the prognosis is very good and I am feeling much better, so I will hopefully be back in Dundee very soon. It has been 18 months since I arrived at

Dundee Football Club and ever since then I have felt as if I was part of a big family. Just a month ago, life has put Debora and me in a difficult situation and it is in these situations when you can see how people really are. I will never be grateful enough to every supporter, for every email and every card I have received. You have all helped me to find out how fortunate I am. All this support is an incentive to me to make sure I return to Dundee as soon as possible.

"I feel very proud of belonging to Dundee Football Club and I have felt very protected during this uncertain time. Jimmy and Peter Marr and Ivano and Dario Bonetti have displayed remarkable behaviour in a situation that had nothing to do with football. I would like to name – one by one – all of my team-mates, but you all know them. I want to thank each one of them for their support and their affection. I am really looking forward to being back in the dressing-room.

"On my behalf, I can say to you that I will work hard to be back with the team and available to Ivano as soon as possible. I would also like to thank every single person in the club. And, of course, thank you for everything Jim (Thomson, Dens stadium manager, who had recently visited Artero in Spain). I will always have Dundee Football Club and the City of Discovery in my heart."

But Dundee were now struggling without Caniggia and things took a turn for the worse in October when they were knocked out of the League Cup by lower league Ross County. The Dingwall outfit's starting line-up ironically included former Dundee hero Brian Irvine.

The big defender was proving to be an inspiration for Javier Artero, having successfully resumed his own top-flight career after being diagnosed with multiple sclerosis in June 1995. Eventually the doctors told Artero he had a relatively mild form of the disease, and he strove to carry on with his football career in the same way that Irvine had done.

Artero drove across Europe to restart his career following his spell of recuperation in Malaga and immediately went out to train with his team-mates. He said: "I have been away from Dundee for two months but all the time I have been speaking to my team-mates on the phone. Also, I don't have words to express how grateful I am to all the supporters and Dundee people who have wished me well. It was a hard experience and now I am looking forward to starting training. I can't wait to just get on with my life and it is good to feel like a football player once more."

Further high-profile signings like Georgian international Temuri Ketsbaia and Chinese skipper Fan Zhiyi were brought in on big wages to stem the tide but they failed to improve results. Ketsbaia first looked set to link up with his countrymen Georgi Nemsadze and Zura Khizanishvili back in June when he said he wanted to quit Wolves and try his luck in Scotland. Dundee were put off by the 33-year-old's £500,000 price tag but went back in for the player after Nemsadze was sidelined for three months with injury.

Ketsbaia had been put on the transfer list in mid-September by manager Dave

Jones. Wolves were prepared to write off the £900,000 they paid Newcastle in the summer of 2000 for the 'Mad Monk' if Dundee bought out the remaining six months of his contract. Capped 45 times for his country, the shaven-headed 33-year-old became a cult figure during his spell at Newcastle United for a wild-eyed celebration against Bolton in 1998. Ketsbaia scored a late winner and proceeded to remove his shirt before kicking the advertising hoarding in anger at being used as a substitute by manager Kenny Dalglish. He took inner rage to a new level and became known as "the Premier League's angriest scorer".

"I am so glad to be here and to have finished my time with Wolves," said Ketsbaia, who turned down counter offers from MLS outfits New York Metro Stars and Tampa Bay Mutiny.

"Every new manager that comes to a club has his ideas about which players he wants and I never got a chance to show what I could do. For a while I put up with it, played in the reserves, but then I decided enough is enough and the situation has not been a happy one. That is behind me now and in Dundee I feel I have joined a club which has real ambition. My friends Georgi and Zura have told me much about what is going on here and it is clear the management and the directors do not want to merely survive, but to challenge in the SPL. The number of internationalists here is proof and while it will not happen in a day, it can happen. I believe I can contribute to what the club are trying to build and am happy at this stage to be working with a continental coach who understands my game rather than another British manager."

Fan Zhiyi's signing ceremony at Dens Park was shown live on Chinese television and the club were already capitalising on the commercial potential of the "Chinese David Beckham". Fan was 31 and had grown up watching the old English Division One in Shanghai before he was spotted by Terry Venables during England's tour of China in 1996. Venables signed him when he took the Crystal Palace job in 1998 and 100 million people tuned in to watch the China captain playing against Sheffield United.

Things were looking good commercially and Dundee were trying to strike a deal to sell the television rights of their home matches to China's main station.

Dundee director and commercial manager Jim Connor also got in touch with Chelsea and Aston Villa for some background on the way they sold the likes of Gianluca Vialli or David Ginola to their fans. Talks were held about opening a Dundee FC shop in Shanghai while the club's website included a Chinese language section after receiving more than 300,000 hits on the day he signed.

Dundee became the second most popular club in China (behind only Manchester United) but the popularity wasn't matched back home when plans were finally submitted to Dundee City Council in November for the 30,000-seater stadium. The application provoked a host of objections, including a protest group which set up a fighting fund to pay legal costs and recruit a town planning consultant. Members of Caird Park Golf Club swung another blow when they added their voices to the chorus of disapproval and voted at their annual meeting to oppose any changes.

On the pitch the Dark Blues were still playing good football but they ended 2001 out of the top six after a slump in form and were struggling for any degree of consistency.

The new year started with a grim warning from Scotland's First Minister that the country's Euro 2008 bid would only proceed if there was clear evidence it was economically viable. Jack McConnell said he was not prepared to adopt a "fingers crossed" attitude and take a risk on new stadia which could end up as white elephants.

A political spat broke out when SNP leader John Swinney said there was no excuse for any further delay and told him to "show some leadership" and grasp the massive opportunity.

It was becoming apparent there was a similar lack of leadership at Dens Park. A Scottish Cup third round draw against Falkirk was followed by a disappointing SPL display in going down 4-2 to relegation-threatened Motherwell at Fir Park.

Ivano was back home in Italy and missed the defeat, which left Dundee sitting uncomfortably on the edge of the relegation zone.

A bewildering plot twist followed in the wake of the defeat. Dundee were about to be dragged through the courts after want-away midfielder Patrizio Billio was taken to Ninewells Hospital with concussion and made allegations he had been assaulted outside Dens Park. Police were already investigating the alleged assault. Billio's car was also targeted by vandals while parked outside the stadium, the locks being squirted full of glue.

Billio hadn't played for the club in over a year following a contractual dispute, which also involved fellow player and countryman, Marco de Marchi.

Chief executive Peter Marr was forced to apologise in the wake of the alleged assault after appearing to suggest the district was a hot-bed of crime and violence. Marr was reported to have talked of assaults being part of life in Dundee, with the Hilltown being singled out as an area where violent attacks were a daily occurrence.

Councillor Fiona Grant said she was "quite incensed" by the comments because it was simply not true that people were walking the streets in fear of being assaulted. "I think it is a regrettable incident both for the Hilltown and the city of Dundee as a whole considering the negative publicity it has drawn in the past few days," she said. "After seeing some less than measured reports of Mr Marr's comments I contacted the police to get figures on crime in the Hilltown and, apparently, only three assaults were reported in the past month. Obviously one assault is too many, but when we are looking at an area which 20,000 people live within walking distance of each other we see some perspective to the figures.

"I would hate for there to be a perception of the Hilltown as a place where people walk the streets in fear of assaults which take place on a daily basis, because this simply is not true. There are many positive aspects of life in the Hilltown which I hope will continue to be looked at, not just some bad publicity. The people who live there enjoy a strong spirit and I don't think they will let this overshadow the good aspects of the area."

Marr hastily got in touch with civic leaders following the negative publicity to assure them that his views on the city of Dundee were nothing but favourable. He said the remarks were taken out of context and he would not allow his family to continue to stay in Dundee if he thought it was a violent place.

Billio's case was then raised in the Italian parliament when Prime Minister Silvio Berlusconi was urged to put pressure on the authorities to fully investigate the incident. Antonio Gentile, a senator with Berlusconi's Forza Italia party, suggested the Prime Minister put pressure on London and Edinburgh, as well as FIFA and UEFA, because his co-nationals should be "protected from illegal conduct". He urged the government to "take a clear position regarding the Italian citizens who were the subject of an attack during their Scottish experience with Dundee".

Berlusconi, the AC Milan president, whose club once had Billio on its books, and sports minister Giuliano Urbani, were asked to "shed some light" on the situation. The Italian FA was already involved in the player's dispute with Dundee FC after Billio appealed to the country's players' union for support after being frozen out by the club. Billio returned to Italy, with the blessing of the club, after receiving a two-week sick note.

Marco de Marchi then said he was afraid to walk the streets following his team-mate's alleged assault. De Marchi made the revelation in an interview that was carried by a number of national papers in Italy and which further angered his bosses at Dens Park. De Marchi said: "I hardly go out now, but yesterday I did and I saw two guys looking at me suspiciously. Perhaps they were curious because my face is in all the newspapers here, but when I saw them come closer I was frightened and I lengthened my stride."

He said the manager's attitude towards him changed after he got injured and expressed hope that some kind of arrangement could be reached to get him out of Dens Park.

The Dark Blues were now consulting their lawyers about accusations of mistreatment which were made by both de Marchi and Billio in the Italian newspapers and on TV.

There were then further unwanted headlines which prompted chief executive Peter Marr to fly back to Dundee from his home in Mallorca to try to calm the storm. Dundee had just parted company with Italian fitness coach Luca Frediani in hostile circumstances and his club car and house were repossessed after he allegedly refused to return the keys.

Anglo-Italian businessman Giovanni di Stefano then reared his ugly head again with a suggestion he was bankrolling Dundee and helping to pay the wages of the club's expensive foreign stars. In an interview with a national newspaper, he would not confirm or deny having invested money in Dundee, and asked the interviewers to draw their own conclusions. Di Stefano appeared well informed about events at Dens Park, including the alleged attack outside the ground on Patrizio Billio and the ongoing contract dispute.

He used the word "we" to describe the club's problems with Billio and de Marchi and suggested the pair should pack up and leave Dens and try to start afresh elsewhere.

"He is very internet-literate and keeps himself up to date with what is happening here, but he has no connection with Dens Park," said Peter Marr.

"Like anyone else, if he wants to get involved here he is welcome to come up and sit round the table with us and tell us how he wants to get involved. The board of directors would have a look, and if it is in the best interests of Dundee FC we would take it on, but we have had no personal contact with di Stefano for two years."

Marr rubbished any talk of a crisis and gave his backing to his under-fire manager. "There has been a lot of speculation about Ivano's position at the club, his not being here and people saying we have fallen out with him but I would say that's total nonsense," he said. "We are 100% behind Ivano and Dario and hope to see them take the club forward. I realise the last few weeks haven't been very pretty but we are not unduly worried. So just to make it clear there has never been a fall-out between us and Ivano and Dario. They are 18 months into a three-year contract."

Marr said the club still planned to extend the deals. He said: "It's a matter of sitting down together. We know where we are on that and hopefully we can sit down early in the year and finalise things. It (the delay in signing the new deals) is because everybody has been busy doing other things - Ivano has been planning ahead and looking at the players here at Dens. His trip to Italy was planned well in advance and it is club business not his wedding - I tried to talk him out of that but he wouldn't listen to me! He has been in Italy quite a lot recently because he is planning for next season. There is a lot of work to be done because we have a lot of players out of contract at the end of the season and have been planning ahead.

"Over Christmas and New Year he and Dario worked really hard for this team. He never had the chance to see his family. They (Ivano and Dario) have not been away any more than they were last year. I think that's actually the first game Ivano has missed this season, while Dario has missed a couple. I don't stay in this country but my life is here, while they live here but their lives are in Italy and they have quite a bit of responsibility back there. They have their mother and father to look after and sometimes they have to return and do various things. But, at the same time, when they are here they are working day and night, seven days a week."

Marr made a point of highlighting Ivano's work with the younger players at Dens and also pointed out that the Dark Blues were not having the best of luck with injuries. "At the start of the season you think if things are going to be okay then the top six is a sensible target to aim at, and possibly a place in Europe too," he said. "But after the season we have had so far with injuries, I would be happy with a top-six finish, though it would be nice to do even better than that. I think we are on course. It's disappointing at the moment but I am sure things will get better shortly."

They didn't.

Tayside Police charged two men in connection with Billio's alleged assault at the end of January. Paul Marr – Peter Marr's son – who was now the club's director of football was charged along with his long-time friend Danny Rice, who he grew up with in Fintry.

Back on the pitch, new goalkeeper Julian Speroni was proving the benefits of Ivano's globetrotting management style but storm clouds were gathering at Dens Park.

Dundee managed to squeeze past Falkirk at the second time of asking in the Scottish Cup before going on a disappointing sequence of five games without a win. The poor run included a derby defeat against Dundee United at Tannadice and being dumped out of the Scottish Cup in the fourth round by First Division Partick Thistle.

Ivano returned to Italy to marry fiancée Erica following the cup exit and there was mounting speculation about his future as he missed three games whilst on honeymoon.

Peter Marr then broke ranks and went public. He immediately put contract talks on hold and said Dundee fans were concerned because they "have not been seeing the kind of football they were getting last season".

However, he made it clear the Bonetti brothers were still the men to lead Dundee to a top-six place.

"I am aware that there has been criticism recently, but I am sure that the majority of the fans are still behind Ivano and Dario and what we are trying to do here," he said. "However, I know some fans have been critical and I respect their views. They are concerned and we know it's because they have not been seeing the kind of football they were getting last season."

He said he expected there would be times in the future when Ivano missed games but he believed Dario was more than capable of stepping up in his absence.

"I live in Spain and when I am over there I am on the phone to my brother Jimmy three or four times a day about our business here," he said. "It is the same with Ivano and Dario and the important thing is not where Ivano is, it is communication and making sure things get done properly. I know that when Dario is in charge, training is done the right way and if he is in the dugout on his own he is more than capable of taking tactical decisions.

"They are in the middle of a three-year plan and, while some of what's gone on recently has been a learning experience for them, they are doing well. I would also say that I keep hearing this talk about things going wrong this season, but we have the same points as last season and, while it isn't going to be easy, we can still make the top six again and everyone is working hard to get there."

Marr also scotched rumours that he was planning to sell up his controlling share in the club to a consortium of Irish businessmen. "Whatever happens this season, myself Ivano and Dario will still be here next year fighting to get us as high up the league as possible," he said. "We eat and sleep Dundee, and I am disappointed anyone should question my long-term commitment to the club."

Cracks were also beginning to show in Scotland's Euro 2008 bid. The SFA were now struggling to meet the stadium criteria and went cap in hand to Ireland. The countries then agreed to submit a joint bid for the tournament despite a split in the ranks over the number of grounds which were being proposed.

Ivano returned to Dundee from Italy in March and immediately came out fighting before resuming his touchline duties with victory against St Johnstone at Dens.

Solicitors representing the Dark Blues director of football Paul Marr and Fintry man Danny Rice were also on the defensive at Dundee Sheriff Court. Not guilty pleas were lodged on behalf of Marr and Rice, who denied assaulting Billio as he left Dens Park with de Marchi.

Marr also denied charges that he entered the club's former fitness coach Luca Frediani's flat and removed items, including two satellite decoders, clothing, champagne and £790. A four-day trial was fixed for June 24 to 27. Neither Marr nor Rice was present in court.

Also absent was Ivano who went away again later that month on "club business" and missed the defeat against Dunfermline at East End Park.

Dundee failed to make the top-six split but Ivano returned to Italy again in April to reassess his signing strategy following the collapse of the ill-fated SPL TV deal. The SPL's proposals to set up their own channel on a subscription basis were eventually sunk by Rangers and Celtic who voted against them. With Sky TV's offer of around £45 million for a four-year deal already rejected, a financial crisis was looming large on the horizon for Scotland's top flight clubs. The remaining 10 clubs proposed to resign from the SPL with two seasons' notice and begin the countdown for the league to be reformed with or without the Old Firm.

Peter Marr blasted Rangers and Celtic for scuppering the SPL TV station. He said: "Celtic and Rangers can pick faults in the SPL TV plan, but they have to come out and show us all what they see as the way forward. I don't see what the Old Firm can put forward that would be better than what was already in place and this will damage some of the other clubs in the league. The SPL has the rights to their games, so they can't automatically set up their own station, but we all need to know what their thinking is."

Ivano arrived back from his homeland and discovered Marr had been just as vocal about his manager's future which he said he was now unsure of given changes in his personal life. There was then a clear-the-air press conference called by Ivano where he told reporters his future was at Dens Park and insisted he had no thoughts about leaving. The press conference did nothing to dispel suspicions that he and the club were not entirely working in harmony, although it did appear as if he would be remaining in charge.

He described the suggestion the impending birth of his first child might lead to him quitting the club as "a joke" and said the only way he would leave would be if he was sacked.

"I have heard on the radio and read in the papers much speculation about my future," he said. "I don't care about speculation but I am speaking out because I want the fans to be clear about my situation. There is supposed to be a problem because my wife and I are waiting for a baby. It's a joke. My wife has said to me she will enjoy coming here with the baby next season and I look forward to bringing my family to Scotland. There is no problem with that. I think 100% I'll be here then. I don't want to leave. I still have a year left on my contract and the only reason I have not signed a new one is because of the financial situation. I hope this week we will know more about that and I will be ready to sign a three, four, or five-year extension. Then, of course, it depends what the club want to do, whether they have the same idea. If my future changes away from Dundee then that will not be because of me – that's for sure. Beyond next season I don't know what is going to happen. But I enjoy it here and it would not be my decision to leave."

Ivano blamed the poor season on a severe injury list which included Georgi Nemsadze, Zura Khizanishvili, Juan Sara, Beto Carranza, Javier Artero and Marcello Marrocco.

"This is like Celtic being without Larsson, Lennon and Hartson," he said. "It would be difficult for them to play without players of this importance and so it has been for us. "This is the answer to the question – why didn't we get into the top six?"

A reporter suggested he had been luckier than most managers to have been afforded the resources to bring in players such as Claudio Caniggia and Fabian Caballero.

"I am not lucky," he said. "If you spend £1 million on a Ferrari then there is a problem which leaves you having to use a Citroen then you are unlucky. To be clear, the reason why I've been in Italy is to try to build a really competitive team for next year. And that is not easy because of the financial situation affecting Scotland, not just Dundee. One way or another we have to be ready to be competitive and that is the only reason why I've been away, not only in Italy but in one other country also. Like every manager in Scotland, I hope to know very soon what the budget for next season will be. I have four players in mind to bring to the club but it depends on whether the money is there."

Ivano said the budget put down for next season would determine whether Dundee would be going for third place or bringing through young players at the expense of results.

Peter Marr welcomed his manager's commitment to staying at Dens Park but said he would not be rushing into re-opening contract discussions. "I am delighted Ivano is making these noises and indicating he is staying, but in the present situation it is prudent we keep our options open," he said. "We'll give him the chance to bring his family over and get settled in next season then take things from there. We had a lengthy chat today over other matters. He did mention that he wanted to know about the budget and I explained that at this stage I could not give him an exact answer. We know what the worst case scenario would be but that could change.

"We will get an update on the TV revenue situation at an SPL meeting tomorrow. But when we sit down on Friday we still won't know exactly how the club is going to be placed."

The anger against Celtic and Rangers was similar to the growing level of discontent against the new stadium after more than 300 objections were made against the proposal. Dundee councillors, however, voted to approve the plans following the public consultation, despite appeals from objectors who addressed the quality development committee. The council received 143 individual letters of objection, along with a petition containing 191 signatures, which was received from the Magdalene Area Tenants and Residents Association. There were objections from the Mill O' Mains Residents Association, Dundee Federation of Tenants Associations, Douglas and Caird Park golf clubs and the Save the Caird Park group.

The final document for the joint bid with Ireland was later signed and sent off to European football's governing body with the backing of Manchester United manager Sir Alex Ferguson. The glossy synopsis of the bid document said that a choice would be made between proposed new stadiums in Dundee, Aberdeen and Easter Road in Edinburgh. The brochure listed St Johnstone's ground in Perth and Arbroath FC's Gayfield as two of Scotland's 21 approved training grounds which were earmarked for Euro 2008.

Well-placed sources said Dundee was the Scottish Executive's number one choice for a new stadium because the Edinburgh bid was "too Central Belt" and was included as "window dressing". First Minister Jack McConnell also hinted the Dundee stadium project was a preferred option when he said that not being in the Central Belt was a "distinct advantage".

Sports minister Mike Watson was also a Dundonian and a Dundee United supporter whose pivotal role in the bid was being seen as advantageous for the city. Although the proposal was given outline planning permission there were still legal obstacles to clear with regards the legally-binding conditions attached to the original purchase.

It now appeared likely that Ivano would also be looking for a new home.

The writing was on the wall when Dundee moved to distance itself from comments he made against referee Willie Young following a 2-1 defeat to Motherwell. Ivano launched a verbal attack on Young following the final game of the league season and suggested the referee would be celebrating Dundee's defeat.

"I hope this is his last game, that he is retiring now," he said. "Every time he was giving free-kicks he was looking at our bench. It is a joke. I think he parties the night after Dundee have lost."

It was an amazing outburst, and, although it wasn't the only reason, it helped convince Dundee's directors that a change of management was necessary. Paraguayan manager Francisco Ocampo, who was in charge of Sol de America, then held talks at Dens Park with Jimmy Marr and Jim Connor about the manager's position.

Ivano returned to his homeland but was unable to make it back to Scotland after being asked to appear before the general purposes committee of the SFA to explain his comments.

Dundee's director of football Paul Marr did make it to the dock. During a trial at Dundee Sheriff Court, Billio and de Marchi alleged Billio was butted by Fintry man Danny Rice after a confrontation with Marr outside Dens Park. The two long-time friends from Fintry eventually walked free from court. The sheriff found Marr not guilty of assaulting Billio. The assault charge against Rice was found not proven. Two further charges against Marr of stealing property from the flat of the club's former fitness coach and attempting to pervert the course of justice were also found not proven.

During the trial, both the Italians were accused of fabricating evidence in a bid to secure a cash settlement before tearing up their contracts and quitting Dundee.

Sheriff Alastair Stewart said that he found the case against Marr and Rice "unsatisfactory" and in particular he dismissed what he described as unreliable evidence given to the court by de Marchi.

There was a huge sigh of relief following the verdicts. Paul Marr said he was delighted and relieved the matter was over which would allow him to get on with his life after what he described as a "very difficult" six months.

Dundee fans were also now awaiting the board's verdict on the Bonetti era. Former manager Jim Duffy was strongly linked with the job during the summer but Ivano stressed he would be back for pre-season training following a holiday in Italy.

"Like the fans, I have had enough of these stories," he said. "What can I say? There are two days left of my holidays then I will be there."

However, he said he didn't organise the club's pre-season trip to Romania and claimed it was Peter Marr who should be asked about signings.

Ivano did go back to Dens but it wasn't for long. Peter Marr issued a statement following his return and said it had been decided to "mutually terminate" Ivano and Dario's contracts immediately. Ivano later insisted it was he – and not the Dundee board – who finally decided that the time was right for him to go.

"I want to make one thing clear," he said. "It was my decision to terminate the contract and I did it in a friendly way. Peter Marr did not sack anyone. I was shocked to hear this."

Marr later criticised Ivano for his lack of regard for Scottish football. He said the Italian's time as a player in Italy's top flight with Juventus and Sampdoria had affected his attitude and subdued youth development at Dens.

"It is important to get someone in who respects the Scottish game," he said. "Ivano sometimes didn't and that may have been due to his time in Serie A. Ivano concentrated solely on the first team and we want someone who will concentrate on the whole club. We have tremendous talent in our youth team and it is important to embrace all of the squad."

Marr did however praise Ivano for bringing plenty of colour and class to the club. He said: "Some of the players he brought here were tremendous – not just for Dundee but for Scottish football. It was tremendously exciting at times and it is unfortunate that it did not last three years. But he got married and his wife is about to have a baby and all that certainly changed Ivano."

Midfielder Temuri Ketsbaia was tipped as a potential replacement, before Jim Duffy returned to take over the Dens Park hot seat for what was a second time. Duffy was a Dundee legend who would easily take his place in the club's greatest-ever team. In a decade of ill-advised shoulder pads and mullets, Duffy was the cultured bald eagle whose defensive play in the 1980s drew comparisons with Liverpool captain Alan Hansen. He was the Scottish Players' Player of the Year when he signed for Dundee from Morton in 1985 and only a wealth of talent in his position stopped him from achieving full international caps.

Duffy gave everything for the cause and his leadership qualities were just as impressive before his Dundee career was cut short by a knee injury at Ibrox in 1987. He caught his studs in the grass playing against Rangers on the Saturday and the surface of his knee cap being broken off was among the list of injuries he suffered. He was a married man with a pregnant wife and son to support and he broke down in tears when he was told he would could no longer play football.

The popular Duffy was afforded a testimonial against a Premier League Select before returning to Glasgow where he was asked to join Gordon McQueen as assistant manager at Airdrie. He went for a jog 10 months after his injury and played in a reserve game for Airdrie which left him in agony afterwards – which put any thoughts of returning to the back of his mind. Duffy became the youngest manager in Britain a few months later when he took over as Falkirk boss and he took The Bairns to within a point of being promoted to the Premier League. He quit the job in November 1989 following just 13 months in charge.

Duffy walked away from the job after being overruled by club chiefs when he demanded they suspend a group of first-team players that got into a pub fight. He immediately regretted his decision to quit but left and bought a pub before being given the chance to train at Love Street by St Mirren manager Tony Fitzpatrick. Duffy joined in five-a-sides and got fully fit during his time in Paisley. He eventually fought his way back to play the game he loved against medical advice. But he then discovered he couldn't play for St Mirren because he wasn't registered, and insurance money had also been paid out following his injury in 1987.

Dundee, who had cancelled his registration, had first refusal on his services if he did return and he was so determined to play again that he struck a deal with the Dark Blues. He signed on until the end of the season and paid back the insurance money to the club. Duffy returned to the Premier League with Dundee in 1990 and by chance his first game was a 2-2 draw against Rangers at Ibrox where his career had been struck down three years previously. The Dark Blues were relegated, despite Duffy's performances earning rave reviews.

Duffy didn't get the contract he wanted and signed for Partick Thistle before eventually returning for a third time to Dundee, who were by then managed by fedora-wearing Simon Strainrod. Duffy combined his playing duties with a role as the charismatic Englishman's assistant before taking over as player/manager in 1993, during a period when the club nearly went bust.

Duffy was one of Scotland's rising managerial stars and he guided First Division Dundee to the 1995 League Cup Final which they lost 2-0 to Aberdeen. Ron Dixon had left his directors to fend for themselves by the time Duffy led the team out at Hampden and the Dark Blues were living a hand-to-mouth existence. Dixon paid little attention to affairs at Dens before eventually selling up. Duffy used to pay for washing powder to clean the players' gear and reimburse petrol expenses. He also worked miracles on a shoestring budget and brought through players including Neil McCann, Jim Hamilton, Iain Anderson and Gavin Rae during his spell in charge. He inherited a squad of under-achievers when he left to join Hibernian in 1996 but was sacked after just 13 months with the Easter Road side adrift at the bottom of the league.

A link with ex-Dundee team-mate Graham Rix prompted a move to Chelsea as youth coach where his influence was significant in soon-to-be England captain John Terry's development as a defender. Duffy then joined Portsmouth after Rix was appointed manager there. He stepped down from the job just six months before he was asked by the Dens Park board to make a surprise return to Dundee in the summer of 2002 for a second stint in charge.

He said he was inheriting a really good squad which he bolstered with the signings of Nacho Novo and Jonay Hernandez, along with the significant re-signing of Julian Speroni. But Temuri Ketsbaia, Beto Garrido, Walter del Rio, Alessandro Romano, Khaled Kemas, Kiko Torres, Gerardo Traverso, Umberto Fatello and Massimo Beghetto were shown the exit door.

Dundee rebels Patrizio Billio and Marco de Marchi also at last had their contracts terminated after the club asked football's governing body to step in and resolve the bitter and long-running dispute. A Dundee spokesman said the club was pleased FIFA had resolved a "crazy situation" and they were no longer paying the pair £25,000 a month to "damage its reputation".

"The contracts have been cancelled and the players have gone," he said. "We are very pleased this chapter is now over. Compensation is still an issue which will be addressed in the future. The benefits to Dundee is we are no longer paying their wages. The players have been taking £25,000 a month to sit and snipe from the sidelines for the past couple of years. Here are two guys who were taking £25,000 a month from the club while seeking to damage its reputation in this country and abroad. It was an unsatisfactory situation all round and the sooner it was brought to an end, the better. That money can now be reinvested in players who are actually committed to the Dark Blues and getting results for the teams."

Peter Marr expressed relief they were now gone but said that only time would tell if one of the darker chapters in the club's history was finally over. He said: "It has also been a difficult time personally with the very public trial of the alleged assault on Billio. It took up a lot of time that could have been spent on better projects.

"We have done a lot of work during the summer trying to stabilise the club in the very unsure future of football in Scotland, especially in the SPL, but things seem to be taking shape now and the new manager has been working very hard with the players. Billio and de Marchi have left the club after FIFA cancelled their contracts but we are not sure if this is the end of the matter – only time will tell."

Marr said he was convinced things would change for the better under Duffy who brought in a new set of rules which left one player going on a shopping trip for a pair of trousers. "I noticed a huge change about the club when Jim had only been a couple of days in the job," he said. "The first thing he did was employ the skills of a translator so not one of our many foreign players were in any doubt as to what will happen. He softened them up by saying they could call him Jim, then hit them with a list of dos and don'ts. Casual attire will be tolerated, but it must be smart.

"When he said no to jeans, one foreign player said he didn't own trousers. He was told in no uncertain terms he was earning more than enough to get out and buy some. I didn't feel it was my place to tell Ivano how to dress, so I'm delighted at Jim's approach to this. He also told the players training will revert to the traditional morning slot, with everyone training together."

Marr said when Ivano was appointed the theory was he'd use his contacts to bring in big players with others being sold off to balance the books. "Ivano was good at bringing players in, but he couldn't get them out," he said.

"The idea of employing Ivano and his brother Dario was my idea. But it just didn't work out the way I hoped. You have to be big enough in this game to hold up your hand when things don't work out. However, I must say I've been tremendously impressed with the way Jim Duffy has gone about things in the short time he's been back with the club."

Dundee City Council's petition to the Court of Session for permission to use Caird Park for a new stadium was granted, subject to the joint Scottish-Irish bid being successful.

But just a month later the dream went up in smoke when UEFA's Executive Committee awarded the honour to Austria and Switzerland. When the Celtic joint bid failed in December, Dundee and Dundee United talked of "alternative possibilities" and refused to dismiss the ground-sharing proposal outright.

The plan did fizzle out but there was more spark on the field as Duffy led Dundee to a top-six finish and the Scottish Cup Final in his first season back in the hot seat. Dundee qualified for Europe for the first time in 29 years despite a 1-0 defeat to Rangers.

But it was the return of Giovanni di Stefano to the fold that would create just as many headlines as Dundee's impressive performance at Hampden.

Di Stefano, his son Michael and a large entourage of guests watched Dundee for the first time as they came very close to denying Rangers victory and the treble. He was also a surprise guest at a party afterwards at the city's Apex Hotel, where he was introduced to the players and the club staff by Dundee owners Peter and Jimmy Marr.

"We are having a party, not to celebrate getting beaten by Rangers but to celebrate a very good season," said Peter Marr.

"Rangers, and Alex McLeish, gave us the respect we deserved and Mr McLeish's decision to pull off an attacking player and replace him with a defender to try to snuff out the threat posed by Fabian Caballero showed that we had them worried. It's been a season worth celebrating. I can't praise Jim Duffy and the players enough for getting us here."

Di Stefano had launched abortive bids to buy into Norwich and Northampton Town before being arrested by Italian police in connection with an investigation into alleged fraudulent trading.

He was remanded in custody by magistrates in Ipswich after being deported from Italy on fraud charges allegedly involving hundreds of thousands of pounds.

Di Stefano praised the Marr brothers and Dundee director Jim Connor for their support during his difficulties and pledged that he would repay the favour if ever required.

He said: "Dundee Football Club are my friends and if, as and when they require assistance I can provide, I will not shy away from my responsibilities. Jimmy Marr has received criticism but, in my opinion, the guy deserves a knighthood. He has smiled through a lot of troubles and I admire him for that. Any time he and Peter, or Dundee Football Club, need me they just have to call, as I have been able to do in the past when I needed their support."

He said that during one of his personal and professional crises, Peter and Jimmy Marr, and Jim Connor phoned his wife "four or five times a week" to offer support and assistance. He said: "I'll never forget that. They know they can count on me. We have retained our friendship."

Dundee's White Knight was set to saddle up.

CHAPTER TEN

A Fishy Plan To Reel In Paul Gascoigne

Gratitude can turn a meal into a feast, a house into a home and a stranger into a friend

Giovanni di Stefano

GIOVANNI DI STEFANO charged through the doors of Dens Park in August 2003 and clarified his position concerning Iraqi dictator Saddam Hussein and al-Qaeda founder Osama bin Laden. The Anglo-Italian businessman, who spoke with a strong Cockney accent, was to become a director of the club at long last, following a meeting in Northampton with Peter Marr and Jim Connor. Dundee rejected his investment in 1999 before he attempted an aborted takeover attempt at Norwich City in 2001 when he tried to get his son installed as a director.

Di Stefano was back in Dundee and was now being offered a seat on the board despite his links with Arkan, Robert Mugabe, Osama bin Laden, Saddam Hussein and Slobodan Milosevic. The self-professed "most investigated man in the world" immediately scratched two names off the list of potential season-ticket holders at Dens Park.

"You will not see Saddam Hussein here," he said. "You will not see bin Laden here. If we do, we'll collect the reward, pay off our overdraft and buy Beckham."

Di Stefano was unveiled at a Dens Park press conference and promised to regularly challenge Rangers and Celtic for trophies and become the third force in Scottish football. He brought with him an inscribed paperweight which would be displayed in the club boardroom. The paperweight, he said, summed up his feelings on the day he "knew would come".

"It's just the words that are important," he said. "It says here: 'Gratitude can turn a meal into a feast, a house into a home and a stranger into a friend' and I hope I will be a good friend to Dundee Football Club.

"I do, of course, have another profession and I must comply with the requirements of that profession but other than that Dundee Football Club certainly will have 100% effort from me.

"I have had a relationship with the club for the past four years. We've been living together. Now is the time for the marriage. You can't always live together. Sometimes the in-laws complain about that."

Although it wasn't clear what financial contribution he would actually be making to the club he pledged to support manager Jim Duffy in recruiting new signings. Di Stefano said if the right player was to cost him £1 million then it would be "no problem". He also revealed plans to construct a new south stand at Dens, in place of The Derry. He said: "Two years from now you'll be seeing a new south stand which will include a community project. I've already said today to Mr Marr and Mr Connor that it is a priority for me. I want to go ahead. If that means I have to fund it, then I have to fund it."

Never one to shy away from controversy, di Stefano joked that the new construction would be named the "Nicholas van Hoogstraten Stand" after the convicted killer. In 2002, van Hoogstraten was jailed for 10 years over the death of former business rival Mohammed Raja, who was stabbed five times before being shot in the head in 1999. Di Stefano sprang Mr van Hoogstraten from jail by overturning his manslaughter conviction.

The businessman maintained his silence when asked how much money he would be injecting into Dundee and also declined to answer what percentage of the club he owned. He denied he was acting for any other individual or group of individuals and he also laughed off suggestions of indecency in his financial affairs.

He said: "There has been an enormous media interest in something that would normally be by the by. They can suggest what they like, but I think I've been the most investigated man in the world and here I am."

Di Stefano then denied he was an unsuitable suitor for Dundee after being asked about his links to several high-profile legal clients including Serbian warlord Arkan. "I do not shy away from the fact Mr Raznatovic (Arkan) was a client," he said. "He was my friend. And I have not shied away from Dundee, I have stayed very loyal. I have made football investments elsewhere but all that's gone and I'm just interested in Dundee Football Club."

Di Stefano said it wasn't in Dundee's interests for him to become involved in the club when he first approached them in 1999.

"At that time there was a potential shadow of a doubt," he said. "But that was unjustified and we all knew that. In a democratic society when there are allegations they must be dealt with. Which they were, very, very successfully. We must now move on."

Di Stefano said he wanted Dundee to challenge the Old Firm's stranglehold on Scottish football and would be actively working to remedy such ills.

"We will be competitive," he said. "We need to do something about that otherwise we can't have a credible league in Scotland. The league is currently a two-horse race but now it's certainly going to be three."

Di Stefano also called for a new British competition to replace the Scottish and English leagues.

He then went into some detail about how he was to going to assist the club in the future. "I have had a sit-down with Jim Duffy and discussed the situation with him," he said. "We already have a very strong team and I can't speculate. But if he feels the need to have a specific player and the price is right then I won't shy away from my responsibilities."

The Dark Blues were first brought to the attention of father-of-five di Stefano by one of his sons, Milan, who became a Dundee supporter while attending school in Scotland. "I presented the idea to my father who found it quite inviting," said Milan. "Part of me did think it would never happen, but there was always the hope. And, as you can see, it has happened. I am still a big fan. I don't think I'd be here otherwise."

Di Stefano said the whole city should be grateful for what Peter Marr had done for Dundee.

Marr, in return, welcomed his new recruit. He said it could be a good acquisition because he would provide financial expertise, commercial know-how and connections from across the world. Marr said di Stefano would be taking a small shareholding and not a controlling interest in the club and stressed that his contacts were of prime importance. Marr said the club was looking to tap into di Stefano's footballing contacts, which included a stake in Italian club Lazio and experience of Serbian football with Obilic.

He said: "The experience he's got in the legal world, financial world and also in the football world are things that are useful when you are running a football club. Then there is also the financial aspect, and we are dealing with a guy who is operating at a higher level than we do at present. If that leads to investment that would be great, but we have not talked money. Whatever happens, Jimmy and I intend to remain in control at Dundee."

Marr also denied a suggestion that di Stefano's links with some of the world's most infamous figures would bring disrepute to Dens Park.

"I think he'll always be controversial, that's the kind of guy he is," said Marr. "But he is a lawyer, he acts for some of the biggest people and in the highest courts and he's accepted there."

Both the SFA and the SPL said they saw nothing in the rules which would exclude him from taking his seat on the board, despite his colourful career.

Dundee FC Supporters' Association secretary Fraser MacDonald said he trusted the judgment of club owners Peter and Jimmy Marr "implicitly". Mr MacDonald said he believed the new arrangement would have the backing of the majority of fans and said many of the allegations surrounding di Stefano were 'hearsay' and should not be held against him.

He said: "Some people criticised the decision to bring back Jim Duffy to the club, and even questioned the decision to bring in Claudio Caniggia.

"Over the years they (the Marrs) have been forced to make a lot of difficult and controversial decisions; on each occasion they have been proved correct. There's no doubt they have the best interests of Dundee Football Club at heart, and the supporters are behind them. From what I have learned, Mr di Stefano has a number of contacts in world football, and if he can bring attractive footballers to Dens the fans will be interested. If he is prepared to invest in the club then the Marrs should be congratulated for attracting investment at a time when a number of other clubs in Scottish football are unable to do so."

Mr MacDonald admitted he was concerned about the adverse publicity Dundee's links to di Stefano would bring, but said most fans were more concerned with success on the pitch.

Dundee started the season very positively with a 3-0 away win against Motherwell, before getting ready to travel to Albania to go up against KS Vllaznia in the UEFA Cup qualifying round.

Dundee Civic Trust were also looking towards Europe to save one of the city's most remarkable treasures, which was at risk of being lost forever.

Nearly 20 years previously, following a successful public appeal, the living room ceiling at Carbet Castle in Broughty Ferry was removed and preserved just before the last remaining sections of the former jute baron's mansion were demolished to make way for a housing development. Commissioned by the Grimond family, the intricately-detailed ceiling was created in 1871 by Charles Frechou, whose other great work was the ceiling of the Paris Opera House. Sandwiched between heavy timbers and polystyrene layers, the ceiling had remained in the care of Dundee Civic Trust, who had been relying on generous benefactors for storage.

But the building where it was being stored was scheduled to be demolished and the trust feared it could not meet the cost of another move, even if somewhere to store it was found. The trust was considering an approach to the French government to see if they could help.

Help of a much different kind was on the table ahead of Dundee's trip to Albania. KS Vllaznia indicated some 700 tickets would be set aside for the away support and Dundee were also offered the services of veteran comedian Norman Wisdom's official translator.

Wisdom was a comedy hero in Albania where his films were the only ones by Western actors permitted by dictator Enver Hoxha to be shown during the Cold War. Charlie Chaplin had called Norman Wisdom his "favourite clown" and the octogenarian film star was hugely popular in Albania, where his films were still regularly shown on TV.

Before the match a spokesman for the Albanian Embassy in London dismissed claims that Vllaznia's home city Shkoder was one of the most dangerous places in Europe.

The spokesman responded to reports which suggested Shkoder was a place of dirt, disease and squalor, riddled with gun-toting locals, and a place where lawlessness flourished.

"I have heard something about these stories, but I have not seen them," he said. "What I can tell you is that the situation in Albania is calm and I do not think there would be any problems for fans. We have had many football clubs and national teams coming to our country and we do not have problems with them and we would be happy to see any fans come on this trip. All I would recommend to your supporters is that they remember that there is a 10 Euro charge on entry to our country, but British citizens do not require a visa and are very welcome."

Vllaznia club president Myftar Cela was murdered in neighbouring Montenegro just weeks before the match and the British Foreign Office warned against travel in the Shkoder area.

A Dundee spokesman said the club would be doing its homework and assessing the situation but stressed they would not be panicked by the scare stories. He said: "This is not the first time we have heard such tales about places where we were headed. The same was said about Serbia when we played Sartid in the Intertoto Cup two years ago, and about Bucharest for our pre-season trip last summer. We were even told there was a danger al-Qaeda would attack when we were in Trinidad in January. But when we got to all these places, our welcome was warm and the treatment we and our fans received excellent. Of course we are aware of the concerns that have been expressed about this area of Albania and, for the sake of the team and any fans who want to travel, we will be doing our homework and assessing the situation. In doing that, we will consult the proper authorities and obtain accurate information, not rely on scare stories."

The 150 or so Dundee fans that braved the trip found a place that was sad and poverty-stricken. Under communism it had been at the centre of the Albanian economy. But following the collapse of the Soviet Union the assorted industries Shkoder had boasted collapsed, and its skilled workforce had largely headed for the capital Tirana.

There might have been concerns about Dundee supporters travelling to the region but the only problems were in negotiating the 120km trip from Tirana over bumps and potholes. The journey involved overtaking cattle, finding a way past flocks of sheep with their shepherds, villagers on horse carts and people riding donkeys and mules.

A Steve Lovell goal just before the break and a Nacho Novo strike five minutes after the break secured a deserved win over Vllaznia in the Loro Borici Stadium. The second goal knocked the stuffing out of the home side who rarely threatened. Dundee's players ran down the clock in the second half, knowing they had one foot in the first round draw proper.

Dundee then returned to league action with a home match against Dunfermline where a Lee Wilkie own goal and a late strike from Stevie Crawford gave the visitors maximum points.

There was more bad news when Dundee's financial position was laid bare. The club's annual report and accounts for the year to May 2002 was posted in August 2003 and revealed the club posted losses of £6.6m in the final year of Ivano Bonetti's colourful reign.

Dens chairman Jimmy Marr admitted the financial position of the club remained "extremely difficult" despite a period of "stability and realism" following Jim Duffy's arrival.

Marr said: "The loss for the financial year and balance sheet bear out the financial cost of pursuing the policies adopted in this year and the previous year. Following the employment of Jim Duffy as manager in early July 2002, the club has enjoyed, in my opinion, a period of stability and realism. Notwithstanding this playing success, the financial position of the club, and football in general, remains extremely difficult. Our debts are the result of striving for that success."

Dundee residents were in the grip of similar financial misery. The Citizens Advice Bureau in Dundee revealed it was dealing with more than £2 million worth of debt in the last financial year which was more than double the previous year's figure. The average amount owed by Dundee residents, in the year from April 2002 to March 2003, amounted to £13,128, not counting mortgages.

The "stability and realism" Marr highlighted seemed entirely at odds with the club's approach to bringing in new faces before the transfer window closed.

Dundee put in a £500,000 bid for Motherwell's young Scotland international James McFadden which was refused, before they upped the offer to £600,000 which was also turned down. Di Stefano made the bid after Duffy expressed his admiration for McFadden although he was caught slightly unawares when a move to sign the player was promptly launched. That sparked discussions behind the scenes between the pair, where Duffy made it clear that he would call the shots on team affairs and decide the make-up of the squad.

Di Stefano said: "There will, indeed, be some interesting news within the transfer deadline, but we as a board and Mr Duffy do not make rash signings simply as a PR move. I could very easily have signed two, three or four top players this last week but whether the manager would have played them or not would have been a different matter. Mr Duffy will decide whom, when and if any players are signed and we will all be guided even by the price levels he suggests. He knows best.

"As a result of our meeting there will be some developments but the transfer window is August 31, 2003. We have a home game on Saturday and a UEFA Cup game on August 28. Let us all please concentrate on those two games and allow the manager to do his job within the framework and new budget at his disposal."

McFadden was still a transfer target, along with Celtic's Mark Fotheringham and Chelsea striker Carlton Cole. But Duffy was remaining tight-lipped on the funds available to spend.

Dundee put defeat by Dunfermline behind them and won 2-1 at Dens against Livingston before booking their place in the UEFA Cup first round with a 4-0 home defeat of Vllaznia.

Some of football's biggest names began to be linked with a move to Dens Park before the transfer window closed, including the most naturally gifted English midfielder of his generation.

Claudio Caniggia's Dundee spell might have been history but di Stefano was signalling his intention to create some more by signing another of the 1990 World Cup's most iconic stars.

Manager Jack Charlton handed Paul Gascoigne his first team debut as a substitute for George Reilly in a 1–0 win over Queens Park Rangers in April 1985 at St James' Park. He spent three more years at St James' Park before signing for Tottenham for a British-record £2.3m.

Just like Caniggia, Paul Gascoigne was also 23 and a relative newcomer to the international scene when he went to the World Cup in Italy in 1990. After lighting up the tournament, Gascoigne's tears famously flowed when he picked up a booking in the semi-final against West Germany. The yellow card would have ruled him out of the final against Argentina, had England progressed. But England suffered penalty shoot-out heartache after extra-time.

Caniggia had already endured a similar fate 24 hours earlier in Naples when he also picked up a semi-final booking against Italy following a deliberate hand-ball.

Gascoigne came home a national hero and dead-cert millionaire. He nearly wrecked his career the following year in the FA Cup Final where a rash tackle on Nottingham Forest's Gary Charles damaged the cruciate ligaments in his knee. The injury meant Gascoigne's planned transfer from Tottenham to Lazio was put off for a year until May 1992. He spent three years in Italy before Rangers broke their transfer record in 1995 to bring him to Scotland. The Geordie lad played some of the best football of his career at Ibrox, and scored 39 goals in 103 games. In March 1998 he returned to England to play for Middlesbrough under Bryan Robson, where he eventually received treatment for stress, depression and drink problems.

He was left out of the England squad for the 1998 World Cup before joining Everton in 2000 and going on to have disappointing spells with Burnley, Boston United and Chinese club Gansu Tianma.

Dundee wanted to bring Gascoigne to Dens as player/coach and were hoping that having some of the finest fishing beats on his doorstep would reel in the angling addict.

Duffy said: "What I would say is that, so far, we have only given what you could call a note of interest. We have contacted him and his people and let them know that, if he would consider coming back to Scotland, we would be seriously interested in having him. At this stage, we have gone no further than that and we will have to see how the thing develops, but I do realise that because it is Paul Gascoigne there is huge media interest in even that much.

"He is a player who can lift the team, have a very good effect on those around him and is always hungry for the ball. Whatever other benefits there could be, that's all that interests me. He plays football the way we want to play it and, as well as appealing to us, I think that might appeal to him."

Duffy said Gazza's passing style would blend perfectly with the way his team was playing, which he believed might persuade him to return to Scotland for the second time in his career.

"I am sure he will have other offers involving more money than we can come up with, but, if he did come here, he would be playing a style of football he likes," Duffy said.

"He is in the latter stages of his career, but with the Caniggia signing we have already seen what coming to a club like Dundee can do for a player who many people said was finished. Claudio ended up going to a World Cup and, while Paul's situation is not identical, this is something that could benefit him."

Duffy suggested the prospect of a quiet life back in Scotland and being able to go about his daily business unobstructed by inquisitive eyes could appeal to the 35-year-old.

Things were looking positive when the midfielder asked for more details after Dundee pledged to find him a house near one of the many well-stocked fishing lochs just outside the city.

Dundee chairman Jimmy Marr stressed, however, that the club would not be held to ransom. "We are not going to break the bank to get him," he said. "We did that with Caniggia and we are not going to do it again. It has to be a sensible offer."

Gascoigne instead took up an offer in Abu Dhabi and signed a one-year deal with Al Jazira of the United Arab Emirates as a replacement for George Weah.

The Dark Blues also lost out in a bidding war for James McFadden on deadline day whilst a move to sign giant striker Peter Crouch from Aston Villa also failed to get over the line.

Dundee failed to sign any player before the window shut. That was despite twice increasing their offer for McFadden, who eventually joined Everton for £1.5m in the final hour.

Duffy said: "The possibility of signing Paul Gascoigne was something that we looked at, but have not been able to do. There is nothing suspicious in any way related to our decision to end the interest – it is simply the case that we will not be pursuing the matter any further."

Di Stefano revealed how approaches to Georgi Kinkladze, and two international players who were with top flight clubs in Spain, had also collapsed in similar circumstances.

Di Stefano said: "As all supporters will know, the club has been unable to sign any player within the transfer deadline. This is through no fault of mine or Mr Duffy. The manager was given a substantial budget within which, at his total discretion, he could sign players. We offered first and foremost £600,000 for Mr McFadden. We increased such to £750,000 and, on Tuesday of last week, to £1m plus an augmented salary. In fairness to Mr McFadden, he was ready to come to Dens Park. His chairman stated quite openly that unless he received 'silly money' the player would be kept until the January transfer window. But we all now know that he signed for Everton for a reputed £1.5 million.

"Mr Duffy also made a more than generous offer to Mr Paul Gascoigne to join Dens as a player/assistant coach.

"After some thought and proper consideration, Mr Gascoigne preferred Al Jazira Football Club.

"The manager has been negotiating with Mr Kinkladze – even up to 11pm on Sunday night – and an increased salary from £5,000 to £8,000 per week was not sufficient to tempt him to Dens Park. It is apparent most prefer to play for the English clubs as opposed to Scottish clubs."

Di Stefano said he would be taking up the matter with the SFA of how to make it more attractive for players to come to Scotland following the transfer deadline disappointments.

He said: "A number of players we approached had no problems with the financial package offered but simply the location and state of Scottish football. I do not have a quick or easy answer, but I will not give up our search for top quality players to play for our club within the SPL."

Di Stefano said Dundee also tried to sign two La Liga stars.

He said: "Mr Duffy also negotiated with a top player from Atletico Madrid (Dani) and was actually at Edinburgh Airport, but that player failed to turn up. After a hundred excuses from both the agent and Atletico, that came to nothing. We then negotiated for a Brazilian player from Deportivo La Coruna (Djalminha). I received a telephone call on Friday in Monte Carlo asking whether I was willing to pay €1.1 million per annum for the salary.

"I approved such, and stated even if it was more it would be okay. On Friday, Saturday and Sunday, we sent our representatives to negotiate with Deportivo La Coruna, because it was clear that the player had personal matters to resolve with the club without which he was not willing to move. Those matters were not able to be resolved, despite the president of Deportivo missing the Sunday game to deal with the matter

"Mr Duffy also has made several other lucrative offers to other players, all of whom preferred other countries to Scotland. To say that I am not upset, disappointed, even angry at how things have turned out is an understatement. However, I am angry at the manner upon which in the world of football men can sign binding contracts and then simply change their minds."

After the ambitious moves to land Gascoigne, McFadden, Dani and Crouch, they had high hopes of securing Djalminha and Kinkladze before those deals also went up in smoke.

"We made two exceptional offers for two players – however, for a variety of very frustrating factors totally outwith our control, neither deal has gone through," said a club spokesman.

"In both cases we believe the players were very keen to come to Dundee – and had said as much. In the case of Djalminha, great progress had been made but an internal problem between his club (Deportivo La Coruna) and him could not be resolved before the transfer deadline. Georgi Kinkladze spoke frequently to the club over the past week and expressed the opinion that he liked the style of play that manager Jim Duffy has adopted at Dens. However, he believes that his immediate future lies in the English Premiership. Despite these refusals, though, we will regroup and look to other options."

Talent was arriving from across the globe elsewhere in Dundee however. Manuscripts were being received from Australia, Spain, Ireland, Wales and England (as well as from across Scotland) for the third round of the Dundee Book Prize. Requests for application forms were also being received from America, reflecting a growing interest in the book prize which celebrated the city's literary heritage.

Giovanni di Stefano had little to write home about following the transfer misery and he said the priority now was to mount a proper challenge to Celtic and Rangers in the league.

He said: "This does not mean that our quest for players has ended. All who know the transfer rules will be fully aware that we can sign any player who is free, without a club or on free transfer. That player, however, will not be able to play in UEFA (Cup) games.

"My main concern, however, is a real and decisive challenge for the SPL. We are in fourth position. We have seven points. We are five adrift from Rangers and two from Celtic. The quest for players continues. I am of the view that players left without a club will now be more attracted to Scottish football and the budget remains the same."

One player who was without a club was former Italian international striker Fabrizio Ravanelli.

The White Feather was in sight.

CHAPTER ELEVEN

He Scores The Goals On The Telly

I would rather be playing Perugia than Juventus, Milan or Lazio.

Giovanni di Stefano

FABRIZIO RAVANELLI was flying the flag for silver foxes long before George Clooney became the poster boy for going grey gracefully.

Born in Perugia, Italy, in 1968, Ravanelli began his career with his hometown club. Affectionately known as the White Feather, in recognition of going grey aged just 14, which was a family trait, he broke into the Perugia first team in 1986 and stayed until 1989. He quickly earned a reputation as a goal-getter of quality and was snapped up by Avellino before making another quick switch to Casertana in the same year.

In 1990, he moved to Reggiana, where he remained for two seasons before joining one of Europe's elite clubs, Juventus, where he played alongside some of the world's greatest talents. He more than held his own among the likes of Roberto Baggio, Gianluca Vialli, Andreas Möller and Alessandro Del Piero, becoming one of Europe's most prolific marksmen in the 1990s. His accuracy in front of goal became as famous as his celebration. Ravanelli would run away after scoring and pull the front of his shirt over his head, which was something children were soon copying in playgrounds across Turin, and then across the footballing world.

He won the UEFA Cup in 1993 and in 1994-95 played a key role as Juventus swept all before them and won the domestic double and the following season's Italian Super Cup. The silverware continued on a grand scale with Marcello Lippi at the helm and Ravanelli went on to score in the 1996 Champions League final victory against Ajax in Rome.

Ravanelli earned 22 caps for the Italian national team between 1995 and 1999, scoring eight goals, and was part of the squad that went to Euro 1996 in England. He made just two appearances at Euro 96 as Italy were dumped out in the first round, but he returned to England in August and signed for Bryan Robson's Middlesbrough. Ravanelli was already well-known in the UK for his famous goal celebrations and occasional appearances on Channel 4's well-respected Saturday morning show Gazzetta Football Italia.

The White Feather's arrival at Middlesbrough stunned the continent. The Italian top flight was still Europe's best and the English Premier League was a long way away from the billion-pound global brand it is today.

But former Manchester United hero Robson was putting together a cosmopolitan side and Ravanelli arrived on £42,000 a week and was paraded alongside Brazilian international stars Emerson and Branco. They would later be joined by another Brazilian, midfield magician Juninho. The big-name signings would set the ball rolling for what became the mass migration of players to the Premier League.

Ravanelli was disappointed at being sold by Juventus but the new challenge didn't faze him and the £7m transfer fee quickly looked like a bargain on the opening day of the 1996-97 season. Ravanelli fired a memorable hat-trick against Liverpool in a 3-3 draw. He lit up the league during that first season, scoring 31 goals in all competitions for Middlesbrough. His outbursts were just as regular as his goals. He frequently let his team-mates know what he thought of them and was involved in several training ground bust-ups. He branded his team "relegation certainties" during a festive interview with an Italian newspaper, where he also ridiculed what he described as Bryan Robson's "truly tragic" decision to give the players time off after Christmas when they had just dropped to the foot of the table.

His talking on the pitch, however, took Middlesbrough to two cup finals. He started both games as Middlesbrough went down 1–0 to Leicester City following a replay in the League Cup Final before further heartbreak in the FA Cup against Chelsea in May.

Ravanelli's Christmas doomsday prediction proved accurate as Middlesbrough were eventually relegated, despite the big signings and big wages. Ravanelli packed his bags. There were rumours that he wanted out of Teeside as far back as November but with relegation confirmed he moved to Marseille for the 1997-98 season. He helped the French giants finish second in the league and qualify for the Champions League but then moved back to Italy in January 1999 and won his second Italian league title with Lazio.

His goals also helped the club to Italian Cup and Italian Super Cup glory but he later found himself behind Claudio Lopez, Hernan Crespo, Marcelo Salas and Simone Inzaghi. He was soon on the move again after being left on the fringes of the first-team in Rome and joined Derby County on a free transfer, signing a two-year deal in 2001.

Ravanelli was still able to command wages of £38,000 a week, despite being beyond the age of 30, but would again suffer the agony of relegation in his first season back in England. Things started well as Ravanelli hit seven goals in his first 10 league games, but Jim Smith's team found life extremely tough in the Premier League. The bright start fizzled out and Derby won just eight of their 38 league matches and were relegated against a backdrop of financial turmoil, with the club battling a rising tide of debt.

The Italian accepted a short-term wage cut during his spell at Derby and his contract was allowed to run down with the club back in the doldrums of the second tier. Derby were still paying back what he was owed long after he had left and he took until the following season to get fit again following a problem with his Achilles.

Ravanelli was getting back to sharpness when he asked former Derby team-mate Craig Burley to help find him a new club somewhere in the Midlands region where he was staying.

Dundee at the time were looking for free agents to bolster their squad following the failed attempts to snap up Gascoigne, McFadden, Dani, Crouch, Djalminha and Kinkladze. Dundee were also monitoring Ravanelli's situation but the 34-year-old wouldn't have known his arrival in the UK some seven years earlier had already impacted upon the Dark Blues.

Stephen McGargle was recommended to Dundee by Bryan Robson after failing to make the breakthrough at the Riverside following the arrival of Ravanelli and Juninho. McGargle's trial period at Dundee was largely forgettable, despite the glowing endorsement from the former England captain, and he was eventually released without fanfare.

Dundee drew 1-1 with Kilmarnock at Rugby Park at the end of August before holding talks with Craig Burley's agent about signing the former Scotland international on a permanent deal.

Burley's agent Gordon Smith said: "Jim (Duffy) has expressed an interest and Craig said to me he would be interested if it was the right deal. I spoke to Jim at the end of last week and we agreed to have a meeting to have another chat about it. We've got common ground on this and it remains just to tie things down. Craig was holding back and waiting for the transfer window to close because he knew it would be the best time to be in a position where you could sign for anybody. He is one of the best players you can pick up. He's just sitting and waiting for the right move."

Burley upped sticks and put pen to paper at Dens Park in time to be involved in the squad for a televised clash against his former club Celtic. Duffy said: "It's great he's agreed to join us, and it represents another move forward for Dundee to get a player of his stature. We have a talented squad and Craig is going to add good competition to it. We have some real quality in midfield, but the time to make signings like this is when things are going well. There are good players in there, like Gavin Rae, Georgi Nemsadze, Barry Smith and Garry Brady, but all the players know that to keep the jersey they have to keep performing."

Dundee wanted Ravanelli to join Burley but again the sticking point was the fact his family were now based in the English Midlands. The Italian had indicated he was willing to take a pay drop to sign for Coventry and stay close to home.

Ravanelli's former club Perugia were ironically drawn against Dundee in the first round of the UEFA Cup, which Giovanni di Stefano described as better than "Juventus, Milan or Lazio". He was deadly serious.

Perugia had already raised eyebrows across Europe when they signed striker Al-Saadi Gaddafi in the summer who was the son of the Libyan leader Colonel Gaddafi. Shortly after the transfer had been made, sanctions imposed by the United Nations in the wake of the 1988 Lockerbie bombing were lifted when Colonel Gaddafi accepted responsibility for the Lockerbie bombing and paid compensation to the families of the victims.

The deal was the latest brainchild of controversial Perugia president Luciano Gaucci who was also pursuing the idea of signing a female footballer.

Gaucci was no stranger to controversy after threatening to release the Korean Ahn Jung-hwan from his club for the crime of scoring the goal that eliminated Italy from the 2002 World Cup.

Di Stefano said he had the greatest respect for Gaucci who got into football after making his fortune from a thoroughbred horse stables.

Di Stefano said: "Luciano Gaucci is a real man, a man not afraid to speak his mind and it is such an honour to be able to play against his club. I have the greatest respect for him. I would rather be playing Perugia than Juventus, Milan or Lazio."

Before the first leg had even kicked-off, Dundee fans were putting arrangements in place to get to the second leg in Perugia and travel agents said they were being inundated with inquiries. The club was still to receive confirmation of their ticket allocation despite the deluge. However, they were encouraged by the response, which suggested they would be backed by an army of travelling fans.

It was little wonder the fans were excited. This would be the club's first foray into the UEFA Cup proper for almost 30 years.

The most popular routes to Italy seemed to be to fly to Florence or Rome on low-cost airlines and then travel on to Perugia. Both the club and the Dundee Supporters' Association were also looking into the possibility of chartering planes for those who wanted to take a more direct route.

DSA secretary Fraser MacDonald said he anticipated a Dark Blues invasion. "There are a large number of fans who are going to make this trip and there are a huge number of different ways to get there," he said.

"Bargain flights are obviously the preferred option for most fans, with a number of Italian airports you can fly to and a very good train service to take you to Perugia. We have asked the company who organised the flight to Albania to look into it and give us prices and we will just have to wait and see how this option compares."

Ravanelli's Dundee deal, however, was still struggling to get off the runway.

Although he was a free agent, the only way Dundee could afford him would be if di Stefano was prepared to dip into the much-talked-of cash reserves that he had indicated he was ready to invest.

There was more movement however across the city as building work started on a new £23m life sciences centre on the campus of Dundee University.

The Centre for Interdisciplinary Research was being built adjoining the existing Wellcome Trust Biocentre off Hawkhill, effectively doubling the size of the already imposing structure. Some old buildings at the site had already been razed to make way for the centre, which was expected to add a further 180 top flight scientists to a biotechnology and life sciences sector in Dundee which already employed well over 2,000 people.

There was a similar razing in the Midlands where Ravanelli's anticipated unveiling as a Coventry City player was called off. He had been due to sign for the Sky Blues but a media conference at Highfield Road was scrapped after interest from Dundee put the brakes on the deal. The club blamed stalling tactics by the Italian for them pulling the plug.

A spokesman for Coventry City said: "Coventry City has withdrawn its interest in Fabrizio Ravanelli after talks with the former Italian international broke down. Ravanelli had agreed terms with the Sky Blues on Wednesday, prior to Dundee's interest in the 34-year-old. The player and his representatives confirmed today the veteran striker still wished to join Coventry on the original terms offered, only to continue to stall on signing the contract. Therefore, the club has decided not to pursue its interest in the player."

Staff from a Dundee DIY outlet chain were kicking up almost as much of a stink. The smell coming from a wastewater pumping station at King George V Wharf was making them physically sick and environmental health was called in to investigate. Lee Scharf, from Jewson, said: "The whole area is stinking – it's making people feel sick. The harbour area is becoming more or less a residential area. If we are struggling to put up with the smell during working hours, how can people live with it 24 hours a day?"

Scottish Water investigated and said the smell was "septic sewage" triggered by a recent dry spell.

Craig Burley meanwhile was being given a clean bill of health at Dens Park. The midfielder passed a medical and it was looking more and more likely that he would be linking up again with Ravanelli. Speculation continued in the following days and it emerged as the week went on that Ravanelli was now feeling more motivated towards making a switch to Scotland.

Dark Blues manager Jim Duffy and director Jim Connor had held "extremely positive" discussions with the player in Edinburgh. The Italian indicated that he was keen to join Dundee but he also asked for 48 hours to discuss the move with his family. The club consented to Ravanelli's request. Things were moving forward and he agreed to yet more talks with Dens officials who were keen to get him fixed up in time to make his debut against Aberdeen in the league.

Burley gained some much-needed game time in an under-21 match in Airdrie after missing the league defeat by Celtic at Dens Park owing to his lack of match fitness. The visitors had taken the lead early on through Bobo Balde and held on despite playing most of the game with 10 men after Didier Agathe was sent off after just 20 minutes.

Duffy jetted off after the match to watch UEFA Cup opponents Perugia taken apart 3-0 in a league defeat by Parma during what turned out to be a memorable trip in more ways than one.

During his scouting mission, Duffy got himself caught up in the earthquake that had shaken the central region of Italy.

"Let's just say it was a different experience," said Duffy. "When you see the walls of your room swaying back and forward, you know something isn't right, but we came through it safe and sound. It was a worthwhile trip and it was good to see Perugia. They played in more of a British style than I would have imagined, but they're a decent side and it should be a good tie."

Duffy, who was accompanied by Giovanni di Stefano's eldest son, Michael, was luckily none the worse for his ordeal and flew back to Scotland to discover things were just as shaky there. Ravanelli was having second thoughts and indicated a reluctance to move his family from their base in England to Dundee. But di Stefano believed he could still convince him otherwise.

The Dundee director mounted a charm offensive and organised a get-together between the di Stefano and Ravanelli families in London to discuss Dundee's interest. He said he would fly back with the Italian's signature.

"I am cautiously optimistic he will accept," he said. "What Mr Ravanelli has stated is that 'his family will not move from England' - not that he is not prepared to play football elsewhere."

Like the tectonic plates in Italy, things were set to move just as quickly. If a deal was struck during the meeting in London it was unlikely to be in the currency which it had now emerged was at the heart of trade in Victorian Dundee. That same week, historians uncovered evidence that mountains of smelly dung provided substantial "filthy lucre" for the council coffers. The importance of so-called "brown gold" surprised experts from St Andrews University investigating waste management through the ages. Researchers found that manure was an unusual source of massive revenues for Victorian town councils and that some effectively operated cartels to control its trade. Environmental historian John Clark said the local authority in Dundee was among those for whom the pong of dung represented the sweet smell of success.

"There was a surprising obsession with it," said Dr Clark. "It was seen as gold, and not only sold, but traded on."

Di Stefano had also struck gold. The Anglo-Italian's powers of persuasion appeared to have worked when the Dens director told the club to call a press conference following the meeting in London. Ravanelli was expected to put pen to paper on a two-year deal.

"Mr di Stefano met Fabrizio at his (di Stefano's) home in London this afternoon as arranged," said a club spokesman. "Mr di Stefano said the meeting was 'extremely positive' and, as a result, he has instructed the club to call a press conference for Monday. We will carry out his instructions within the course of the next 24 to 48 hours."

Aberdeen were the next visitors to Dens Park in the league. Before the match Aberdeen manager Steve Paterson said he was also given the opportunity to sign Ravanelli but stressed he had "no regrets" at being unable to secure a deal.

"I got a fax from Ravanelli's agent saying he would take a pay cut to come to Scotland, but what he wanted was still at least five times what Aberdeen can afford," he said. "If someone wants to bankroll a deal to let Dundee get him instead, then good luck to them. I'm happier using Aberdeen's money more wisely and trying to bring through more home-bred youngsters."

Ravanelli agreed to sign for Dundee but his family wouldn't be joining him. His wife and children were settled in Derby where his son had recently started school. Ravanelli said: "It's absolutely 100% – I'll be in Dundee on Monday to sign a contract."

Jim Duffy was still cagey, given the failures to get previous proposed deals over the line. He said Ravanelli's lack of fitness would likely delay any debut if he did sign for the club.

"If Ravanelli signs next week it will be fantastic news for the club and the fans and it will be good to work with another good player," he said. "If he does not sign, though, I will not be unduly concerned because, as I have said, we have a good squad here. If, and when he comes in, we will find out what his fitness levels are like, but common sense tells you his general fitness cannot be the same as that of the other players."

Dundee's first league victory over Aberdeen at Dens Park for 15 years ensured the feel-good factor was very much in evidence ahead of Ravanelli's arrival. In-form striker Nacho Novo's seventh goal of the season clinched victory after he rolled the ball under David Preece following a quick free-kick from Barry Smith. Dundee looked fitter, stronger and better organised throughout.

Striker Juan Sara said afterwards that new signing Ravanelli would have to "fight for his place like everyone else" but suggested a higher power might decide.

"I am happy with my performance and pretty happy that I had chances to score – that's very important," said Sara, who was starting his first match of the season. "Even if I didn't score it is good for a striker to have chances. I need to play games to get sharp – it's as simple as that. My last full 90 minutes was for Coventry (during a short loan spell) eight months ago. But I believe I am going to get goals for Dundee. I have scored 35 for them in 60 games so that's not bad. I have to be respected for that. I believe in my God so he will decide and I want to play with good players like Nacho (Novo), Fabian, and now Fabrizio Ravanelli."

Argentine striker Fabian Caballero reckoned Ravanelli's impending arrival would strengthen competition for places among the squad at Dens and put his own first-team spot at risk.

"I read in the newspapers that Ravanelli is coming to Dundee, but nothing is concrete yet," he said. "If he does come, though, it will be good for the club. He is a fine player with experience of playing for many big teams and I am sure we can learn from him. At the moment with Steven Milne injured, we have myself, Juan Sara, Nacho Novo and Steve Lovell competing for places. If Ravanelli comes it will become ever harder to get in the team. But that can only be good for Dundee because the rest of us will have to play better to be sure of our places. If we aren't scoring goals the competition will be so strong that we are going to be under pressure."

After all the waiting, the grey-haired Italian superstar finally arrived in Dundee to sign a two-year deal and went on to declare that his fitness was "quite good" despite his spell on the sidelines. Perugia, his first love, were due to arrive at Dens Park as Dundee's next opponents in the UEFA Cup but Ravanelli was keen to point out where his loyalties would now lie.

Ravanelli was ineligible for the match but spoke positively of his hopes of playing in Europe with Dundee in the future if they could get past their Serie A opponents. "Perugia were my team when I was a boy, and I will always like them, but now I am with Dundee and I want Dundee to win on Wednesday," he said.

Although he had not played competitive football all season, he said he had been training hard and was fully fit despite understandably lacking in match sharpness. "I need to do more work with the ball, but this is normal," he said. "My fitness is good and I am looking forward to being with Dundee. There has been much talk, and now I just want to get on with playing."

Duffy expressed his delight at Ravanelli's arrival to bolster the ranks but said he was entirely focused on preparing for the first leg match against Perugia. The Italian side had just picked up a point against European champions AC Milan and Duffy said the performance left him in no doubt about the size of the task facing Dundee. "It's great that this deal is now done and we can get down to playing," he said. "I'm happy to have Ravanelli here, but, for now, all we are thinking about is Perugia. They had a fabulous result yesterday when they drew with Milan. You are talking about a team capable of holding the European champions, so that really whets the appetite for Wednesday. Of course it's going to be hard, but weeks like this, with a big signing and a huge game, don't come around too often and we are really looking forward to what lies ahead."

The Bird & The Feather

Dundee publicly said the Ravanelli capture was initiated by Duffy but secured by Giovanni di Stefano, although privately others within Dens Park were suggesting otherwise.

Duffy said he had "no problem" with the signing despite the fact there appeared to be some friction between the pair over the length of the contract which had been offered. Di Stefano said there were "absolutely no differences between me, the club or Mr Duffy and there never will be" and stressed all transfer moves were at the sole discretion of the manager.

Duffy privately believed the deal offered should only have been until the end of the season. "He (Ravanelli) is primarily Giovanni's decision but, at the end of the day, it is my decision on who plays in the team," said Duffy. "If I was going to stamp my feet and have a major tantrum, I would have done. But I have no problem with it whatsoever.

"We identified some players and Craig Burley was 100% my decision. This one was not 100% mine but I have no problem with it whatsoever. It is a gamble, there is no doubt about that. But every player you bring in is a gamble. Ravanelli has a fantastic pedigree, is a proven goalscorer and has played at the highest level. He is not a player who runs all over the place, he is a penalty box player and perhaps that is something we have been lacking. If he is fit and gets the hunger which we hope he still has then we think he can do a good job for us."

The Dark Blues were getting a player who had won 22 international caps for Italy and been involved in transfer deals totalling more than £12 million during his career.

The White Feather had now landed and former boss Ivano Bonetti quickly joined him and Giovanni di Stefano in nailing his colours to the mast ahead of the visit of Perugia.

Despite the degree of animosity that followed his exit from Dundee, Ivano said there was never any question of him not giving his full backing to his former charges. "Whatever happened when I left would never affect my rapport with the fans and I still have great respect for the players at Dundee," he said. "They are good people and I want to see them succeed against Perugia."

In the build-up to the match, Dundee fans were dreaming of another big name joining Ravanelli when di Stefano said he wanted to make a bid for Juventus midfielder Edgar Davids.

He said he would stump up the cash to make the deal a reality during the January transfer window if Juventus were willing to listen to offers.

One of the greatest and most recognisable players of his generation, Davids stood out due to the protective goggles he wore after undergoing operations for glaucoma. He had won the Champions League with Ajax in 1995 and the Dutch league three times. While with Juventus he had also won three Italian league winner's medals. The tough-tackling Dutch midfielder had fallen out with manager Marcello Lippi, however, and was out of contract the following summer. So far, he had refused to sign a new deal.

"There are a number of players we are negotiating with, and who we would look at bringing here," said di Stefano. "If Mr Duffy identified Davids as a player he wanted, then I would see no problem with that. That would, of course, have to wait until January, and would mean a transfer fee. But again I do not see that has to be a problem, but there really is not much I can say about Mr Davids right now, and January is quite a long way off. You might be surprised by where players would want to come, and we must not cheapen Scottish football. A lot has been done to rejuvenate the game in Scotland and, under certain circumstances I see no reason why a player like Mr Davids should not come here."

Di Stefano amazingly told Duffy to go to Italy to convince Davids to come to Dundee.

At the time Edgar Davids was an integral part of the Netherlands international side. He was also on wages of £90,000 a week and was attracting interest from Barcelona and Chelsea. Duffy – likely sensing the chances of getting Davids to swap his penthouse flat on the outskirts of Turin for a tenement in Tannadice Street were somewhat thin – managed to get out of the trip and instead got back to reality and returned his focus to the UEFA Cup clash at Dens.

"All I would say on signings is that my number one priority is to fix up players at this club who will be out of contract, and who have been doing a great job," said Duffy. "I want them to stay and it is important we take care of that. That apart, all I am concentrating on is what should be a great occasion against Perugia. This is a game that is almost right up there alongside the cup final and we want to go out and do our best to win it."

The Italian side won 2-1 despite a close-fought game under the Dens Park floodlights. After a goalless first half, Marco Di Loreto opened the scoring for Perugia five minutes after the interval, only for Lee Wilkie to hit back with a terrific header on 63 minutes. It looked like Dundee might take something from the match, but Massimiliano Fusani's 85th-minute strike ensured the Dark Blues would have to score at least twice in Italy to progress.

Duffy still refused to rule out pulling off a shock despite the odds being stacked against Dundee. "Now the pendulum swings very dramatically towards Perugia," he said. "We still have to believe we have half a chance, but we are up against a top-class side. They are in a really good situation. But in the second leg they might want to sit back and see the game through. Knowing their manager and their work ethic, I don't think they will switch off, but sometimes the manager's message does not get through to the players."

Perugia president Luciano Gaucci appeared to suggest the return leg was a formality when he said he was already dreaming of getting a big tie in the second round.

"In our Intertoto and now UEFA Cup games we have scored 10 goals and conceded one," he said. "The figures speak for themselves. Now we must be careful not to lower our guard, confront the second leg with the maximum attention and determination and go through to the next round. The dream would be to get Roma in the draw and the prestige would be double or treble if we were to get a result against them. Playing Liverpool would be good, too. We are capable of doing well and getting results against the big teams, whereas we can struggle against lesser opponents."

Gaucci did not witness the game first hand but said that the man-of-the-match title might not be appropriate for games featuring Perugia in the near future.

"By mid-October there will be a female player at Perugia," he said. "I am convinced that she will do well. It will be one of the best players in the world, either the first or the second, and she will be capable of competing in Serie A. I want to make Perugia known all over the world, that's the objective."

Di Stefano said people were now taking Dundee and Scottish football seriously following the capture of Ravanelli and Burley and the commendable showing against Perugia.

Ravanelli praised his new team-mates after the UEFA tie and diplomatically stated that he would not rule out the possibility of a miracle happening in the return leg in Perugia.

"It was a very good performance from Dundee," he said. "We played very well, especially in the first half. "It was a good match and we were strong and created chances. This was a very good test for Dundee because Perugia are a quality team and were good tactically. Their coach Serse Cosmi is a good friend of mine so I know his teams are always strong. But for me this showed Scottish football is improving because Dundee were close to Perugia and perhaps deserved a draw. Everything is possible in football so I believe we can go to Italy and win the match. That would be fantastic. It will be difficult but not impossible."

There was similar glowing praise afforded by another superstar when Dundee's new £1.3m Maggie's cancer caring centre at Ninewells Hospital was officially opened by Sir Bob Geldof the following day. Sir Bob said the centre was "an instant landmark" after being designed by Frank Gehry who was widely rated the world's greatest architect for his pioneering work on projects like Bilbao's Guggenheim Museum and the Walt Disney Concert Hall in Los Angeles. Band Aid and Live Aid organiser Sir Bob was no stranger to the big stage himself but Ravanelli would have to wait a little longer for his own return to the spotlight.

Despite a serious injury to striker Steve Lovell, picked up in the defeat against Perugia, Duffy resisted the temptation to throw Ravanelli in against Rangers at Ibrox in the league. "I won't be playing Fabrizio at all at Ibrox, as the simple fact is he is not ready," he said. "It's not fair on the player himself and I won't play him just for the sake of it."

Duffy also shot down fresh speculation over reports of a move for Georgi Kinkladze. "I encountered four agents dealing with Kinkladze, so, as far as I'm concerned, he is just one quarter of a representative for the player," said Duffy. "This latest report is rubbish because I am now only interested in dealing with the squad I have."

Ravanelli missed the 3-1 defeat at the hands of Rangers at Ibrox, where Dundee were level with just five minutes to go against a side which boasted a 100% record in the league. Rangers went ahead through Shota Arveladze in the second half before Nacho Novo equalised for Dundee on 76 minutes when he converted from close range. Dundee's defiance evaporated towards the death and they succumbed to the inevitable when substitute Paolo Vanoli struck a fierce 30-yard drive straight into the top corner. The Ibrox Bears were still celebrating when Arveladze got his second of the game and finished off Dundee's chances of wiping out Rangers two-point gap over Celtic at the top.

Dundee's plans to stage a closed-doors match to boost Ravanelli's fitness were then further mired by having an under-21 game and a number of players absent. Duffy warned Dundee fans that the next game against Hearts was far too early for Ravanelli and also Burley who had not played competitively for five months.

"Fabrizio needs a bit of work and some form of game," said Duffy. "Because of that he cannot be considered for Hearts on Saturday. But after that we have two weeks until the next league fixture, against Partick Thistle, and I'll organise a closed-doors match during that time. I don't want to build up the fans hopes, as I know they are desperate to see these players playing for us. However, they also have to be fit enough to play in these games, so it may need a bit more time."

Ravanelli's Dundee debut might have been heavily delayed but it was nothing compared to the wait for the club's commemorative shirts which finally arrived after 18 months. The proposal, first mooted by chief executive Peter Marr in April 2002, was to mark the 40th anniversary of Dundee's legendary 1962 championship win. The names of Liney, Hamilton, Cox, Seith, Ure, Wishart, Smith, Penman, Cousin, Gilzean and Robertson made up the greatest team in Dundee's history.

The Dundee team of 1961-62 became all-time heroes when they won the Division One title and reached the semi-final of the European Cup the following season before losing to AC Milan. The legends will live forever in the folklore of Dens Park and Marr had wanted to mark the anniversary by giving 3,500 supporters a special jersey as part of their season ticket package. However, the plan was dogged by delay after delay, with the club having to apologise time and again for not fulfilling their end of the bargain. Dens officials said the reason for the hold-up was they did not consider the quality of merchandise manufactured by the original Spanish supplier to be up to scratch.

However, the attire eventually turned up at the club shop just before Duffy arranged a closed-doors friendly against Hearts to give Burley and Ravanelli valuable game-time. Duffy wanted to use the match as part of his team's build-up for their return trip to Perugia and also included Beto Carranza, Barry Smith, Lee Mair and Dave Mackay in the squad.

Jonay Hernandez would also feature in the match after Dundee asked him to miss the 24,000-mile round trip to South America for Venezeula's friendly with El Salvador. "There's a big gap between the last game and the next one and, with Perugia coming up on Wednesday, I want to keep the players ticking over," said Duffy. "We advised the Venezuelans we wanted to keep Jonay and asked that if that was a problem could they let us know. "We have heard nothing so we are presuming it's okay that he is missing the game over there."

But the hand of Lady Luck struck again.

Ravanelli missed training in the build-up to the match and it appeared likely he would be unable to take his place in the starting line-up after he was struck down with a virus.

"If they (Burley and Ravanelli) were able to play, and that's a big if, in the practice match then there's a chance they could be involved against Partick a week on Saturday," Duffy said. "But if you've not played in five months, a couple of weeks' training doesn't make you match fit. Remember, when we put players through a full pre-season training we then give them four or five games to get properly sharp for competitive fixtures."

The closed-doors friendly wasn't the only match in the spotlight. Dundee's UEFA Cup preliminary round away leg with Vllaznia became the subject of a match-rigging investigation in Albania along with Dinamo Tirana's 4-0 defeat by Lokeren.

UEFA asked for a report from the Albanian Football Federation which had accused Vllaznia and Dinamo of fixing the matches to make money from betting. An investigation by the country's governing body into the first-leg tie in Albania, which Dundee won 2-0, was held after suspicious betting patterns emerged in the Balkans. Not only was the suggestion that the outcome of the matches was arranged, it was alleged the fixing went as far as to ensuring the exact scorelines.

Ravanelli managed to recover against the odds and finally wore a Dundee shirt for the first time alongside Burley at Murrayfield, during a largely forgettable goalless draw.

The Dark Blues fielded a mixture of youth and experience, with kids such as Duncan McLean, Bobby Linn, Dougie Cameron and Calum MacDonald playing. Burley was on the pitch for an hour and Ravanelli also managed to get 75 minutes under his belt.

"It was a good workout," said Duffy afterwards. "Hearts had quite a strong side out, but the important thing was for players like Fabrizio Ravanelli and Craig Burley to get to know the other lads and to get a game under their belts.

"This was only their first game together so we're not going to go overboard about it. They've both still got a bit to go, however their general fitness is okay. But they need match sharpness."

The White Feather's Dundee career was up and running.

SPL Table, October 4, 2003

		Pld	Pts
1	Celtic	8	22
2	Rangers	8	21
3	Hearts	8	14
4	Dunfermline Ath.	8	12
5	Dundee	8	11
6	Motherwell	8	11
7	Hibernian	8	11
8	Livingston	8	9
9	Kilmarnock	8	8
10	Aberdeen	8	7
11	Dundee United	8	5
12	Partick Thistle	8	2

CHAPTER TWELVE

One Night In North Lanarkshire

It was my quickest ever hat-trick, and I will take more confidence into Saturday's match.

Fabrizio Ravanelli

A "NEIGHBOURS from hell" project in Dundee was being hailed as a powerful method of dealing with problem tenants. A model of Dundee's nuisance neighbours centre was being used in a bid to cut anti-social behaviour in Manchester, which had more incidents than anywhere else in England. The Dundee centre in St Mary's was dubbed the "sin bin" and was working with families to examine and change the behaviour patterns that caused problems with their neighbours.

Similar mediation looked likely to be needed after reports emerged suggesting the SFA would refuse to endorse di Stefano's appointment as a Dundee director. The SFA general purposes committee were obliged to approve any boardroom appointment and consideration of the case was to be discussed at a meeting the following month. It emerged the SFA were alarmed about alleged aspects of his past and might consider him to be "not a fit and proper person to hold such a position within association football".

Di Stefano had allegedly already lodged a guarantee with the club's bankers to cover a seven-figure portion of the considerable debts. He had also played a part in the signings of Craig Burley and Fabrizio Ravanelli, with the big-money salaries they were both commanding. It was suggested that rejection from the SFA could be ruinous for Dundee, although the SFA's rules wouldn't stop him financing the club without actually being on the board.

Di Stefano came out fighting and said he would not take such a slur lying down. He angrily threw down the gauntlet to his critics. "If there is anyone who believes the best interests of Dundee Football Club and Scottish football would be served by my resignation as a director, then take me to court and prove it," he said. "Prove, that I am not 100% committed to Dundee. Prove that I have not already invested considerable sums and had substantial bank guarantees accepted. Prove that I have not given a commitment to stay here for the long term. Prove that I am not a fit and proper person. And prove that my interest in this club is not utterly simple and benign. I am here to put money in to Dundee, not take it out. I want to see the team my son loves succeed, nothing else. If you haven't got the guts to take me on in court then buy me out."

Perhaps unsurprisingly, given the club's far-reaching debts, Dundee came out in support of their White Knight and claimed he was being harshly treated.

The off-field drama was then put to one side as more than 2,000 Dundee fans travelled to Italy to watch the UEFA Cup campaign wind up with defeat in Perugia. Ivano was now working as a pundit for Italian television and was a surprise guest as Dundee trained at the stadium before the match. Although he was still in a legal dispute with the club following his exit, he spoke with directors Giovanni di Stefano and Jim Connor and was given a warm welcome by his former players.

One player who didn't shake his hand was Lee Wilkie, whose Dundee career almost ended after a furious training-ground dispute during his former manager's spell at Dens.

Ivano wished his successor Jim Duffy good luck before speaking again of his growing respect for Wilkie's international team-mate Gavin Rae, who he had once rated at £10m. He also said his shopping list would include Rae if he ever got back into management. "If I became a manager again I would bring Gavin here," he said. "I have watched him on TV since I left and I still say he could play in Serie A. I am not working here – but I am a fan. It is good to see the staff and the players, and I will be very happy if Dundee win."

Ivano also visited the team hotel in the countryside which Dundee were sharing with Colonel Gaddafi's son Al-Saadi, who had booked almost half of it out for himself.

Ravanelli was ineligible and worked out on his own on the touchline while the main squad trained on the pitch. But the work he put in proved he was ready for a starting berth against Partick Thistle.

Ivano predicted his countryman would be a success in the SPL. But he responded diplomatically when he was asked by a journalist if Ravanelli could become a new Claudio Caniggia.

"Claudio was a one-off," he said. "Most players lose pace as they get older, but he will still be fast at 90. Ravanelli can do well for Dundee, though, if he is still hungry. At 34, he is not too old to play well and he has been a quality striker."

Ivano joined the fans before the match in Italy and it was evident he was still immensely popular with a section of the support who chanted his name and greeted him like a returning hero. Ravanelli also ingratiated himself with the Dundee faithful during the trip and was happy to chat, sign autographs and have his picture taken with supporters. He proved himself to be an absolute gentleman in his exchanges with the adoring legions.

Most fans did not go straight to Perugia because direct flights were difficult and expensive. The vast majority touched down in places such as Rome, Florence, Bologna, Pisa and Ancona before travelling to Perugia. One incident witnessed in the city centre summed up the carnival atmosphere. A couple of fans asked a police officer for help because of a lack of taxis and the fact they were unsure where their hotel was. The officer, in perfect English, told them to wait as he borrowed a radio from a junior colleague. The officer then arranged for a spare police van to take them, and others, to their hotel.

Before the match, Dundee fans appeared to be everywhere. Most of them congregated on the steps of a church overlooking the square as they belted out Dundee and Scotland anthems, as well as chanting former manager Ivano's name and Gio di Stefano's name, as bewildered Italians looked on. Some locals said Perugia had never seen anything like it, even when the giants of Juventus and Milan visited on league duty. They said they had expected only a couple of hundred to make the trip, not a couple of thousand. Locals lined the pavement to watch what was unfolding as a piper led the fans downhill on a 15-minute walk to the buses which were put on to take them to the Renato Curi Stadium.

The 2,000 fans watched their team go out of the tournament 3-1 on aggregate following a goal on 71 minutes from substitute Massimo Margiotta. Perugia were well-organised and Dundee struggled to make an impression on the match and never really looked like being the first Scottish club in history to win away in Italy. One of the more remarkable things about the game was the bitterly cold temperature. Some of the Perugia fans even started fires up the back of the terraces to keep warm.

Despite the disappointing result, and the wintry conditions, the Dark Blues fans received warm praise from all quarters for the way they behaved while on their European adventure. "There's no doubt that they've done the club proud," said a club spokesman. "Anyone who was walking through Perugia will have seen that they were superb ambassadors for the city and Scotland."

He said the celebratory atmosphere the fans carried with them to the continent was a proud moment for everyone associated with Dundee.

Defender Jonay Hernandez, referring to the extraordinary support from the stands throughout the match, said the club's fans were better than those at Real Madrid. "I never thought I would see anything like this, and for a club the size of Dundee to take so many fans to a game so far away is just amazing," he said. "I was at Real Madrid, and they are a great club who will take many thousands of fans with them when they reach finals. There is no way, though, they would take 2,000 to an away leg in the first round in Europe. Dundee are much smaller and for this many to come to Italy to support us tells me we have good supporters. They were amazing – and when we had a look at the pitch one-hour-and-a-half before kick-off, they were already in the stadium singing songs. I am sad we could not give them victory, but for me this was still one of the most beautiful experiences in my life."

The first-team squad were allowed a long lie after arriving back from Italy just after 4am. Duffy said he would be making a couple of changes for the SPL meeting with Partick Thistle at Dens and indicated that this would likely mean a debut for Ravanelli at some stage. "He's in the squad, and is definitely going to be involved," said Duffy. "When he came, his fitness levels were not too bad and he's been doing work to improve further. What he needs are games and, while he may not be ready for 90 minutes, he's fit enough to play a part. His ability and experience come into it as well."

Whilst injury-hit Ravanelli was keen to restore his reputation after a long spell on the sidelines, the reputation of another of the city's adopted sons was already in the spotlight. The man described as the world's greatest living explorer, Sir Ranulph Fiennes, launched his biography of Captain Robert Falcon Scott in Dundee. The book was a "fiercely argued testament" intended to rehabilitate Scott's reputation. Sir Ranulph said he was able to deconstruct many of the "fabrications" made by other writers in recent years which had tarnished the deeds and memory of Scott.

Scott had left the base camp in Cape Evans on Antarctica's coast with four other men in November 1911 during the race to reach the South Pole. They arrived two months later, only to find that Norwegian explorer Roald Amundsen had beaten them. During the 800-mile journey back, Scott and his party perished in bitterly cold temperatures of -44 degrees towards the end of March 1912. Scott was later condemned for leading his South Pole expedition to disaster but Sir Ranulph scotched the suggestion that he was a bumbling amateur responsible for the deaths of his men. Recent findings, he said, proved that it was extraordinary weather which had destroyed Scott's party. Given average conditions for the time of year, he said they would have made it back to base camp. Sir Ranulph said: "Heroes on pedestals have long been prey to character assassination without worrying about historical reality. Historical reality is my priority."

Duffy's priority was three points against Partick Thistle. He warned that nothing less than a win would be acceptable. Ravanelli warned the Dundee fans not to expect miracles when he made his long-awaited debut. He had been at the club for nearly four weeks, slowly building up his fitness. He asked for patience and urged the fans to keep in mind the fact that he had not played competitively since the end of the previous season.

"I want to say to the fans that I am very happy to play for Dundee," he said. "But I want all of my body to be 100% and it will not be easy for me. I want them to support me because I will need it. It will be difficult after four months without a game and I don't know if I will start or be on the bench. But what I will promise the supporters is that I believe in this team, we have a lot of good players and I am sure we can do a very good job.

"I want to play very, very well for Dundee and of course I want to score a goal but for me the main thing is to win the match. Scottish supporters are wonderful and I am sure the players will want to win against Partick to say thank you. This is a capital match, very important, and if we win there is a possibility we will be in a good position in the league. So the first thing we must do is to forget about the Perugia game very quickly and think only of Partick."

Grey wigs, in tribute to the hairstyle of the Italian marksman, had long been sold out in Dundee and had been waiting to be used. After four weeks in the shadows, the wigs, like Ravanelli himself, were about to be thrust into the spotlight.

The White Feather's first appearance in a Dundee shirt was hugely impressive. It might not have been as explosive as his hat-trick-grabbing Middlesbrough debut seven years previously but it was just as memorable for the Dundee faithful.

The fans had conjured up their own chant for the big man. "There's only one Ravanelli. He scores goals on the telly. He's got grey hair but we don't care. Ravanelli is a Dundee Derry boy."

Ravanelli linked well with his new strike partners Fabian Caballero and Nacho Novo as Duffy put out an attacking line up with three up top. The Italian played slightly deeper than he might have done in his pomp but his movement and awareness troubled the Partick Thistle defence throughout the afternoon.

Dundee were put under early pressure on six minutes. A poor clearance from Lee Wilkie looked to have put James Grady through on goal but Dave Mackay was quickly on hand to clear the danger. Ravanelli's first attempt on goal came on eight minutes. Dundee won a free-kick just outside the box and Ravanelli picked the ball up and placed it before firing his 25-yard effort high over the Thistle crossbar. The home side almost opened the scoring just minutes later when Fabian Caballero's drive from just inside the box went inches wide. Dundee looked a little leggy at times, which was understandable given their midweek endeavours in Italy where they were largely under the cosh for 90 minutes.

A lapse in concentration almost cost Dundee a goal on 17 minutes. Gerry Britton's knock-down found Derek Fleming in space but he couldn't beat Julian Speroni from close-range. The Dundee front three were linking up well and the crowd were getting behind the team. Caballero's incisive pass then found Nacho Novo running through on goal, but the Spaniard's delicate chip over Partick goalkeeper Kenny Arthur crept just beyond the post. Ravanelli turned provider shortly after when his header from a Caballero cross found Novo a yard from goal. But Arthur was there again to block the shot and concede a corner. Still clearly lacking match sharpness, Ravanelli was nevertheless showing some nice touches in the opening exchanges and he created another chance on 27 minutes. The striker found Novo with a shrewd pass but Arthur saved Thistle's bacon once again.

Novo almost broke the deadlock on 41 minutes with a rasping drive from just inside the box which was brilliantly tipped over by Arthur, who was producing a goalkeeping masterclass. Arthur was looking unbeatable but Dundee kept knocking on the door after the break and finally broke the deadlock on 53 minutes thanks to some magic from Ravanelli. The Italian showed terrific vision with a penetrating long-range pass from inside his own half which found Novo. The Spaniard took a touch and went round Arthur before slipping the ball home from 14 yards.

The inspiring Ravanelli was heavily involved in almost all of Dundee's dangerous attacking play against a Thistle side which rarely threatened to get back into the game. He nearly created a second when he capitalised on a blunder by defender Jean-Yves Anis inside the box and set up Novo wide on the left. The Spaniard's snap-shot was deflected for a corner.

Dundee kept pushing forward to kill the game off but were thwarted by Arthur yet again when he saved from Novo on 64 minutes from a Jonay Hernandez cross-field pass.

Thistle threw bodies forward at the death in search of an equaliser, but Duffy's side held out against the relegation strugglers for what was a well-deserved three points.

Ravanelli spoke to reporters afterwards and said he had enjoyed his Dundee debut, despite lacking a little in terms of fitness levels. He said: "My performance was not bad and I gave a very good ball for Nacho's goal. It was a great result for us after the disappointment of losing in Perugia earlier in the week. I enjoyed it, but it was my first game in four months and I fully expect to be stronger in the future."

Ravanelli then turned his attention to the city derby against United which was up next at Tannadice and was a match that he was expecting to start. "I realise that the game against Dundee United is an important one for both city clubs and I am looking forward to it," he said.

Dens Park boss Jim Duffy said afterwards there was "no doubt" Ravanelli needed more minutes under his belt but predicted he would be "top class" in three or four games time. He said: "I think Ravanelli was steady. "He needs games but he gave a steady performance. He's still got to get to know the players, but the most important contribution to the whole game was his weighted pass through to Nacho. That's the kind of quality he has. He can assess things. In three or four matches' time he'll be top class, and we'll need to give him that time. His presence on the pitch can draw other players around him and that gives other players a little bit more space."

Dundee midfielder Gavin Rae said he was also impressed with Ravanelli's debut. "It's been a hard week, coming back from Italy," he said. "Obviously we didn't play that well over there so the main thing was to get the points and we did it. Having a game in midweek may have been a factor in Thistle putting us under pressure, but any team can push any team at the end. Barry (Smith) made a brilliant block near the end. He slotted back in at centre-half because Lee Mair was injured and did brilliantly. I also thought Ravanelli did well. He held the ball up and created a few chances. He's obviously a quality player. He showed even without being match fit that he can contribute."

Ravanelli's signature was looking good value.

But it was the signatures of the commanding officers of a German U-boat which surrendered in Dundee at the end of World War 2 that were racking up just as many headlines. The find happened at a dinner that week aboard the frigate Unicorn to mark the centenary of the Royal Naval Reserve and the 206th anniversary of the Battle of Camperdown.

The Unicorn's visitor book, which dates to 1929 and contains the signatures of illustrious figures including King George VI and Queen Elizabeth II, was passed among the 100 guests. The book was then handed back to the Unicorn governor and honorary historian, Lieutenant Commander Roderick Stewart, to be placed safely back inside its cover, when a small slip of paper fell out from between the blank pages at the back. It carried two German signatures from the U-boat, U-2326, which surrendered in Dundee, before her captain and executive officer were brought aboard the Unicorn.

Mr Stewart said: "There is a memorable photograph taken at the time of the two officers leaving the Unicorn, the executive officer ruefully rubbing his head having just bumped it hard on the low entrance port. The officer in the foreground of the photograph is a Dutch interpreter, who presumably failed to translate 'mind your head'. We were given a copy of the photograph by Captain Colin Keay, whose father Captain Willie Keay was the Unicorn's captain at the time, and it is good to have the story completed by the discovery of these two signatures."

Meanwhile, Dundee's own commanding officer was going to war with Ivano. After the victory against Partick Thistle, chief executive Peter Marr expressed anger at the conduct of his former employee when he visited the team before the match against Perugia.

Things looked harmonious when Ivano appeared at the club's training session and was seen to embrace some of his former charges as they left the field. However, Marr claimed he also turned up at the team's hotel and urged numerous players not to sign new contracts because he could help them find clubs in Italy.

"It was totally unprofessional of Bonetti to appear before the game," he said. "He was at the pre-match training session and at the hotel. He upset our manager Jim Duffy, he totally upset our pre-match build-up and it was unethical of a professional person to do that type of thing. He shouldn't have been near the players. We also believe he tried to tap as many as seven of our players and we'll be reporting him for acting illegally. I spoke to one of the player's agents and he confirmed it to me. Jim Duffy spoke to a couple of players and they confirmed it as well. If we get absolute proof, then we'll be reporting him because he is not a licensed agent. In Perugia the club officials stayed at a different hotel from the players in order to give them some peace and to concentrate fully on the match. I didn't go near the training so why should he appear there? I think it's totally ridiculous. What would he have felt about someone doing that to him? His car even followed the team bus up to the stadium and he tried to get in behind the bus."

Ivano and Giovanni di Stefano did hold talks in Perugia to try to thrash out a compromise over money the Italian claimed he was still due from his time at Dundee. But Marr insisted he had no legitimate reason to turn up at the hotel.

"They should be concentrating on the game and nothing else," he said. "None of the fans went near the team. He just totally disrupted the whole thing. No one should be talking to the players on the day of a big game about moving to Italy."

Marr saw Ivano at the stadium but didn't shake his hand. It had been clear that there was no love lost between the pair following their bitter split during the close season of 2002.

"I didn't speak to the man all the time I was there," he said.

"I saw him at the stadium but I didn't shake his hand. I've no time for the man at all, given the way he treated me in the summer. I have tried to talk to him a few times over that period but he wouldn't speak to me. I talked to his wife more often than I talked to him."

Although many of them had chanted his name in Italy, Marr said the feelings of the supporters towards Ivano would be completely different if they "knew the truth".

"I think when everything's done and dusted and the fans find out some of the things he's done, which will come out eventually, that will be knocked on the head," he said. "They will maybe see him in a different light. The season that he left he did no preparation whatsoever for the following season. We had to do it all. Some of the things he did were outrageous. I think fans will see him in a truer light. The last six months he was here were incredible. I had to keep the peace and make up stories as to why he wasn't here."

Marr also alleged he discouraged players from signing new deals for the club. "For instance, he told Julian Speroni not to sign for us," he said. "If it hadn't been for (former director of football) Paul Marr persistently pushing Julian to sign for the club he wouldn't be here. Khaled Kemas was also told by Ivano not to sign for Dundee and he was supposed to be our manager."

Ivano hit back – not for the first time – and stressed he didn't care what Peter Marr said. But he denied tapping players and defended himself against all claims of disrupting the training camp during his visit.

"I am not in a position to offer anyone jobs – this is completely untrue," he said. "I do not care about what Peter Marr says. If I were working as a manager in Italy then the first thing I would do is try to buy good players, but what is strange about that? I know some good players very well from my time at Dundee. That is not the situation, though. It was really a joy to see the players and I had a talk with Jim Duffy, too, and he is a really nice guy. I can't understand why I should not meet them. I had two wonderful seasons with some of these players. I am not saying anything about Peter Marr and did not speak to him in Perugia but I had a wonderful chat with Giovanni di Stefano. Dundee now has a person in power to do well for them and I am really happy about the new situation."

Dundee fan Alan Cheghall helped found a new chapter of the Dark Blues legion after the match. Alan was chosen from hundreds of Norwich Union employees to take part in a 17-day African adventure with Raleigh International. He and around a dozen colleagues visited the remote desert village of Purros in north-west Namibia to spend 10 days helping to create a school playground. During a briefing before the trip, the group were told that items taken for granted in Britain could make a great deal of difference to the lives of the villagers in Purros. Understanding the global significance of sport, and football in particular, Alan contacted Dundee to see whether the club would donate a set of strips for the school he was to visit. The club was happy to oblige so Alan set off with a dozen strips and a couple of footballs.

He said: "The people out there really have got nothing compared to us, so when I took out the strips they went down a storm. For a people who live out in the desert, they all know their football and one of the things they wanted us to do was build a five-a-side pitch. We had a kick-about later and I scored the first goal on the pitch in my Dundee top."

Craig Burley was also turning out in a Dundee top and he played for 90 minutes and scored in the under-21 match against Partick Thistle to put him in contention for the derby. Burley said: "I've never felt so frustrated since signing. When my contract expired at Derby during the summer, I trained harder than ever to ensure I'd be in peak condition for my new club. I lost 10lb in weight and am now lighter than when I started out. Unfortunately, I tore a calf muscle on my Dundee debut in the under-21s, hence the reason for my delay in playing for the first team. However, I'm feeling great now, although it's up to Jim Duffy when he bloods me.

"As a kid at Chelsea, all there seemed to be was London derbies. Then there was the derby to beat all derbies when I joined Celtic. I've been extremely impressed with the quality of player at Dens. However, my former Derby colleague Fabrizio Ravanelli is even more impressed. I knew Scottish football was better than it's portrayed in England – he didn't. However, he does now."

Duffy had a decision to make over Burley. There was a chance that his hand might be forced however as injuries to Tom Cowan, Brent Sancho, Stevie Milne, Steve Lovell and Tom Hutchinson had left bodies thin on the ground.

"Craig is getting closer to the required fitness level but ideally he needs another match under his belt," said Duffy. "However, when you have injuries like we do at the moment sometimes you have to take an extra gamble."

Duffy also spoke for the first time about what happened in Perugia. He said it was "unethical" that Ivano turned up at the team hotel the night before and the day of the game. He said: "I have no problem personally with Ivano Bonetti. I have no issue with his coming to the stadium and speaking to some of the players but he should not have then come back to our hotel and continued having conversations with people so close to a big game."

Before the derby, the city's Lord Provost set his sights on the SPL when he blasted plans to stop schoolboy signings from playing for their school teams as "garbage". John Letford, who was also co-founder of the Sunday Boys' League in 1965-66, said the SPL was "right out of order" after proposing a blanket ban. "People like Davie Narey and John Holt were involved in the game at schoolboy level, indeed players from both Dundee and Dundee United played for their schools while S-signings," said the Lord Provost.

"Schools come first. There were never any problems. Relations were good and both clubs work well with schools. You just have to look at Scottish clubs these days – hardly a Scottish name among them. Their laddies are sitting on the bench every week, if they're at the game at all. The SPL are right out of order with this one. They're certainly not helping develop the laddies by thinking of this ban."

The SPL was expected to decide on the matter at their board meeting on November 20 and both city clubs declared their intention to vote against the tough new proposals.

The "laddies" would be on the bench for the live TV clash at Tannadice where Dundee hadn't defeated United since November 2000 when Caniggia was among the scorers.

Ravanelli was left speechless after being mobbed before the game as he walked the 100 yards down Tannadice Street from Dens. The man who was used to running a gauntlet of hate from rival fans before big derbies in Italy was even asked for his autograph by star-struck Dundee United supporters.

"That wouldn't have happened in Italy," he said in disbelief.

Ravanelli started the derby against United in front of just almost 13,000 fans. Dundee were the brighter of the two sides despite their recent Tannadice record and almost went ahead while some of the away fans were still taking their seats.

Nacho Novo should have given Dundee a dream start inside just 20 seconds but his poor chip was caught by goalkeeper Paul Gallacher when it appeared easier to score. Fabian Caballero then put Gallacher under slightly more pressure with a fierce drive from a tight angle a couple of minutes later which he did well to keep out.

United finally started to get to grips with the game and pantomime villain Billy Dodds should have done much better when he sent a header well wide in front of goal. The former Dundee striker was constantly jeered by the away fans throughout who had never forgiven him for signing for their rivals. They mocked his every touch and even taunted the United fans with the chant: "You signed Billy Dodds, You signed Billy Dodds, We signed Caniggia, We signed Caniggia, You signed Billy Dodds."

Ravanelli looked dangerous despite still struggling for match sharpness. He curled a left-foot free-kick just wide before Dundee's pressure paid off on 19 minutes when Novo was pulled down inside the box by David McCracken. Novo sent Gallacher the wrong way to give Dundee the lead after the referee pointed to the spot. Dundee continued to dictate most of the play during a frenetic first half. The front three of Novo, Caballero and Ravanelli were involved in most of Dundee's best moments. United looked a completely different proposition after the restart and almost equalised but Julian Speroni showed quick reactions to deal with Jim McIntyre's forceful header. Dundee threw on Craig Burley for his Dundee debut in place of the injured Jonay Hernandez before Ravanelli rolled back the years and spun brilliantly before firing a drive just wide.

United decided to take a gamble and threw more bodies forward in search of an equaliser despite Dundee looking dangerous on the break. The decision was rewarded on 56 minutes when Jim Paterson picked out McIntyre with a perfect cross from the left which he glanced with his head into Speroni's bottom left-hand corner.

Dundee didn't let their heads go down and responded well to being pegged back when a dangerous Ravanelli cross caused panic in the United ranks. Gallacher and Chris Innes got themselves in a tangle in the box but the ball was eventually cleared to safety before Fabian Caballero could swoop.

Play by now was raging from end to end in typical derby fashion and United's Andy McLaren and Dundee's Gavin Rae both missed good chances to score. With a quarter of the game remaining, United's Alan Archibald sent a fierce drive whistling just inches over the crossbar from the edge of the box.

Not to be outdone, Dundee then went even closer when Caballero's cross took a deflection and struck the United crossbar with goalkeeper Gallacher beaten. Gallacher then kept United in the match when he pulled off a brilliant double-save from Novo's close-range strike on 79 minutes. Republic of Ireland international Owen Coyle had a chance to win the game for United at the death but he put his header over the bar and the teams left with a share of the spoils.

After the match Ravanelli told the fans that the goals would come and expressed his desire to become a Dens Park hero. "I really like it here and I wish I had come to Scotland when I was younger because the football is good and the fans are wonderful," he said.

"I had other offers but the Dundee one was the best and I have no problem with playing in Scottish football. I have played in a lot of derbies and this was just as enjoyable as the others, although we are disappointed we could only draw because I feel this Dundee team has a lot of possibilities. I have not scored yet either, although I learned when I was at Juventus that that is not so important as long as I am helping the team. The goals will come. I would love to be a hero here."

Dundee was already proving to be a popular place for heroes. A big-budget Bollywood movie called Cape Karma was being filmed in Dundee, Perthshire and Angus. It was being made by the company behind the cult football flick Bend It Like Beckham.

Award-winning director Pankaj Advani – who shot the first digital film in India – decided to make the entire movie in Tayside after being shown the region's attractions by TayScreen. Executive producer Sumit Kumar said: "Dundee has huge connections with India. The first Indians arrived in Dundee and many of the jute barons owned houses in Broughty Ferry. The message of the film is that fate always repays you for what you do. It is a message that crosses cultures and borders."

The Bollywood team would have struggled to script the next chapter in Ravanelli's Dundee story any better. It all happened in the unlikely setting of North Lanarkshire. A midweek league cup tie against Clyde at Broadwood in front of just

1,701 fans would ensure that his dream of entering his name into Dundee folklore would come true. Even more impressive was the fact that Dundee went into the game without eight players, while another two or three played despite being less than 100% fit.

"We have got boys like Gavin Rae, who are never normally injured, out right now and it just seems like everyone is getting hurt," said defender Lee Wilkie. "I've never been involved when so many people have been out and it is obviously a handicap. It's happened, though, and we just have to get on with it. We do have the injuries, but we will still have a lot of good players and we believe we can get through. We had a good run in the Scottish Cup last season and the boys loved it. Reaching the final showed we can do well in the knockout competitions and we want to stay in this one for a few matches."

Duffy said he fully expected Dundee to defeat their First Division opponents and go into the draw for the last eight. Despite the bodies stacking up on the treatment table he said he would accept no excuses.

"This has certainly given me a different kind of problem and it is one I don't like," he said. "You expect to pick up injuries, but you do not expect so many at one time and the squad is a bit thin. None of the players who missed yesterday will be fit for the games this week and Hernandez and Rae are definitely out for Wednesday. On top of that, we also have a situation where Fabrizio Ravanelli and Craig Burley are still searching for their match fitness. They are probably up to about 75% right now and it is asking a lot of players to be playing 90 minutes in those circumstances, but we are going to have to. Clyde have done very well and are a strong, physical side. But we have good players in the team and we will make sure there is no nonsense in the heads about being tired after the derby. Selection-wise we are all over the place in every department of the team. But I am not looking for sympathy nor will I use this situation as an excuse. The injuries we have means there is now an opportunity for one or two people and I expect to see them rise to the challenge. I believe we have enough good players available to us to go and play anywhere, providing that our attitude is right and it is up to the guys coming in to prove they should be in the side and make it difficult for me to leave them out once everyone is fit again."

Clyde player/manager Alan Kernaghan lined up in defence but had to do without on-loan Dunfermline Athletic wing-back Chris McGroarty and dropped John Potter to the bench. He said: "With Nacho Novo and Fabrizio Ravanelli, they are bound to cause us problems, but my side will try to be organised and go about the game in a sensible manner."

On the night, Ravanelli conjured up a magical hat-trick within the space of six minutes after taking the game by the scruff of the neck following his arrival as a second-half substitute.

Duffy rang the changes after the derby draw. Callum MacDonald made his first start for Dundee alongside new signing Craig Burley. MacDonald and Burley replaced injured pair Jonay Hernandez and Gavin Rae, while Ravanelli was replaced by Juan Sara up front. Dundee were on the back foot almost immediately when Clyde took the lead within two minutes when Pat Keogh converted a cross from Jack Ross with his head from 12 yards. The Dark Blues equalised within two minutes when Nacho Novo pounced on the rebound after Juan Sara's shot was cleared off the line by Mark McLaughlin. Both sides continued to push forward and the match was end-to-end stuff, with Clyde goalkeeper Bryn Halliwell making saves from Novo and Caballero to keep the scores level.

Dundee dominated proceedings after the restart. They took the lead on 66 minutes when Lee Wilkie picked up the ball on the halfway line. He carried the ball half the length of the park before coolly slipping it past Halliwell from 10 yards after playing a neat one-two with Caballero.

Just like Ivano's wonder chip against Aberdeen on Caniggia's debut, this would be another stunning goal which would be overshadowed by the appearance of a superstar substitute.

For a man whose time in English football was best remembered by a hat-trick against Liverpool, Ravanelli conjured up another treble to win the game almost single-handedly. He entered the fray on 70 minutes and quickly snuffed out Clyde's hopes of performing an upset when he put the game beyond them with goals on 73, 74 and 79 minutes.

The legs might not have been as sprightly as they once were, but he looked sharp as a tack. Ravanelli replaced the misfiring Caballero and just three minutes later he got his first when he took a return pass from Novo before smashing a left-foot shot into the back of the net. Sixty seconds later he made it 4-1 when he was quickest to react to a rebound after Juan Sara's effort was spilled out by Halliwell.

The goals kept on coming in a staggering finale and Clyde weren't to be left out of the frenzy. On 78 minutes, substitute Mark Gillhaney gave his team some hope by firing past Julian Speroni from close range. However, Ravanelli had the last word when Dundee raced back up the park a minute later and the Italian fired low past Halliwell from a Sara assist to make it a six-minute hat-trick.

Amazingly, he could have had a fourth, blasting the ball off the post in the last minute.

The Clyde website's match report said: "In the end it was a very depressing night for Clyde. "If Clyde are serious about challenging to make the step up then this scoreline was a major wake-up call. Clyde simply couldn't pass the ball well enough and retain possession to trouble an average SPL team. Far too many weak passes or dreadful first-time passes with poor crosses ruined otherwise great endeavour. In the end class told in the shape of Mr Ravanelli."

'Mr Ravanelli' walked into the Clyde dressing room immediately afterwards and asked his opponents to sign the match ball before leaving with it proudly clasped under his arm. Things got more surreal when Ravanelli said the game at Broadwood brought back memories of playing for Juventus in a UEFA Cup game in the 67,229-capacity Stadio delle Alpi.

"I recall one game against CSKA Sofia when Juventus won 5-0," he said. "Every time I touched the ball I scored and I got all the goals. It was important for me to score three tonight. It was my quickest ever hat-trick, and I will take more confidence into Saturday's match. I now want to score at home before our fans. When I was on the bench I was focusing on the match because the manager had told me before the game that I would rest but if the match was not so easy then I would come on. Now I will give the ball to my children when I see them. I need a month more to be fit as I am still not 100%."

Manager Jim Duffy was, naturally, delighted with Ravanelli's hat-trick.

He said: "I am very pleased as he has only been here for a short time and has been short of fitness. He looked sharp tonight, though, and maybe that was because he was not asked to run about earlier. I decided to see how the game would go and if we needed the extra talent he would be introduced. Clyde are a notoriously difficult team to beat, so to go there and get five goals says a lot for the players. I prefer to keep things low key, but I feel on this occasion they deserve the praise they got.

"Obviously, there was Fabrizio's hat-trick, but there were a lot of good performances and I was particularly pleased that we finished the game with three young players in Mark Fotheringham, Callum MacDonald and Bobby Linn on the park and doing well. With the squad we have, it is always going to be difficult for these boys when everyone is fit, but our injuries have given them their chance and it is nice to see them take it."

Ravanelli's team-mates knew they had witnessed something special. Some were in a state of shock in the dressing room and young defender Callum MacDonald said he was still struggling to take it all in. He admitted he would never forget his Dundee debut.

"I've just been sitting in the dressing-room thinking that to make my debut on a night when Ravanelli hit a hat-trick is almost unbelievable," he said. "His finishing was superb, and just to be on the pitch with a player of his ability is great."

Team-mate Garry Brady described Ravanelli's hat-trick as "a bit of a stunner". He said: "Ravanelli came on and got the three goals in seven minutes and that speaks for itself. He's a great guy. I have met a few players who have played at a high level like he has and you expect them to be a bit big-time, and with his stature you would expect the same. Both he and Craig Burley, though, have been great and they mix well and get on with the lads. Their attitude has been great and instead of being big-time they are the total opposite."

The White Feather had, as promised, written his name into Dundee folklore.

CHAPTER THIRTEEN

Beware Of Italians Bearing Gifts

It was a gamble that didn't pay off.

Peter Marr, Dundee FC owner

A LINK-UP between the SFA and Safeway prompted the bizarre sight of Scotland fans huddling together for warmth as they camped overnight in a supermarket car park at the start of November. The SFA appeared to believe selling tickets for the Euro 2004 play-off against Holland in the fruit and veg aisle was a good move, and Tartan Army foot soldiers queued up outside Safeway in freezing temperatures in Arbroath Road to be first in line when doors opened.

Ravanelli's heroic exploits against Clyde was the warm-up which earned him a starting place at the expense of Fabian Caballero when Dundee returned to league duty against Hibs. Hibernian midfielder Stephen Glass was born in Dundee and said he had been watching developments at Dens with interest. He predicted Ravanelli would become a huge success at Dundee.

"I was brought up on Dundee derbies and never imagined the day would come, like last Sunday, when I would be sitting watching Fabrizio Ravanelli playing in one," said Glass. "He is a fantastic player who, I think, will do really well in Scotland. "Dundee have other quality players, too, with Novo and Nemsadze obvious examples. It is not just the foreigners either – in Gavin Rae and Lee Wilkie they have two excellent young Scots.

"We have to worry about ourselves, though. We've won our last two games and want to build on that. Hibs might not have as big a name as Ravanelli, but we have a lot of talent, with Derek Riordan very impressive against Queen of the South. It should be an interesting game."

Off the park, Ravanelli was proving just as popular. Inundated with requests for interviews since his arrival, Ravanelli had refused very few and had spoken eloquently and enthusiastically about the club and the city. He appeared to love life in Dundee. What was also apparent was he was keen to tell that to anyone who would listen.

On the pitch, Dundee and Hibs were a little less polite, leaving absolutely nothing in the dressing room as they threw everything at each other for 90 minutes. Ravanelli picked off where he left off at Broadwood with another influential display alongside youngster Bobby Linn, who was given the job of partnering him up front. Linn was making his first-team start at Dens with Dundee still struggling for bodies.

The away side started positively with Derek Riordan's 25-yard effort well held by Julian Speroni. Ravanelli looked sharp and almost scored his first league goal when he met Nacho Novo's cross, but his header was brilliantly tipped onto the post by Daniel Andersson. Dundee were looking dangerous before Craig Burley was sent off on 24 minutes, being shown a straight red for a bad tackle on Tom McManus.

Bobby Linn had already been booked for a foul on Ian Murray and Duffy made the sensible decision to take him off after just 29 minutes to save him following Burley down the tunnel after the occasion clearly got the better of him. The loss of Burley and the over-excited Linn didn't reduce Dundee's attacking menace and they went in front despite being down to 10 men.

When the goal came it was courtesy of the perfect Ravanelli assist. The on-song hitman turned provider when he used his head to play a Barry Smith cross into the path of Nacho Novo, who fired in his 13th goal of the season at the second attempt. Hibs pushed men forward to make their advantage count but were denied an equaliser thanks to a couple of superb Julian Speroni stops prior to the break.

Dundee tightened things up after going a man down but still retained an attacking threat on the break and should have gone further ahead after the restart. Andersson was forced to deny Novo twice, along with strikes from Ravanelli and Barry Smith, as Dundee looked like adding to their lead despite the numerical handicap.

Hibs kept plugging away and equalised from a controversial retaken free-kick on 81 minutes from Derek Riordan. Riordan's first 20-yard effort was saved by Speroni only for referee Kenny Clark to order the kick to be retaken because he hadn't blown his whistle. Riordan's second effort cruelly veered over the top of the Dundee wall and in off the post.

It was backs to the wall at the death as Dundee held on to preserve a point with Speroni again called upon to save from Colin Murdock. Ian Murray then headed over from close range but Dundee escaped with a point.

Duffy was furious Hibs had been given a second bite at the cherry and wasn't happy with the referee's performance. He told him to hold his hands up and admit he got it wrong. Duffy said: "I never get involved with referees because they have an unenviable job but we are all scrutinised nowadays and the ref has to put his hands up and say: 'I made a mistake'. I think he made several. There were so many decisions that were wrong and, if Kenny Clark is honest with himself, he'll say he had a bad game. If referees can't accept criticism they shouldn't be in the game. They will circle the wagons and say everything is all right. But, if there were more honesty, then they would admit they had a bad day. The fourth official comes and tells me to sit down and calm down, but I genuinely don't think they appreciate the effort and passion that's involved in football.

"We are criticised for making errors and if referees are part of the excitement of football they have to be prepared to accept that, too. It was a crucial decision at a crucial time of the game and it was a wrong decision – simple as that."

Nacho Novo agreed with his manager and had received a yellow card for protesting. "Yes, it was a disappointing decision and it was a shame for Julian," he said. "But I also believe we should have had one or two penalties. In particular, there was one right at the end of the match when I could have scored the winner but was pushed when I tried to hit the ball."

The following evening Dundee's heroes of the past were celebrated when a sportsman's dinner was held at the Invercarse Hotel to mark the 30th anniversary of the 1973 League Cup win against Celtic. Dundee famously won the match 1-0 with a goal on 75 minutes from Gordon Wallace who chested down a Bobby Wilson free-kick with his back to goal and fired the ball low past Ally Hunter. Ten former players attended and shared memories of defeating Celtic at Hampden during an energy crisis and appalling weather which saw the kick-off brought forward to 1.30pm and the 27,924 attendance was, unsurprisingly, the lowest-ever for a League Cup Final.

The subject of ticket sales prompted an ugly spat between Dundee and Dundee United the following week. It was described in some quarters as "The Battle of Tannadice Street". The clubs got involved in a row over an unpaid bill, with verbal bickering played out on the back pages. It made for strained relations between the neighbours. Claims and counter-claims were made over Dundee's failure to meet the deadline for a payment of £83,000 due to United from ticket sales for the derby.

United went public with their decision to contact the SPL, before Dundee responded by expressing "sympathy" that the Tangerines were so desperate for cash. A Dundee spokesman said United were informed the reason for the delay was the club was switching banks but gave assurances the cash would be forwarded next week.

"I am genuinely sorry to learn Dundee United have financial problems," the spokesman said. "There has been speculation for some time that was the case and today's events confirm this. They have our sympathy. We were contacted by a Dundee United director last week who asked us to do him a personal favour and pay the money early – that is before the deadline – as they were having difficulty meeting their financial commitments. We indicated we could not pay before the deadline as we were in the middle of changing banks, which is a major undertaking.

"We did, however, give an assurance that the sum would be paid next week. There was further contact yesterday from another director seeking the money and again we explained about the bank changeover. There was then a further conversation with (United chairman) Eddie Thompson and he was given repeated assurances that the money would be paid. We can't move any faster and we will settle this debt. We have made a promise and we will keep it."

Dundee United spokesman Malcolm Brown said the complaint was nothing to do with a lack of cash. "That is a cheeky comment and it is not Dundee United who owe £83,000," he said. "Also, Dundee FC know nothing about the financial situation at Tannadice. We have reported Dundee to the SPL because of non-payment of gate money. The sum was due to be paid yesterday. There was no indication when the money would be paid and we did not want a repeat of what happened following the February match when they took three months to pay."

When informed the Dark Blues had promised to pay the money the following week, Brown said he viewed this as vindication of their actions. "If it is the case then we are delighted that our policy of going public and informing the SPL has worked so well," he said. "If we had been given a definite date for payment do you think we would have gone through all this hassle?"

The final word on the matter was left to Dundee director Jim Connor. "United must be very much in need of a victory if they view this as a success," he said.

The Dark Blues returned to Dens the following week for a match against a Motherwell team which had controversially escaped relegation the previous season. Motherwell had brought in big-names like John Spencer, Andy Goram and Roberto Martinez to challenge the Old Firm, but the experiment failed disastrously. The club went into administration in April 2003 and finished bottom of the SPL but they escaped relegation when the league rejected an application from the First Division champions Falkirk to share a ground while their new stadium was being built.

Duffy said: "If you look at Motherwell this season, their record speaks for itself. They have gone from being a team who, technically, should not have been in the league to just a point behind us with a game in hand. In the last few matches they have been particularly impressive – at home they've drawn with Rangers and were unlucky not to win. Away, they have beaten Aberdeen and Dundee United and scored a few goals, so they deserve the respect we will give them. Very often when you have as many injuries as we've had there is a dip in form, but the boys have been playing well. They have also been battling very hard in games and that has not often been something that has been associated with Dundee over the last few seasons. The boys are aware of how good Motherwell's form has been and they will be prepared for them tomorrow."

Both sides tried to play a passing game and attacking football. Young forward Bobby Linn was told to calm down and he was given another chance to impress alongside Ravanelli up front for Dundee. The Dark Blues enjoyed the bulk of possession in the first half and Ravanelli missed a gilt-edged chance from just five yards when he pulled away from his marker. With the goal gaping, he sent a free header over the crossbar from a dangerous Garry Brady cross.

Ravanelli again showed a touch of class shortly afterwards. He held off Stephen Pearson and Scott Leitch before finding Juan Sara with a curling pass. But the Argentine striker – performing in an unfamiliar midfield berth due to the lack of available bodies – lost control at the vital moment and the chance went a-begging. Motherwell then punished Dundee's poor finishing when they took the lead six minutes into the second half, slicing Dundee wide open with some accurate passing. Steven Craig intelligently darted across his marker and put the ball into the far corner of the net from David Clarkson's near-post cross.

Dundee players and fans shouted for a penalty when Nacho Novo latched on to a through ball from Fabian Caballero and rounded Gordon Marshall. Novo stayed on his feet when he might have gone down after being hampered by the goalkeeper.

Ravanelli then threatened twice in quick succession. First he blasted straight at the goalkeeper from 16 yards before watching a free-kick being deflected wide afterwards.

Motherwell held on and Duffy admitted they deserved to take all three points. "We didn't deserve to win," he said. "Motherwell deserved their victory – there is no doubt about that. They were the team with the bigger appetite, whereas we were poor in so many departments. The only area where we were not bad was defence, where the two Lees did well and young Dougie Cameron had a steady debut. We are missing a lot of players but the ones who go on the pitch are the ones you have to concern yourself with and they have to do better. We passed the ball to the opposition so often and it was not like us. If you don't pass crisply you won't create, and Gordon Marshall didn't have much to do. It was not good enough."

Motherwell manager Terry Butcher was in brighter spirits and looking towards European football. "I've told the players to steady up," he said. "We can't afford to be paying European bonuses. That's four away wins and four clean sheets. I think I'll retire now. Seriously, it wasn't the best game, but it's a case of never mind the quality, look at the result."

Motherwell were given top marks, something which wasn't afforded to Dundee MP Iain Luke who was on the receiving end of a tongue-lashing from talent show judge Simon Cowell. Mr Luke was one of 12 MPs who signed an early day motion attacking Pop Idol and described the criticism handed out to some of the show's contestants as "discriminatory and unfair". The show's "Mr Nasty" hit back in typical fashion from the judging panel on the Saturday night live show when he said he gave the MPs "nil" in the wake of the criticism. He said: "These kids could wipe the floor with an awful lot of MPs."

Dundee's manager Jim Duffy then turned "Pub Idol" when he opened a bar on Shore Terrace, which was promising to bring a little bit of Spain to the City of Discovery. He poured the first pint but might have needed something stronger when conflicting messages started coming from within the boardroom.

There was financial trouble on the horizon.

Dundee fans were told to expect to see their club go into administration by the beginning of the following week at the latest.

There was confidence Dundee would survive the worst crisis in its history, but it would likely mean the exit door for a host of big name stars at Dens Park. Peter Marr said the situation was serious and drastic action would require to be taken to save the club from extinction with debts reportedly spiralling to over £13 million. The appointment of an administrator appeared inevitable but Marr pledged to do everything in his power to save the club that he and his brother Jimmy rescued six years previously.

Nobody could have predicted things could have gone so bad so quickly, but it was immediately clear that things were not harmonious within the boardroom at Dens Park. "I want to reassure the fans that every possible effort is being made to safeguard the future of the club, and as soon as we can say more about how that will be done, we will do it," said Marr. "We are fans as well. We love this club, and the last thing we want is to see Dundee get into any more financial difficulty. Whatever we do will be designed to bring the club through the difficult period it faces. We hope to emerge from this stronger and fitter."

However, Giovanni di Stefano expressed surprise and played down any talk of a crisis. He said there would be no need for the club to go into administration. "This is the first I have heard," he said. "For it to go into administration would require a board meeting to be called and that has not happened. I have not spoken to anyone about administration and the bank have not notified us about it. What would be the point of administration? There is no point. The liability this club has to the bank has been well publicised, but this is just the sort of rumours we've been having to deal with. First they were trying to say I am not a fit person and now this.

"There are ongoing liabilities and there is an inherited tax debt of approaching £1 million – I think the exact figure is something like £700,000. But I have given an undertaking to the Inland Revenue to pay that and they have accepted it. I'm in court in London today and I'll be in Italy to see my son play football this weekend. I sponsor his school team and like any dad I want to see him play. I do not know when I will be back in Dundee, but that is only because right now it is not necessary for me to be there. If that was to change I could be there within a day and would be."

Di Stefano insisted he would completely refuse to agree to any proposed motion to put the club into administration. Behind the scenes, the other three directors were ready to overrule him to save Dundee.

The fans were in a state of shock but turned out in numbers for the journey to East End Park in a show of solidarity at the next league game against Dunfermline. Duffy said he was confident that what was happening at boardroom level would not affect his team on the park.

The fans gave them huge backing and Dundee started brightly. They almost took the lead on seven minutes when Juan Sara's header from a Jonay Hernandez free-kick was cleared off the line by Gary Dempsey. Three minutes later, Fabian Caballero headed just wide, before linking up well with Nacho Novo to free Ravanelli on the edge of the box. Ravanelli's curling effort was deflected inches wide of the upright. The Dark Blues dominated the first half and should have gone in ahead.

But Dunfermline took control of proceedings after the break and took the lead on 52 minutes. Darren Young's delivery to the edge of the box was left by veteran Craig Brewster. Scotland striker Stevie Crawford used all his guile and experience to evade Lee Mair's challenge and he fired the ball home from 16 yards out. The impressive Crawford later added a second after 64 minutes when he powered home a bullet header from 16 yards after getting on the end of Barry Nicholson's free-kick. Things almost got worse for Dundee but Young was denied a third for Dunfermline when the ball broke to him inside the box. Speroni did well to block the shot. Dundee kept battling right to the end and managed to keep the score down.

Ravanelli and his Dundee team-mates had had a day to forget on the pitch but the storm clouds were gathering for the whole club. Things were about to get much worse.

At the end of the Dunfermline defeat Ravanelli waved to the Dundee fans, which appeared to suggest it was the final time they would see him in a Dark Blue jersey. He was asked afterwards by reporters if it was a goodbye gesture. He said: "I don't know, but I read in the newspapers that it is a very bad situation and there are many possibilities for letting players go. When I arrived I was told there would be a good future for me at the club, that it is a good team to play in Europe and that we would be trying to win many matches and compete with the Old Firm. Now I find I am not very happy. I have been given assurances by Giovanni di Stefano and Peter Marr and I would want to stay here.

"I love Dundee and I love the fans. I have a two-year contract and I want to believe in Mr di Stefano and Mr Marr, that they can get us out of this situation. Nobody comes into the changing room and tells us what happens – it would be nice to know. It is very difficult for me to try to play well and concentrate with all the financial problems. Every player enjoys playing at Dundee. It is a fantastic club and I have enjoyed my time here."

Just a few hours after the Dunfermline game, Dundee author Pat Kelly stood at the spot where President John F. Kennedy was killed in Dallas 40 years previously. Mr Kelly joined mourners on the grassy knoll where a short memorial service was conducted before joining delegates to discuss the assassination at a major conference. The JFK researcher was invited after contacting one of America's most acclaimed forensic pathologists, Dr Cyril Wecht, in a bid to uncover the truth behind the 1963 assassination. Dr Wecht was one of the few people in the world who had actually inspected the relevant evidence in the JFK case, including the President's blood-stained clothes. Dr Wecht was one of the most consistent critics of the "single bullet" theory, believing one bullet could not have caused seven wounds to the President and other occupants in the car. Dr Wecht said: "If President Kennedy's body were to be exhumed at this time, we would have a good chance to reconstruct the head wounds to determine whether he was hit in the head by two different shots."

There would soon be just as many questions hanging over Dens Park.

A press conference was called at the start of the week. Peter Marr urged fans and the local business community to rally round and help save the club from impending closure. He confirmed he had put the club into administration and it was up for sale for as little as £1 to Giovanni di Stefano, or anyone else who could clear the debts.

"Obviously this is not a nice thing to have to do, but we will be working hard with the administrator to bring the club through this," he said. "I feel sorry for staff, players and fans that it has come to this, but we feel this is the best course of action. The last few days have been difficult because it has been in the open that it was going to happen, but I've not been able to say anything and let the fans know what is going on. Now we will be depending on the fans to support us as they always have done and we need the business community, many of whom are Dundee fans, to stand up and be counted."

Marr said he would be keeping the chain of events which would follow the decision strictly private, but it was expected there would be job losses in the coming days. He said the outlook was extremely serious but not quite as grave as many feared. Marr also made it clear that several millions of the debt were sums owed to him and his brother Jimmy which they would be writing off.

Despite the club's predicament it was clear that Marr was no longer expecting di Stefano to ride in on a white charger to save the day. It was also abundantly clear that the two men were not now on speaking terms. "I haven't heard from Giovanni since Thursday and I do not expect to," he said. "He obviously has nothing to say to me and I have nothing to say to him. We thought Giovanni di Stefano would be the answer. However, various discussions were held and time has now run out without those discussions bearing fruit."

Marr said the last straw that broke the camel's back was a demand from the Inland Revenue. HMRC had threatened a winding-up petition within a week over an unpaid tax bill of £750,000. Following talks with the Bank of Scotland, Marr said the decision to enter administration had been made in an effort to protect the club.

Marr didn't pull his punches when reporters asked him how the club had accumulated such massive debts, which according to some quarters were said to be as high as £23 million.

"Paying players too much money," he said. "We based it on bringing in players and selling them on. It was a gamble that didn't pay off."

Marr said the club had failed to sell players and generate enough income while fellow director Jim Connor said the loss of TV revenue had also been a huge blow.

"It's a relief in some ways that it is now out in the open because it's better than carrying on and trying to put on a brave face," he said. "It's a cry for help from us."

A war of words broke out when di Stefano said he would continue to pay Ravanelli's wages and hotel expenses to help keep him at Dundee. He said: "I have just spoken to Mr Ravanelli and, as far as his playing contract is concerned, his salary and expenses are paid by me and he will continue to play for Dundee Football Club without the costs to the administrators, if they so desire. I will continue to pay, as I have done, his salary and his hotel expenses."

Dundee later expressed a degree of shock at di Stefano's comments, with a spokesman stating the club was not aware that he had started to pay the Italian's salary. He also said di Stefano was offered the club for £1 but suggested the rest of the board did not trust him to come up with the promised cash injection even if he had bought them out.

"I can confirm that control of the club was offered to Mr di Stefano for £1," he said. "But, in return for total control, he wanted the Marrs to walk away completely from the club in which they have invested millions. They could not, as directors, have the confidence that the promised investment by Mr di Stefano would materialise. Since he became a director in August we have had three months of totally unfulfilled promises of investment. It reached the point where the club had to take action to safeguard itself."

Di Stefano then made a series of allegations that sullied the fragile relations even further. He accused the Marr brothers of calling in the administrators because major creditors the Bank of Scotland would ensure their other companies were treated more leniently than the football club. This was dismissed as "utter nonsense" by Dundee who said it was well-known that the Marr brothers' businesses were intertwined closely with the club. But it was "simply wrong" to say that administration was dependent on anything other than the club's position.

The ugly spat continued to be played out in public.

"Dundee will not survive administration because no administrator will be able to sustain that kind of situation," said di Stefano. "This isn't a Motherwell, with a John Boyle figure prepared to write off his losses. Here we are talking about a number of trade creditors. I know people will try to make me a scapegoat, but let's be clear – it was not me who accrued the debt with the Inland Revenue. It was not me who accrued these liabilities."

Peter Marr went on the offensive after being accused of not keeping di Stefano informed. "Giovanni is all bluff and bluster," he said. "He has known since last Tuesday that we favoured going into administration. He failed to attend a board meeting on Friday when the decision to apply for administration was passed unanimously. He can talk all he wants, but we see this measure as the only way forward."

Di Stefano also claimed he put up a personal guarantee to pay the unpaid tax bill of £750,000. Again Marr came out and denied that had actually happened.

Despite the row, the other directors amazingly insisted the door remained open to di Stefano.

Manager Jim Duffy said not knowing if his job was safe was worse than knowing – even if it is bad news. "The main thing is to get it resolved so everybody at the club knows where they stand," he said. "I can't pre-empt what will happen, whether or not the club is going to go forward and survive. It might include me, and it might not. Cost-cutting is cost-cutting and no one is safe. We will just have to wait and see if that is the case, and if it is then we will have to deal with it."

Dundee chartered accountants Henderson Loggie then attempted to spell out what would happen and said the administrator would come in with a blank sheet of paper.

"Anything is possible, including the sale of any of the club's assets," said a spokesperson. "He has the power and the authority to make decisions and that could include the decision to unload the most valuable players. The board, while it would not be dissolved, would be helpless to intervene. The administrator would have the power, alone, to make the decisions."

The last Dundee chairman whose tenure was not surrounded by controversy later expressed his sadness at the plight of his favourite club. Graham Thomson, who became a director at Dens Park in 1972, enjoyed a brief spell at the helm from 1986 before the club was taken over by businessman Angus Cook in the late 1980s.

Mr Thomson, who still owned shares in the club, said it was a "very sad day, not only for Dundee FC but the community as a whole" as the club had played a vital part in many people's lives. A successful businessman who was deputy president of the former Timex in the city and a former president of the Chamber of Commerce, Mr Thomson said a football club must be run as a business with particular attention paid to wages and salaries. He said it appeared that wages had been allowed to spiral out of control.

"We kept a very, very close eye on this in my day," he said. "They were very strictly controlled as that is the only way of running a successful business. You have to be able to balance the books at the end of the day."

Mr Thomson said youth development could now provide the route to the club's salvation. "I always felt it was one of the key policies during my time to bring through the youths," he said. "I was a great believer in developing our own talent. My hope is that all the young players and apprentices will be looked at favourably because they are the future of the club."

Administration would herald the biggest earners going first and one of the candidates to be first through the exit door was Ravanelli.

The former Italian international said he was bemused and bewildered that, just two months after joining the Dark Blues, his Dens career looked over before it had really got started.

Ravanelli had hugely impressed his team-mates with his work-rate and dedication during his short spell at the club. Some people thought he might not take Dundee seriously but he was proving to be exactly the same as Claudio Caniggia when it came to professionalism. Ravanelli was also taking some of the club's youngsters, like Duncan McLean, under his wing and working with them on the training ground to pass on his experience. He was also happy to socialise with the rest of his team-mates and his party trick was being able to drink a bottle of Bacardi Breezer with a straw in about one second flat.

Sadly, for Ravanelli, last orders had been called.

CHAPTER FOURTEEN

The Darkest Hour

Often the club has to keep things private and confidential for legal reasons, otherwise many other 'wolves' would be on our door far sooner than they have.

Peter Marr

DUNDEE officially went into administration at lunchtime on November 24, 2003. An application was made to the Court of Session in Edinburgh. Tom Burton and Fiona Taylor, from the accountants Ernst & Young, were appointed as joint administrators.

That cost good people their jobs and left many local businesses out of pocket.

Mr Burton said: "This move stops the clock running on the club's debts and gives us the ability to restructure its operations and debts. However, the company is in a critical financial position and solutions to its problems will not be easy to find. The company has some £20 million of debt and is losing £100,000 per week. This cannot be allowed to continue."

Peter Marr had jetted off to Dubai following the announcement and the following day it was left to Duffy to break the news that Ravanelli's short-lived time in Dundee was over. A member of the board perhaps should have read the list, but it was left to the manager, who tried to make the best of an impossible situation.

The White Feather was among 20 players and coaches who had their contracts scrapped, along with a warning from the administrators that more far-reaching cuts would follow. The sight of grey-faced young men emerging from Dens Park after being told they could not be kept on was a memory that would not fade for a considerable time.

Craig Burley, Georgi Nemsadze, Fabian Caballero, Juan Sara and Beto Carranza were sent packing, while young players like Barry Forbes and Gavin Beith were also sacked. Youth development supremo Kenny Cameron, goalkeeping coach Paul Mathers, assistant physio Robbie Raeside, European scout Javier Artero, and community coach Kevin Lee also left.

There were more than a few tears elsewhere when five members of the office staff including long-serving commercial director Jim Connor were also given their marching orders. Connor – who remained a member of the board – agreed to see out the week before clearing his desk.

The sacked players were also told that they would not receive any wages for the month, despite being just three days away from pay day.

First to emerge through the door after the meeting was Fabian Caballero. "I'm finished," he said.

"It is very sad. I was very happy here and the fans were very good to me. I do not know what I will do now. My wife is pregnant but I do not know if I will go back to our home in Paraguay or stay here. I do want a club as soon as possible. I want to train and I want to play."

Juan Sara didn't hold back when he came out. Peter Marr was in his sights.

"I hope the people who have brought the club into this position are sitting happy in the sunshine now while we are being sacked," said Sara.

"But I am disappointed at how this has been handled and very angry. Peter Marr was in charge and he has to pay for putting the club into this situation, not the players. I don't understand the law here. I cannot believe that employees can be sacked like this. You come into work one day and they tell you that you are sacked, you have no rights, you no longer have a contract, you are not getting your money and to go home. This decision – taken by people in suits, not football people – is not fair. The club owes me a lot of money and they know that."

Georgian midfielder Georgi Nemsadze was slightly more philosophical.

"The news is bad, but this is life and you have to be prepared for whatever happens," he said. "I have many friends here and I enjoyed playing for Dundee. I had one and a half years of my contract left, so I was not ready for this and it is a very bad situation."

Goalkeeper Jamie Langfield had joined Dundee as a boy, eight years previously. He said he was finding it difficult to come to terms with such a big part of his life being over. He said: "It's a sad day for me because this club has been a part of me for a long time and it's the same for a lot of boys in there. It was an emotional meeting and there were a few tears shed inside, but we appreciated that it was Jim Duffy who told us. We could see how hard it was for him."

Langfield and the other members of staff were told that they should not expect severance pay.

Goalkeeper Julian Speroni managed to escape the death knell but he spoke of his anguish at seeing so many of his friends forced to leave through no fault of their own. "This is a terrible thing and with Christmas just a month away they're asking players to leave with no money," said the Argentinian. "It is not just experienced players – we are also talking about young boys. It is the 25th of November and they might not get money for this month even."

Speroni said he was not sure if he would continue to get paid, despite escaping the axe, and he expressed fears for the club's existence going forward.

Striker Steve Lovell, who would also be staying, was forced to comfort the departing Nemsadze.

He said: "The manager read a list and it was honourable on his part that he wanted to be the one to tell us. I was sitting next to Georgi when the news was announced so I put my arm around him. He is a top lad and it's going to be hard because we are all about to lose friends. I experienced similar situations at Portsmouth and Bournemouth. It happens to football clubs, although it really should not have got this far."

Ravanelli was similarly grim-faced when he came out of the emotional meeting. He immediately expressed his intention to contact the man who brought him to Dens.

"I will speak to him (di Stefano) and I want to believe his intentions are good because he brought me here," he said. "This is very disappointing for me because I think when I arrived here there was a very good programme for the club and myself but that is obviously not the situation because the club is now in administration and I'll lose money."

Duffy would be staying on but he was clearly distressed. He looked ashen-faced as he told reporters that informing the players they would be leaving was "just awful" and easily the worst thing he had ever had to do.

"I personally told the players, along with Jim, and it was difficult for both of us, very emotional," said Duffy.

"I am not their employer so it was not strictly my job to tell them and I would rather someone else had to do it. But I felt it was important that it came from me and they realised I was only relaying the information. I genuinely feel devastated – shattered. I am remaining at the club for the moment anyway, but that is not any consolation. I am not being melodramatic, it's just that this has been a very, very difficult time."

Dave Mackay was also kept on by the club but he said he would welcome the chance to ask Peter and Jimmy Marr for their take on events.

"Only a couple of weeks ago I, along with Lee Mair, was offered a three-and-a-half-year contract," he said. "I cannot understand how they could be offering us that then all of a sudden it comes out the club is £20 million in debt and going into administration. It's a pity Peter and Jimmy Marr weren't the ones to break the news about who was going to us because that would have allowed myself and others the chance to ask just how Dundee have ended up in this state."

Releasing high-earners Georgi Nemsadze, Fabrizio Ravanelli, Craig

Burley, Fabian Caballero and Juan Sara was bad enough but the most galling aspect was so many kids had to go. Some were lost to the game before they'd been given a chance.

However, in a further twist, it was being suggested that Ravanelli might be dramatically reinstated, following the intervention of di Stefano. Fraser Wishart, the assistant secretary of the Scottish Professional Footballers' Association, was also at Dens that day to offer advice to those who were sacked.

"The players that left today have not been paid for this month and I think that is important to note," he said. "I have asked the administrator to go back to the creditors, the bank and the directors of the club to see whether they will honour that month's contract.

"The administrator runs the club from now on and he's been given monies from the bank to keep the club alive until January. I think what he's planning to do is look at the situation over the next few months and hopefully sell a couple of players to help the club get on to an even keel. Whether there will be further cuts or full liquidation, I don't think anyone knows."

Administrator Tom Burton said the cost-cutting measures were just the beginning of the job which was now happening in order to save Dundee. He said: "We have taken the first step towards this end by ensuring that Dundee Football Club has sufficient playing staff to fulfil its commitments, whilst taking action to significantly reduce the cost to the club. Regrettably, this means that 25 of the 70 full-time staff employed at Dundee have had their contracts terminated. The effect of reducing the numbers of full-time staff by a third has served to reduce the club's wage bill by 45%.

"It is important to stress that this action only begins to address the challenges faced by the club. We have started the process of stemming the week-by-week losses but there remains considerable work to do to secure the long-term viability of Dundee Football Club. Administration does, however, give us the opportunity to take these necessary actions and we are encouraged with the support being shown by creditors, staff, fans and Scottish football in general at this difficult time."

Dundee fanzine editor Robin Grimmond said the situation was worse than the dark days of playing First Division football and talk of mergers with city rivals United.

"We've been pretty low before," he said. "There was the merger talk and that seemed bad enough, but while I'd never want a merger this seems even worse. I don't think talk of a merger is going to come back. I doubt it would get the support to be viable and I think it would kill both clubs.

"It's bad enough for the supporters, waiting to hear what is happening, but it must be terrible for the players, staff and manager. I think that once the figures have been looked at there will have to be some cutting away at the playing staff, but we still have to stay in the Premier League and survive."

Mr Grimmond said it would be very hard to blame Peter and Jimmy Marr for the club's downfall after they saved it from extinction when Ron Dixon threatened to close the doors.

"We might never know the make-up of that debt," he said.

"The Marrs came in and saved the club from extinction, then there was the gamble with the Bonettis that didn't pay off. It is a hell of a lot of debt for any club to be in, and something has gone far wrong, but I don't want to apportion blame. I have no reason to believe the Marrs don't have the best interests of the club at heart. They are doing this to save the club rather than just walking away."

The Dundee Supporters' Association set up a fighting fund to help the club after deciding they couldn't just sit back and do nothing. Chairman George Knight said: "It's more important than ever that we do everything within our power to ensure the club's future. Whatever effort we make and however much we raise, it's better than just sitting back and accepting the situation."

Steps were also being taken to establish a supporters' trust but legal complexities meant it could take up to 12 weeks before it could start accepting donations.

In the meantime, DSA were setting up a bank account to raise money and kicked the fund off with a £1,000 donation from its own coffers.

Mr Knight said: "At the end of the day Mr di Stefano can still come in and now, more than ever, we need to see the colour of his money. As an association we reserve judgment on whether or not this will happen. Mr di Stefano talks a lot but this is action we need now to save the club."

Dundee and Tayside Chamber of Commerce and Industry said the contribution Dundee makes to the local economy should not be underestimated. Chief executive Mervyn Rolfe said: "It's terrible to think that we now seem to be in serious danger of losing one of the city's football teams. However, this isn't just a football team but a part of the heritage of our city. It's also an important business.

"If the club goes down completely, then it means the number of away supporters visiting Dundee and spending their money will be halved. Dundee's demise would be a significant loss to the city."

There was also sadness expressed from the House of Commons. Dundee MP and lifelong fan Iain Luke pledged his support and assistance to the cause.

The manager was then given the unenviable task of trying to lift the spirits of his shattered players before the next trip to Livingston on league business.

"For a few days it has been quiet and there has not been the same joviality," said Duffy. "I usually try to add humour to the proceedings to make it more enjoyable but it has not been a time for that. However, today we have attempted to get the spirits up a bit. I have tried my best to pick everyone up and we should be able to adopt a positive approach at Livingston, although it will be very difficult. We can still go 4-3-3 if we want to. I can ask them to do so, but there will be some guys who don't have experience of that.

"And when everyone is fit I still feel confident we can compete at the better end of the SPL.

"I would have to say, though, that Georgi Nemsadze and Fabian Caballero in particular were massively instrumental in our success last season. There are a lot of players missing but those two especially were fixtures in the team and are top-class players. Without them we will have to change the way we play a bit."

Defender Lee Mair said he was gutted so many close friends were now out of work. "It's been very hard, I'm not going to pretend it hasn't," he said. "For me, seeing boys like Gav Beith, Fracas (Barry Forbes) and Kris Brash go, was very tough because I came up through the ranks with them.

"Worst of all was Jamie Langfield going, because he and I shared digs for three years, then had a year living at Gavin Rae's house. We are best mates. He knows this is just a setback and, with his ability, he will come through, but seeing him go was tough to take.

"In saying that, it is much harder for the boys who have lost their jobs. What they have gone through is much worse than those of us who have still got jobs, and to be told you can just go home 'and don't bother coming back tomorrow' must be the worst feeling ever. They have not even got any money for the time they worked this month.

"I'm still getting paid and, while I know what's happened to them is not my fault, it still leaves me feeling guilty. I know a lot of the other boys feel the same. We've been told our wages for the next couple of months are guaranteed and we can't really understand why they couldn't have given the boys some of that money. But that's the administrator's job and he knows what needs doing better than me."

Dundee played out a 1-1 draw with Livingston in their first game after going into administration. Mark Fotheringham's equaliser six minutes from time brought unbridled joy from the stands which appeared to be as much down to relief as it was celebratory.

"I have never experienced anything like this before – it has been a terrible week," said Fotheringham. "Fifteen players went and that included the likes of Fabrizio Ravanelli and Craig Burley. They were great guys to have around the dressing-room, people with bags of experience.

"For me as a youngster, it is great to learn from people like them or Georgi Nemsadze or Fabian Caballero. They are away now, though, and I am sad to see them go, even though I have an opportunity to come into the team. A few of my friends, the younger lads, lost their jobs, but I guess life goes on and I am sure we will all rally round for them."

With the club in such trouble the fans were asking questions of the board. Radio phone-ins and newspaper hotlines and letter pages were packed with puzzled questions as to why players like Burley and Ravanelli were brought in if the club was on the brink of collapse.

There was just as much bemusement as to why – just a few months earlier – Dundee were very public about their policy of chasing the signatures of the likes of Paul Gascoigne, James McFadden and Peter Crouch, which would surely have proved very expensive.

"GDS (di Stefano) promised to personally pay the wages of both players," Peter Marr told supporters who were clearly puzzled over the club remaining silent on its problems for so long.

"He made repeated verbal promises and gave assurances to the club. I think I also read these promises in the press. Often the club have to keep things private and confidential for legal reasons otherwise many other 'wolves' would be on our door far sooner than they have. In an ideal world we would like to tell fans everything – and be able to ask for your help. But it's not what the fans do with that information, it's what others like the media and third parties can do with it to harm the club. At the moment, Scottish football isn't a world that rewards openness – it punishes it."

Marr said the major portion of the debt was £13.5 million which was owed to the Bank of Scotland.

"The next biggest element is the money Jimmy and I have put in over the years," he said. "We have no intention of taking that out and do not see it as 'debt'."

He also said it made sense for Dundee and city rivals United to now seriously look at sharing a ground to cut costs going forward.

It was perhaps a little early to be looking that far ahead and Marr admitted as much when he said that he could give no guarantees the Dark Blues would survive.

"I hope so, but I can't give you an assurance," he said. "I will do everything I can to make sure it survives and I know the fans will back the club."

Marr also spoke to the fans on Radio Tay's 'Tay Talk-In' Sunday morning show. He admitted that "with hindsight" getting involved with Giovanni di Stefano was a mistake and that there had been no offer from outside parties to buy him out.

There was real concern the club would not survive beyond Christmas.

The supporters' association launched its Dee4Life fundraising campaign where fans demonstrated their support for the club by hosting a number of

"Dee Day'" fundraising events. Many die-hards took part in official activities organised by the supporters' association rather than travelling to Glasgow to watch the side in action against league leaders Celtic on December 13.

Individual fundraisers were held at more than a dozen pubs in Dundee and many fans donated the cost of their match ticket to the Dee4Life fund.

Television and radio reports before Dundee's Christmas fixture against Aberdeen at Pittodrie suggested a mystery benefactor was ready to rescue the club from possible extinction.

However, the claims were rubbished after the game as "very misleading" with suspicions rife that it was another white elephant being flaunted by Giovanni di Stefano.

Manager Jim Duffy said: "If anyone wants to invest, I hope matron allows them out for long enough."

One man who was definitely out was di Stefano.

He eventually resigned from the board in January 2004, after just five months, but indicated he had not turned his back on the city altogether.

He said he was pressing forward with a new company - Dundee City Football Club Ltd - that he envisaged taking over at Dens Park if the current club went out of business.

In his resignation statement, he said he would work to expose "those who sought to destroy football at Dens Park" and repeated his call for Peter and Jimmy Marr to step down as directors.

He said, "It has been stated by both Peter and James Marr that my remaining on the board of directors precludes the club from obtaining short, medium and long-term finance.

"I have no doubt such is not the case. Nevertheless, no opportunity must be waived in the quest for the club to survive. My resignation has not been caused by any factor involving the mendacity published by the media. All will know that I have formed a company called Dundee City Football Club Ltd, which will in due course ensure that football survives at Dens Park.

"My resignation allows me to concentrate on exposing those who sought to destroy football at Dens Park. I will not leave a single stone unturned when investigating what occurred at Dens Park and the surrounding companies and to assist the authorities in a proper investigation into the role played by Bank of Scotland into what can only be a demise in Scottish Football.

"Finally, I call upon both Peter and James Marr to resign as directors of The Dundee Football Club Ltd and Dundee FC Holdings PLC, to assume the liabilities incurred by their management into their own private companies and allow the club to survive under the management of whoever seeks to advance football at Dundee."

Ravanelli returned to his home town and joined Serie A side Perugia until the end of the season which marked the end of the White Feather's Dundee adventure.

"I am delighted to return to my home town and to play for my first club," he said.

Some months later Ravanelli was among a total of 18 former Dundee players and backroom staff who lodged tribunal complaints seeking compensation for being sacked.

The actions were lodged on behalf of the group by the Scottish Professional Footballers' Association and the documentation was signed by club captain Barry Smith in his capacity as the union representative for the players at Dens Park.

The players were claiming a protective award of up to three months' wages as a result of the club's alleged failure to consult them about their imminent sackings.

A spokesperson for the administrator stressed that former players and backroom staff would be treated the same as all other creditors.

Ravanelli might have returned to Italy by that stage, but his name was back in the local press in May 2004 when a man was fined £400 at Dundee Sheriff Court.

The accused admitting failing to provide his name and address to police and resisting arrest after police were called to a disturbance after the derby match between Dundee and United. The offending fan had his shirt off and was shouting. He was asked his name by police and replied: "Fabrizio Ravanelli". His solicitor said his client had given the name of the former Dundee FC footballer as a joke, after having consumed a considerable amount of alcohol that day.

A month later the real Ravanelli was back in the news when the group of former Dundee players won their fight to force the club to pay them wages owed. The club was not represented and the case was not contested after the tribunal heard the staff had "relied on gossip, hearsay and the media for their information".

The tribunal heard they did not know until the day the axe fell, that they were to be sacked, despite the fact that some names were being publicly debated as being on the hit list.

Dundee's fans had raised a staggering £150,000 by the first quarter of 2004 to stave off the threat of immediate closure, which went up to half a million by the summer.

The club managed to battle on until the end of the season.

Owners Peter and Jimmy Marr did what they could and didn't walk away, while the manager affirmed his legendary status by staying put, despite offers to jump ship.

It is only right to point out that Peter and Jimmy lost millions in the process, then spent another seven-figure sum ensuring their mistakes didn't lead to closure.

George Knight, chairman of the Dundee FC Supporters' Association, who headed up the Dee4Life fundraising campaign, said the effort from the fans to save the club was amazing.

He said, "At our AGM at the end of last season, we touted the setting up of a supporters' trust and it was unanimously agreed that we wouldn't go ahead with it because there didn't seem to be any need.

"At that time the mood was extremely buoyant, the club having just been in a cup final.

"Also at that time, Giovanni di Stefano was around the place touting signings like James McFadden and talking of an investment of £26 million. It wasn't necessarily a question of believing that would happen, but at the same time I don't think anyone expected that the situation would turn the other way so dramatically.

"It is ridiculous to look back and think there we were with a big travelling support going all the way to Italy, coming away disappointed that Dundee had been beaten by a Serie A side, and then within six weeks we were in administration and were watching 15 players lose their jobs."

Mr Knight said a turning point was when Tom Burton reportedly wanted to sell Dens and groundshare with Dundee United after realising how dire the financial position was. Mr Knight said: "That news coincided with a derby at Tannadice and there was a boycott by Dundee fans. I believed it would be better to let the club die with some dignity, rather than let it move and suffer a lingering death.

"I think the fans felt the same way because the suggestion of going to Tannadice seemed to have a galvanising effect. Things really got going and that effort to raise half a million pounds was amazing."

Against all odds, Jim Duffy led his depleted Dundee side to a seventh place finish at the end of the season and the Dark Blues came out of administration despite still carrying seven-figure debts.

The superstars were gone. But the memories and, more importantly, the club would live on.

CHAPTER FIFTEEN

Porridge For A White Knight

It's a real shame what's happened to Dundee. I've got sympathy for everyone at the club

Paul Merson

A PHONE call sealed Dundee's fate in 2005, a year after surviving administration. A draw in a final day shoot-out with Livingston sent them through the SPL trap door in controversial circumstances and at an estimated cost of £1.5 million. Hassan Kachloul was playing as an amateur and set up Livingston's equaliser, but Dundee asked the SPL to investigate suggestions the Moroccan had been paid. The SPL board ruled that payments were in line with those professional players were receiving, despite the club's claims the cash was for his role as a "commercial executive".

Dundee, who finished bottom of the league, hoped a guilty verdict would result in a points deduction and see Livingston relegated instead of them. But Livvy escaped being docked points, instead being handed a £15,000 fine, because of their findings that they could have signed him as a professional player anyway. However, it was claimed Kachloul's amateur contract with previous club Reading meant Livingston also had to sign him as an amateur until the summer transfer window opened.

Peter Marr said: "It came down to one piece of evidence – a registration paper for Kachloul, and we couldn't get it in time. The judge was going on holiday and wouldn't give us more time to find that evidence. We also lost time because the hotel where they were hearing the case in Edinburgh had a fire alarm and we were stood outside for three hours. It was only a phone call – one call would have confirmed this registration he had, playing down in England. If we had got it clarified we'd have won the case. That's football – the width of a post or one phone call can seal your fate."

Dundee's former legal adviser unsurprisingly wasn't asked to step in. But Giovanni di Stefano wasn't far from the headlines after suggesting he was ready to stand for election as a Dundee MP, whilst reiterating his intention to return to Dens Park in the future. Di Stefano had recently formed The Radical Party of Great Britain.

"I will either stand in Sedgefield where I have no chance of winning, just to take votes from Tony Blair and maybe let one of the other parties in, or I will fight one of the Dundee wards where I think I have a very good chance," he said. "I have a lot of friends up in Dundee – you might not believe it but I am very popular there. I don't know if I would make a good member of parliament, though. I'm a bit too outspoken to be a good MP. I haven't made up my mind yet which ward I would contest, but as soon as the date of the general election is announced I will decide where I will go."

Di Stefano said he'd be welcomed back to Dens Park with open arms by the fans, despite reneging on investment promises before the club went into administration. "Do you blame me?" he said. "I'm not a mug, I'm a business man. Once I saw there were £20 million debts, and Dundee were heading for administration, I wasn't going to throw money at it. Peter Marr has done a great job there but administration hasn't taken the debts away, they've just been restructured. I could have done that, funding was in place with the bank. All administration has done is leave a lot of people very angry. I get loads of emails from people in Dundee who want me back at Dundee FC, and I will be back, although not while they are heavily in debt. They are going to be my club eventually. I'm the only person who can run the club properly, in a business-like way. It can be a healthy club again once the debt is scaled down."

Peter and Jimmy Marr ended their formal association with Dundee by resigning as directors in 2007. Their 10-year association with the club cost them as much as £10 million. Peter admitted a sense of relief at finally reaching the end of the road and said their time in charge dragged on too long. He said: "When we came in I said we'd stay five years and we probably stayed five years too long. However, despite the problems, I am satisfied we are leaving with the club heading in the right direction."

Chairman Bob Brannan led Dundee back from the brink and managed to strike a deal with the Bank of Scotland to wipe out the club's £7m debt in 2008.

The club then took a gamble on Aberdeen-based Calum Melville who answered an advert to join up at Dundee and bankrolled the club to the tune of £1.6 million. Melville, whose family made their money from an oil rig supply business, was listed among the richest young businessmen in Scotland with a fortune, shared with elder brother Stuart, reportedly around £100 million. Initially brought on to the board to help cover what had become a yearly shortfall of around £300,000, Melville quickly decided to provide the funding for a "real go" at winning promotion in 2009-10.

That led to Dundee being the second biggest spenders in Scottish football. but they failed to get out of the First Division after sacking Jocky Scott, despite being top of the table. That move backfired badly as the players, under new boss Gordon Chisholm, were beaten to the title by Inverness Caley Thistle.

The budget reduced during the summer but players were still recruited and contracts drawn up and Dundee continued running at a loss. Melville eventually resigned from the board in September which left the club with a financial headache. HMRC demanded full settlement of a tax bill for £365,000. Melville claimed to have lodged £200,000 and efforts were made to raise the shortfall from supporters, sponsors and the local business community. The other board members suspected that even if they managed to find the money to pay HMRC their troubles would persist.

Without Melville's assistance Dundee were on the brink of closure once again and met Bryan Jackson to begin the process of entering administration again.

Dundee went back into administration in October 2010 and were deducted 25 points, leaving them 20 points adrift at the bottom of the First Division. Brannan was the first of the Dens Park hierarchy to fall on his sword. He said: "For five long years, working alongside Ian Bodie, George Knight, an army of volunteers from Dee4Life and with donations from various individuals such as John Bennett, Alan Hampton and Angelo Kelly, Dundee FC was brought back from the brink of extinction, eliminating a mountain of bank debt inherited from the administration of 2003. It breaks my heart to see its future threatened again. The change of strategy in 2009 has clearly failed."

The 25-point loss was accompanied by a transfer embargo and a warning they could be relegated to the fourth tier unless they exited administration by the end of March. Jackson took control and gave the club a 50-50 chance of surviving beyond Christmas.

Fabrizio Ravanelli said he would be prepared to dip into his own pocket if it helped. He said: "I'm really sad to hear this news. Even though I was not at Dundee for very long, I know it's a great club with very special fans and a great city, and I wish it well. I didn't realise that what happened when I was there could now happen again. It's very sad and I hope for all concerned that it can be resolved. It doesn't matter who steps in, whether it be fans or a businessman or someone else, it's just important the situation is resolved and club is saved. For my part, if it was possible I would certainly be prepared to make a financial contribution, to help them get back to the top of the Scottish game. There are plenty of teams around Europe who carry large debts – you only have to look at Real Madrid and Barcelona. But I would draw a parallel here with Fiorentina in my own country. They were relegated down the leagues (as a result of bankruptcy) but look where they are now."

A petition was launched to have Dundee's 25-point penalty overturned which gathered 15,736 signatures and was signed by some of football's biggest names. Paul Merson and Paul Walsh – both former England internationals who were respected pundits on Sky Sports – said they were happy to do anything they could to help. Merson's former club Portsmouth was eventually relegated from the English Premier League after being docked nine points for going into administration in 2010.

"It's a real shame what's happened to Dundee and I've got sympathy for everyone at the club," said Merson, whose playing career included spells at Arsenal, Middlesbrough and Aston Villa. "I'm happy to sign the petition and I hope Dundee can survive this. Administration is horrible and I hope the fans get behind the team."

Former Liverpool and Tottenham striker Walsh also gave the petition his full backing. "You don't want to see any football club enter administration," he said. "It would be a very sad day for Scottish football if they went under. Hopefully Dundee will receive investment and get back on their feet."

Nacho Novo spoke of his anguish at the situation his beloved Dundee found themselves in and promised he would be signing the petition. He said: "It breaks my heart to hear what they have done to Dundee, it's a disgrace. I will do anything I can to help support this. Dundee is still very close to my heart."

Rangers manager and former United player Walter Smith also pledged to add his name. "I loved to beat Dundee when I was with United, but it is not good to see what is happening at the club at the moment," he said. "They are too important to Scottish football to go out of business and I would urge all football fans, including Dundee United supporters, to sign this petition."

Singer and X Factor judge Cheryl Cole, glamour model Katie Price and Spice Girl Victoria Beckham also played their part as the fans battled to raise the cash to keep the club alive. John MacPhail, a former Dundee player, travelled to the city from Teeside to donate his personal collection of memorabilia to help save the club that give him his first start in the game. The signed photo collection which went under the hammer featured signed prints from some of football's biggest names, including Paul Gascoigne, Geoff Hurst and Alan Shearer. It also featured signed photographs of Cheryl Cole, Katie Price and Victoria Beckham – not that anyone was too bothered about the infinite details of such things; as long as the cash came in.

Born in Dundee, MacPhail played for Dundee from 1975-1979 before heading south where his career highlights included captaining Sunderland to two promotions. MacPhail purchased the prints with a view to keeping them in the family but was keen to do anything he could to help the club which held a special place in his heart. He said: "I owe the club so much, they gave me a fantastic start in my football career. It breaks my heart to see the situation the club finds itself in. To think Dundee could cease to exist is the ultimate nightmare for me. It would break my heart."

Nine players and the management team of Gordon Chisholm and Billy Dodds were made redundant to cut costs, with former player Barry Smith put in charge of the team.

Despite the 25-point deduction, Smith helped the club through a turbulent administration period where Dundee went on a record-breaking unbeaten run of 23 matches. The team ended up in sixth place against the odds, despite having to play 49-year-old goalkeeping coach Bobby Geddes between the sticks in one game due to a lack of bodies.

The fans also turned out in force. They poured through the turnstiles and raised the cash, along with the business community, which eventually saw the club exit administration in May 2011.

Barry Smith, in his final programme notes of the season, wrote: "When we were set the challenge in November to stay in this league we always believed it was possible and despite several obstacles put in our way, we achieved that aim. Everyone can be rightly proud of their contribution to helping the club through this period."

Two years later Giovanni di Stefano was convicted of 25 charges including deception, fraud and money-laundering between 2001 and 2011 after being unmasked as a fraud with no legal training. He was sentenced to 14 years for duping "desperate and vulnerable victims" into thinking he was a bona fide legal professional when he was not registered to work as a lawyer in Italy or the UK. During the trial, di Stefano told of his links to Robert Mugabe, Osama bin Laden, Saddam Hussein and his "friendship" with the daughter of Slobodan Milosevic. London's Southwark Crown Court heard he had conned clients out of millions of pounds.

Di Stefano's Dundee adventure was over.

CHAPTER SIXTEEN

Real Heroes Don't Wear Capes

"I had played in Italy, the best championship in the world, played three World Cups and played in the best teams in Argentina – Boca and River Plate. But I enjoyed my time at Dundee as much as anything."

Claudio Caniggia

SEEMINGLY washed-up and damaged goods when he arrived in the city, Claudio Caniggia's career was ultimately revived during his brief spell in Dundee. He was the biggest name to play in the Scottish Premier League since Paul Gascoigne signed for Rangers from Lazio for a then club record of £4.3 million. The signing caught the imagination of the footballing public across the globe and he ended his debut season being nominated for the PFA Player of the Year Award. He only lost out to 53-goal Henrik Larsson but was unsurprisingly named the Dundee Player of the Year despite leaving under something of a cloud when the end finally came.

Caniggia lit up a season when entertainment seemed more important than results. He was on the verge of taking his life in another direction when he was asked to play for Dundee. He said: "I was thinking of stopping playing football. I was still training on my own, staying fit, and then the Bonettis called me – I knew them from Italy – and asked if I would come to Dundee? I said why not? I decided to come to Scotland and it was great at Dundee. Trust me, with my heart, I really enjoyed my time in Dundee. I could not understand any of the accents but it was a great team."

Caniggia said he knew Ivano and Dario from his time in Italy which "was enough for me to take the decision to go to Dundee". He said: "OK, I didn't know too much about Dundee but the coaches explained all about the city and the people and the stadium and everything so it was no problem. I am Argentine and used to travelling. I had plenty of experience, already 10 years in Europe. It was a small club and I had played in two World Cups but it was great for me – once I got used to the weather! It rained so many days! When I play football, though, it doesn't matter and it was a great place to play football and the Scottish people were wonderful. I had played in Italy, the best championship in the world, played three World Cups and played in the best teams in Argentina – Boca and River Plate – but I enjoyed my time at Dundee as much as anything. I could have gone other places but I am so pleased I chose Dundee."

Caniggia said the fans were right behind him from the moment he joined and there were some really good people at the club who looked after him off the park as well. He said: "I had a great time and the team did really well, too. We had a great team then with Gavin Rae, Barry Smith, Beto Carranza, Georgi Nemsadze and all of those guys. We could win against the best teams and played beautiful games. We finished sixth and it was a great championship."

Caniggia said he will never forget his goalscoring debut against Aberdeen – he got an elbow in the face off the ball straight after coming on the park. "That was my welcome to Scotland!" he said. "It was a good game, though – I really enjoyed it and we won 2-0. Then the home support was fantastic the week after. I was amazed at the great people and the stadium full."

Caniggia also told how he almost joined Celtic instead of Rangers when he left Dens Park in 2001 for Champions League football in a bid to win a World Cup place with Argentina. He said: "Let me tell you, I remember Celtic came to me and Rangers also to speak about moving. I was already 33 years old and I wanted to go to the World Cup. I did when I was 35 because of that. Sometimes it is difficult to leave when you have had a great time but I couldn't miss the opportunity – I wanted the World Cup. Even though I took that decision, the Dundee fans were unbelievable. I can't find the words to explain. I had played in two World Cups already and I knew I had to step up a little bit so I took the chance to play in the Champions League. It was difficult but I want to say to Dundee fans how much I enjoyed my time there. Really, my feelings with the people at the club and the staff who are there every day is very clear, I had great relationships with them all.

"My family enjoyed Dundee very much, too. I like Scotland and the people. I made a lot of friends and my sons made a lot of friends, too."

After he left Dundee he went on to spend two years at Rangers between 2001 and 2003, during which time he firmly established himself as a favourite with the fans. Caniggia scored 21 goals in 78 appearances games for Rangers, including the opener in the League Cup final win against Celtic in 2003. He scored his farewell Rangers goal on the final day of the league campaign, helping Rangers clinch the SPL title by lashing Dunfermline 6-1 at Ibrox. But Caniggia would miss out on a starting place against old club Dundee in the Scottish Cup Final after suffering a back injury. He joined in the treble celebrations after watching from the stand.

Caniggia played well enough in his first season at Rangers to achieve his dream of being called up for the 2002 Argentina World Cup squad. But the dream turned into a nightmare for an injury-hit Caniggia who managed to get red-carded for dissent without even playing a game. Caniggia, then aged 35, had earlier been recalled for a friendly against Wales. His sparkling performance in Cardiff had all but guaranteed his starting spot at the World Cup in Japan and Korea. Fate intervened though. Caniggia was injured following a Chris Sutton challenge and had to be replaced inside the first 20 minutes of his side's 3-2 Scottish Cup Final victory over Celtic. He had already been promised he would start the tournament but now it looked likely he would watch the action at home as he struggled to get back to fitness. Remarkably he made the squad. Caniggia was nowhere near 100% and missed Argentina's first two defeats in the tournament.

He was well enough to take a spot on the bench for the final group match against Sweden but he became the first player to be sent off at a World Cup without actually playing. Caniggia was sent packing in first-half injury time when he complained vociferously from the sidelines after referee Ali Bujsaim had penalised Argentina. The referee told him to sit back down but he continued to berate the Emirati official. He was eventually shown the red card but it was a sad end for a man whose name will always be connected with the World Cup.

Caniggia left Glasgow the following season and reserved a similar verbal blast for Rangers manager Alex McLeish after being released despite the promise of a contract extension. The Argentine would later claim that McLeish – who had replaced Dick Advocaat during Caniggia's first season – had misled him. He also compared his former manager to "Mickey Mouse".

Caniggia rejected a two-year-deal with Monaco because he thought he was staying at Ibrox. He instead ended up at Qatar SC where he won the Prince's Cup before retiring after one last pay day. He received offers to play in Japan and the USA during his years in professional retirement and spoke about wanting to make a comeback in Australia, but nothing materialised.

However, towards the end of 2009, Argentina's 1986 World Cup-winning manager Carlos Bilardo gave him an incredible opportunity to return to the game. Bilardo offered Caniggia the chance to play for Argentina at the World Cup in South Africa at the age of 43, despite having being out of the game for four and a half years.

Caniggia was still in good shape and insisted that he hadn't lost any of his pace. But he couldn't decide what to do. He turned down the offer but would later regret it. "It would've been unbelievable to play at another World Cup," he said.

Caniggia did return to competitive action in 2012 at the age of 45. He lined up alongside several other former internationals, such as Ray Parlour and Graeme Le Saux for FC Wembley in the FA Cup. It was a stunt dreamed up by Budweiser, who were sponsors of the competition. The team, which played in the Combined Counties Premier Division, some eight tiers below the Premier League, were managed by former England boss Terry Venables.

Caniggia scored on his FA Cup debut. The match was just 13 minutes old when Caniggia ran on to a perfect through ball and coolly slotted it beyond the goalkeeper to evoke memories of Pittodrie in October 2000.

The non-league side beat Langford 3-2 to set up a clash with Uxbridge in the preliminary round. But Wembley's FA Cup dreams were shattered after they were mercilessly thumped 5-0.

In 2014 Caniggia was back in the headlines across the world when organisers brought in a "Caniggia lookalike" to take part in a legends game between Argentina and Brazil. Caniggia missed his plane to Sao Paolo for the match but promoters – no doubt realising his box office appeal – pulled a fast one and kept up the pretence that he was still playing.

Caniggia was "substituted" by fellow Argentine and former Newcastle United player Daniel Cordone but the plan was rumbled when fans spotted a tattoo on the ex-Toon man's right arm, which Caniggia does not have. More than 10,000 people watched the match in Brazil and consumer standards officials launched an investigation after the final whistle when the switch was uncovered.

Despite hanging up his boots for good, Caniggia is kept on his toes by his model wife and three children who have become as famous as the Dens Park hero.

Mariana has been married to Caniggia since 1988 and regularly appears in gossip magazines in Argentina. A frivolous spender who jets around the world, Mariana and her husband have remained in the media spotlight through their two younger children, who star in the reality show Caniggia Libre (Caniggia Free, in English) on MTV. The twins Alexander and Charlotte are hyper-extravagant and film the show at the family home in Spain, which is described as being situated in "the neighbourhood of the millionaires".

Alexander is also a singer who has become widely known for hit singles like 2017's Siempre Al Top and Congele Mi Corazón. He has grown popular on Instagram, earning almost a million followers, and is building a career in television. He appeared in the MTV Resistiré reality show, where participants were abandoned on the Chilean side of the Andes mountain range.

Charlotte's television appearances started in 2012 when she took part in the eighth season of Argentina's version of Strictly Come Dancing. She also participated in Celebrity Island on Italian television and Gran Hermano, the Spanish version of Big Brother.

Unlike the extravagance of the rest of his family, the eldest of the clan, Kevin Axel, moved away from the media spotlight at the age of 15 to dedicate himself to painting.

His first exhibition was in Marbella, one of the cities where he lived. In 2010 he made his first exhibition in Argentina at the Borges Cultural Center, Buenos Aires, with his show Born From Nature.

The event was attended by his father and a certain Diego Maradona.

Maradona's great pal Caniggia was inducted into the Dundee Hall of Fame in 2009. He returned in 2018 to speak about his career at the Whitehall Theatre in Dundee. He retains a great affection for Dundee and Glasgow.

Dundee retains a great affection for him too.

CHAPTER SEVENTEEN
Memories Are Made Of This

But the highs – the square in Perugia, 17,000 fans at Hampden, Claudio Caniggia pulling on the dark blue – when they come, you savour them all the more.

Peter Marr

FORMER Dundee owner Peter Marr said he would like to think his time in charge gave everyone connected with the club "a few good memories". Marr said his own memories of watching Caniggia and Ravanelli wearing the dark blue of Dundee will stay with him until the day he dies. But his memories of Giovanni di Stefano are – perhaps understandably – slightly less favourable and he admitted there were just too many lies before everything fell apart.

"'I see you've brought your lawyer,' was how a smiling Giovanni di Stefano kicked off our first meeting back in 1998," said Marr. "Then di Stefano said, 'We won't get a deal done now because lawyers only break deals'.

"Looking back on it years later, it's easy to say we should've seen it coming. Fast forward five years and that lack of foresight would cost us everything. We had finished sixth in Jim Duffy's first season in charge, which wasn't brilliant, but we also made it to the Scottish Cup Final. And 17,000 Dees went to Hampden that day and, at that point, it was the culmination of everything we'd worked for since we bought the club.

"Although we knew things were getting increasingly tight, it was still an enjoyable time. Looking around that famous old ground at a sea of dark blue is something that will live with me forever. It's why Jimmy and I got involved in the first place. These were our glory days and we wanted everybody to share them with us.

"I still remember it was sweltering through in Glasgow, but my wife Anne – an even bigger Dundee fan than I am – wouldn't take her jacket off because she'd worn it for every round. She was sitting there roasting, but that's how much it meant to her. We lost to a Lorenzo Amoruso header, and I still think if big Lee Wilkie, who was suspended that day, had been on the park the Italian never would have got the chance. Rangers were knackered by that point. They'd had a tough finish to the season and if we had just sneaked a goal I think we'd have had them."

Dundee qualified for Europe which Marr said was "an experience that would turn out to be the high point of the whole adventure".

"After that, things came tumbling down very quickly," he said. "Europe was always an ambition of ours. When I was younger and Dundee won the league, I was too young to travel to the away European Cup games. I always remember being envious of this guy who stayed up the road who used to get to go.

"The thing is, when we finally got into Europe off the back of the Scottish Cup Final, I missed the first away game in Albania. Fortunately, we came through that one and we were in the pot for the next round. We ended up getting Perugia, which was a wee bit unlucky really because we wanted to get through, and landing a Serie A team didn't give us much hope of that. We needed the money at this point – we knew it. Things were really starting to pinch.

"We were staying in this wee hotel in the countryside and, weirdly enough, Colonel Gaddafi's son Al-Saadi had about half of it booked for himself at the same time. It sounds mental, but he was playing for Perugia back in 2003. So it was Dundee FC and Colonel Gaddafi's son in this hotel. Absolutely bizarre, but totally unforgettable.

"We took over 2,000 supporters to Italy with us and I'm sure most of them would still say it was the time of their lives. It certainly was for me. Looking around the square and seeing those fans singing and having a drink – I just wanted to rip my club tie off and join them. But I couldn't."

Marr said that by the time Dundee got knocked out of Europe, things were getting really, really bad.

He said: "The bank just kept on giving us money. As long as we signed a personal guarantee, they let us do whatever we wanted to do. Giovanni had first got in touch with us years before. His son, who was at Gordonstoun, had watched us lose 1-0 to St Johnstone on Sky and the next day the club got an email addressed to: Jimmy Marr, Chairman of Dundee United Football Club. Needless to say, I thought it was a wind-up.

"Giovanni was standing as an MEP at the time and was based in Brussels. He invited us over for a meeting. Jimmy, myself and our lawyer went to listen to what he had to say. Give him his due, he put his hands up and said, 'Listen, I come with a bit of baggage'. We didn't realise at the time it was all that carry on with Arkan and that sort of stuff. We didn't realise it was that bad.

"I'll always remember we went out to this Italian restaurant and he headed straight for a table right at the back, facing the door. We never thought twice about it at the time, but later we realised he needed to see who was coming in. I think that's how worried he was at the time. That's when he dropped the 'lawyer' line. And that's when we should have known. After all, he was a lawyer himself."

Marr said di Stefano was going to buy the club "lock, stock and barrel".

"He didn't buy it because of the bad publicity he was getting from a west coast newspaper," he said. "The word was that if he came in the sports council wouldn't give Dundee their grants, and Giovanni pulled out as a result. I think we were getting about a million-and-a-quarter in grants, and he didn't want to put another million-and-a-quarter in to cover that, on top of what he was already going to give Jimmy and I for the club.

"He had basically promised us the money we had invested into the club, and we had quite a few inter-company debts from loans our other companies had made to Dundee over the years."

The deal fell through that time, but, when things got worse in 2003, they got back in touch with him.

Peter said: "Basically, we were clutching at straws. He offered us help and, for better or worse, we took it. Despite everything he's said, he never lost £650,000 from his dealings with Dundee. Any money he put into the club he got back out. By this time, we had stepped aside to let him run the club and he got full access to the books, so to say he didn't know there was debt is nonsense.

"One of the biggest things pressing us was the Inland Revenue. It was PAYE tax. Funny how things go in cycles, isn't it? We were due them a lot of money and, at this stage, Jim Connor was running the club under direction from Giovanni. He had signed Craig Burley and Fabrizio Ravanelli and he was going to cover their wages. When it became apparent he wasn't actually going to pay, Jimmy and I had to put our hands up and go to the bank. We had a meeting in Edinburgh and they advised us to go into administration.

"Giovanni had promised to put in however many millions and it just hadn't materialised. At the end of it all, it was as simple as that. There were too many lies and the whole thing fell apart."

Marr said they had no choice but to put the club into administration.

He said: "Jim Duffy had to tell players they would lose their jobs and the future of the club was far from certain. Dundee Football Club was more than £20 million in debt, Jimmy and I had lost control of the club, and the dream had turned into a nightmare. It was a horrible time. Fortunately, however, the fans were about to come into their own."

Back in 2003, the debt was over £20 million, and Tom Burton, from Ernst & Young, was appointed by the court to act as administrator. His first act was to tear up 25 player and staff contracts.

Marr said: "Me and Jim Duffy worked really closely at that time to try to keep something for the club, because Tom would have binned everybody. We needed to stay in the SPL and we were never going to manage that if he'd really gone to town. The one regret I've got is Jimmy and I didn't go into the dressing-room and tell the players.

"Jim had requested he be allowed to go and do it and we respected that – I still do – but we really should have gone in, too.

"Jimmy and I told the rest of the staff what was going on and what cuts were going to be made, but when it came to the players Jim said: 'They're my players, let me go and speak to them'.

"We got a wee bit of stick for that. I can understand it, but I don't think it's fair. It's hard telling people they've not got a job, but, let's be honest, it happens in everyday life all the time. We get sort of sentimental with football players, but, at the end of the day, they're only doing a job like everybody else. It was a shame on the young lads for sure, I don't think any of them went on to really make it as players after that.

"We did manage to get money for a few boys however. We got fees for Gavin Rae and Julian Speroni, and we also got good money for Nacho Novo. However, typically, he had a clause in his contract, just like Caniggia, whereby he got a percentage of the fee. That was a standard clause at the time – something agents would tack on. You think you're getting a million pounds for a player, but after the player gets his cut and the previous club gets their cut, you're left with a lot less.

"It was a horrible time for the fans as well as everyone at the club, but they were brilliant. They really rallied around, rattling buckets outside the ground for instance. It was an emotional time – everybody wanted to help out where they could. I'd never knock Dee4Life. They had the best interests of the club at heart. But I still think the administrator wound them up with all his bucket-rattling talk. With the seriousness of the debt we had at the time, the money raised from bucket collections wouldn't have come close to plugging the gap and I feel he used the fans for publicity. At the same time, it wasn't just our fans who chipped in, it was fans of other clubs, too.

"Nevertheless, it was Tom Burton who made himself out to be the saviour of the club, but if he was the saviour when we came out of administration, we wouldn't have been in debt. As it was, we still had £7 million, of which £3 million was serviceable."

Marr said he felt the club could service that debt if they stayed in the SPL.

However, they were controversially relegated in 2005, following the Kachloul is he/isn't he amateur affair.

Marr said he still follows Dundee home and away.

He said: "I think I always will. That's the thing about this club; it's in your blood. You go through all sorts as a Dundee fan.

"If nothing else, I'd like to think my time in charge gave everyone connected with the club a few good memories. It certainly did for me. I'll savour those memories until the day I die.

"I hope the other fans that witnessed them feel the same."

CHAPTER EIGHTEEN

He's Got Grey Hair But We Don't Care

From what he had told us he was going to be the new Roman Abramovich, and under his charge the club were going to do great things.

Fabrizio Ravanelli

SIX games ordinarily shouldn't give a player legendary status at a football club. But then again, not every player is Fabrizio Ravanelli.

When the White Feather left Dundee he went back to his home-town club Perugia. He played a further 41 games for them and scored nine goals before retiring from football with a record of 522 club appearances and 190 goals. His national team record wasn't too shabby either with eight goals from 22 games over a four-year period in the mid to late-1990s.

After hanging up his boots, Ravanelli worked as a football pundit for Sky Italia, Fox Sports, and Mediaset. He covered domestic football and the Champions League before taking up the role of youth team manager at former club Juventus in 2011. He remained there until 2013, when he signed a two-year contract as the new head coach of French Ligue 1 club AC Ajaccio. He left after just 12 Ligue 1 matches, following his fifth consecutive defeat. Ravanelli returned to work as an Italian football pundit after his sacking.

In 2017 he sensationally threw his hat into the ring for the vacant Dundee managerial position following Paul Hartley's sacking and insisted he could save the club from relegation. Ravanelli joined Arsenal Kyiv, of the Ukraine Premier League, in the summer of 2018 but resigned after just nine league games saying he couldn't stay there any more.

"Even now I have mixed feelings about Dundee," he said.

"On the one hand I remember the great affection shown towards me by the fans and the people of the city. On the other, having to leave so soon into my stay was very sad and is still a cause of regret.

"I was surprised, too, because of all the promises that had been made by Giovanni di Stefano. From what he had told us he was going to be something like the new Roman Abramovich, and under his charge the club were going to do great things.

"I still love both Scotland and England. You don't have to be in the country for long to know that the fans in the UK are exceptional. For me they are a show within the show.

"It would be nice to go back and if I got the chance to manage in either country, I would be packed up and on my way."

There is a photo which takes pride of place in Ravanelli's home in Italy which will always remind him of the greatest moment of his ultimately brief spell at Dundee. The photo is of him celebrating scoring his hat-trick against Clyde in the League Cup.

He said: "That was the best memory."

CHAPTER NINETEEN
I Wouldn't Have Changed It For The World

You couldn't have scripted it. It would have seemed too ridiculous. But that was what it was like back then.

Peter Marr

SCIENTISTS have suggested memory fades as people get older because the brain runs out of energy. Try telling that to those who were at the heart of what was Dundee's most exciting team since the 1960s and early 1970s. It was a time when Scottish football itself was packed with global talent.

Henrik Larsson, Lubomir Moravcik, Ronald de Boer, Andrei Kanchelskis and Franck Sauzee were among the stars in the SPL before Tore Andre Flo later arrived at Rangers from Chelsea for £12m as sensible spending went out the window in the Old Firm chase for Champions League glory.

Dundee's own glittering array of international talent was just as impressive.

However, it was the signing of Claudio Caniggia which took things to a completely new level and ensured it would be one of the most memorable seasons in living memory. It seems like another lifetime but Caniggia and his supporting cast still look back fondly on their time together at Dens Park when they became everyone's favourite second team.

Some years later Beto Carranza revealed that he turned up at Caniggia's hotel in Asuncion, Paraguay's capital, when he heard he was in town, and they went out for dinner and shared memories of their time together in the City of Discovery.

That affection is shared by the other major players in the Caniggia/Dundee FC story – including former Dundee owner Peter Marr who described the signing of the Argentine legend as "almost unbelievable".

Marr recalled Ivano scurrying up to him not long after he'd arrived and telling him: "Peter, I can get Claudio Caniggia".

Marr said: "I never thought I'd hear those words coming out of a Dundee manager's mouth, and if it had been anyone else I would have laughed. But this was Ivano, and he looked serious."

Marr said he asked how much it was going to cost and admitted he was still half-expecting his manager to burst out laughing and tell him it was just a wind up.

Marr said: "He gave me a figure. 'Go for it, ' I said, and that was that. Claudio

Caniggia signed for Dundee – still makes me smile even now. As usual, the figure I got turned out to be about half of what it actually cost us. He ended up being on really, really big money. But once the deal was done I just thought about what a boost he would give the club's profile.

"I'll always remember it because I was on holiday in Florida with the grandchildren, sitting in a fish-and-chip place in Orlando, and Sky Sports was on, and the banner across the bottom of the screen suddenly flashed up, 'Claudio Caniggia signs for Dundee FC'. I knew it was happening, of course, but you still could've knocked me down with a feather. It was almost unbelievable.

"His first game was away to Aberdeen and I remember looking at the players that weren't starting that day and seeing Claudio, Beto Carranza, another Argentina international, and Georgi Nemsadze, captain of Georgia. I had that realisation, once again, that things had turned around so far in such a short time. Caniggia came on, of course, and scored the winner. You couldn't have scripted it. It would've seemed too ridiculous. But that was what it was like back then. Every day seemed to bring something else you never thought possible."

Marr used to go to Dens as a youngster to watch Charlie Cooke. He said: "Dundee weren't a good team at the time, but Charlie was marvellous. You went just to watch him. You could see the same sort of thing happening around Claudio. It didn't matter who he was playing, he'd be ripping them apart, and he was just this wee guy.

"At that time our average gate had gone up to being on a par with United, and I think maybe even a wee bit in front of them. And that happened within the space of three years. When we got promoted, our average gate would've been about 3,000 and we would have had about 1,500 season tickets. Three years later, we'd gone up to about 8,000 average."

But Marr insisted that wasn't just to do with Caniggia. "There was Nemsadze, who was different class," he said. "He was the captain of Georgia. but he was kind of within our budget, because, although he'd been playing in Italy, he'd been playing at a lower level.

"Then there was Fabian Caballero. He was a fantastic player, and if he hadn't been injured in that game against United, we'd have got big money for him. He'd been at Arsenal when he was younger, but just didn't make it. You could see that quality in him and what happened is such a shame, because he was never the same player after the injury. It didn't help that he was a terrible trainer, mind, and he ate dreadfully. He had a club car and if you ever saw inside it, it was full of sweetie papers. Some people just won't be told.

"Juan Sara never got the same attention that Fabian got, but he was some player, too, and he could take a goal. He missed a lot, too, right enough, but he was in the right place to miss them at least.

"If our plan for Dundee was going to work, we needed to make money selling some of these guys on, but, for various reasons, it didn't happen. In Claudio's case, when he signed on there was a clause put in his contract that meant 50% of any onward transfer fee, he had to get. When we sold him to Rangers, he got half the fee. The other half only ended up covering his wages."

Marr said that when Caniggia was leaving there was "actually a bit of unpleasantness". He said that was a shame after everything that had happened during his season to remember.

Marr said: "I was over in Mallorca – I was staying there at the time – and Jim Connor phoned saying there'd been trouble with Caniggia's agent. He'd been demanding that we sell Claudio to Rangers and was being quite threatening to staff at Dens. I was coming back anyway, so I said I'd meet them in our offices in Hawkhill. At this point, we couldn't afford his wages any longer anyway so if we could've got some money back that would've been great. It was one of these weird situations you hear of more and more these days – Claudio was half-owned by certain people in South America and they wanted money. Whether he owed them this money or whatever, I'm not sure, but he needed a certain amount of money. When I met them, I was trying to get them to reduce their share so I could get more money for Dundee, but it was obvious they weren't for backing down. So I agreed to accept Rangers' offer. What they didn't realise was we had CCTV in our car park, and after we'd shaken hands they went away down and did a wee jig. They danced and held each other in the car park. It obviously meant a lot to them to get that money."

Former Dark Blues captain Barry Smith also reflected on Caniggia's time at the club and described him as "a tremendous talent but an even better person".

For all that the Bonetti era is remembered for the foreign talent, the Italian was admirably loyal to the core of the Scottish players who formed the backbone of his team. Smith was the prime example and was Ivano's captain. He went on to make more than 400 appearances for the club before becoming manager in 2010.

"We had known since around April that Jocky wouldn't be in charge but there weren't any real signs who would replace him," said Smith. "Then, in July, the surprise announcement came it was Italian brothers Ivano and Dario Bonetti who were going to be responsible for improving the squad that Jocky had built. Little did we know then the transformation there would be to what was a successful team.

"There's not much I could add about what has been said about Claudio the player. He was an excellent striker who scored goals and worked hard for the team.

"What impressed me most about him, though, was off the park. The Argentine took time to talk to the young forwards at Dens like Steven Milne and Graham Bayne. Pouring pints in a local pub after a derby win showed how down to earth he truly was."

Smith said the Bonetti project ultimately failed to deliver and the big spending later set the ball rolling on a traumatic period when the club just survived extinction.

He said: "Ultimately, that will always have to be taken into account when looking back on the Bonetti era. But, from a playing point of view, from start to finish with the Bonettis, there was never a dull moment – from the way they arrived at the club, when Jocky Scott left after a successful couple of years, to their quickfire departure. I found adapting to the brothers' ways was the most difficult part of their tenure at Dens. However, I always felt I had to buy into what they were doing to give myself the best chance of retaining my place in the team. In a footballing sense, it is a time most Dundee fans will remember fondly, given the calibre of player that was brought to Dens Park – and I have to admit I'm no different.

"As a kid, you grow up hoping to play with World Cup winners and quality internationals but, in reality, it very rarely happens. I was very fortunate to be part of what was an exciting time at Dens Park. The Bonetti era was short but it had an impact on Scottish football and certainly boosted coverage of Dundee."

Former defender Lee Wilkie said he will never forget the day Caniggia signed.

"I was away with the Scotland under-21 squad and someone told me we were signing Claudio Caniggia, a World Cup legend," he said. "I could hardly believe it. And I have to say he was a class person as well as a class player. He didn't speak much English, but he mixed with all the boys. The only bad thing about Claudio was before a game at Dens you couldn't get into the toilet because he'd be in there having a fag. He used to go in just before it was time to run out, then he'd appear with a big smile on his face and be ready."

Stevie Milne was one of the young forwards who learned so much from Caniggia during the Argentine's short spell at Dens Park. "It's still a bit surreal the whole thing," he recalled. "I remember watching Caniggia in the 1990 World Cup and I was 10. I learned a lot from him as he spent a lot of time with the young strikers. Although his English wasn't great, he was able to get his message across and passed on his knowledge to me. It stuck with me as you obviously listen when someone like him is telling you things."

Milne broke through the youth ranks and into the first team and said that ending up alongside Caniggia was remarkable. "It's something I'll never forget," he said. "We went on trips to Italy, played in Europe, it was an exciting time for a young player. I absolutely loved my time at Dundee."

However, Milne said few of the characters at Dens Park during his eight years at the club were as intriguing as Ivano Bonetti.

"Ivano was an interesting manager," he said. "When he came to the club everything changed. We had players from all corners of the globe turning up. Loads of foreign boys were flooding into the dressing-room but still we had a good team spirit. He instilled a different way of life on the players here too. We switched from morning to afternoon training. Now that might not sound like a big thing to people but it was to us at the time. When you are a youngster you are brought up setting yourself up for morning sessions, it's difficult to change.

"But I tell you what, I wouldn't change that time for the world."

CHAPTER TWENTY

The Dreams We Have As Children

A World Cup star, in a Dundee shirt, at Tannadice, putting us in front – just tremendous.

Graham Smith

LIFELONG Dundee fan Graham Smith grew up watching the likes of Bobby Glennie, Albert Kidd, Keith Wright and Tommy Coyne perform at Dens Park. He admits he's seen it all over the years and has followed the Dark Blues through thick and thin at home and abroad. He has watched his beloved club almost go out of business three times; almost merge with rivals United; buy a player for £1,000 and a set of tracksuits; become the second most popular club in China; give a place on the board to a bogus lawyer dubbed the Devil's Advocate; and sensationally sign two of football's global superstars.

Little wonder then that Graham admits that one thing supporting Dundee has never been over the years is dull.

He said: "I think we'd just finished in fifth place in the SPL under Jocky Scott which was our best finish for years, so it was a bit of a surprise when it emerged that he would be leaving. In truth, we kind of saw it coming and knew there was something going on when the club signed Patrizio Billio, Javier Artero, Jose Mesas Puerta and Francisco Luna apparently without Jocky's knowledge or approval.

"Jocky finished the season and left, and the next thing we know these two Italian guys swept in with their entourage, standing in leather jackets and Dundee FC baseball caps as they were announced as the new management team. Immediately it was clear things were going to get very interesting. Ivano and Dario came with a genuine footballing pedigree having been with the big boys in Italian football and we knew these guys would have serious contacts."

Graham knew things were changing when Juan Sara and Fabian Caballero signed.

"They were two players we'd never really heard of at the time but Caballero had previously been on Arsenal's books so we were quietly confident he would be a success," he said.

"Then one evening I was out with the dog and got a text from my brother who told me that Dundee had just signed the Georgian international captain Georgi Nemsadze. I couldn't believe it and thought he was pulling my leg. Let's not forget this is the team a few years ago that signed a centre-half from Lochore Welfare for £1,000 and a set of tracksuits."

Graham went to watch Dundee in their first pre-season game against Raith Rovers at Starks Park under the Bonetti brothers with more than 1,000 away fans in attendance.

"Caballero and Sara both scored but even as a first outing, a pre-season game at a pedestrian pace, you could see these boys were different class," said Graham.

"Momentum was really building and we played some tremendous football at the start of that season under Ivano and Dario. They kept a Scottish spine running through the team with Barry Smith, Gavin Rae and Willie Falconer as permanent fixtures.

"Having those guys there also helped when the sleeves needed to be rolled up.

"As for Nemsadze? What a player he was. He simply oozed class and composure and went past players as if they weren't there."

Graham remembers after one match, Radio Scotland reporter Chick Young said: 'If this Dundee team are playing at a ground near you, get out there and watch them'.

Graham continued: "Suddenly we were a fashionable team. The wind was knocked out of our sails when Caballero picked up a long-term injury in a derby match against United and almost immediately goals were harder to come by. Ivano started the search for a replacement and the press got hold of a rumour that we were interested in Claudio Caniggia. Ivano knew him, but we thought it was fanciful at best. Basically we didn't think there was a hope we'd sign him."

Graham said his jaw dropped when Caniggia was paraded alongside Beto Carranza. He said: "This guy was a World Cup legend, after all; I remember watching him on TV getting clattered around all over the place by Cameroon defenders and now here he was at Dundee.

"Dundee had brought a world superstar footballer to Scotland. Not Celtic, not Rangers, but Dundee."

Graham said he would never forget Caniggia's debut. He was in the packed away end at Aberdeen where every second person appeared to be either wearing a blonde wig or an Argentina shirt.

"Caniggia started on the bench," he said. "We took the lead with a delicious chip from Ivano Bonetti. Stevie Milne went down injured and I remember watching Caniggia getting stripped and his number 33 going up on the board. The roof nearly came off the South Stand at Pittodrie. Honestly, it was incredible – I hadn't heard a noise like it for years.

"Gavin Rae got sent off in the second half and suddenly it looked like the fairytale might not have a happy ending. We were coping quite well though, then Caniggia skinned Phil McGuire down the left and was mowed down. McGuire was sent off to even things up and it looked like we'd hold on for the win. Then we broke up field with just seconds remaining and Nemsadze slides a wonderful pass through which Caniggia runs on to. He steps by the defender and rolls it into the bottom corner. There was absolute bedlam in the Dundee end."

Graham said Caniggia's goal and overall performance proved to the Dundee fans that he was the real deal and still up there with the best.

"This guy hadn't just come to earn one last pay day," said Graham. "It was almost unreal having the guy at Dens – you could see even at 33 he was miles ahead of most players in the league. He had vision, technical ability, could ride a tackle and his movement was often streets ahead of anyone else. He was just a terrific player and by all accounts he was a genuinely humble guy who spent a lot of time with the young lads at Dens, passing on advice and tips."

Graham's memories of Caniggia's derby debut against United were just as sweet. He said: "I remember the Dundee fans singing his name throughout the match. Just before half-time, Willie Falconer wins a header and puts Caniggia through on goal and boom – he despatched into the bottom corner and it's 1-0 Dundee.

"A World Cup star, in a Dundee shirt, at Tannadice, putting us in front – just tremendous. Just blow the whistle ref, we can all go home happy. Kind of glad he didn't though because Nemsadze's chip to make it 2-0 was also a thing of beauty."

Graham says a big disappointment about that season is the fans never got to see a fit Caballero and Caniggia in the same team at full flight. He said: "Without Caballero's injury, we probably wouldn't have got close to signing Caniggia."

He admits that there was always the underlying concern of where the money was coming from to fund the talent that he was watching every week.

"I think the model the Marrs had adopted was to bring these guys in, showcase them and sell them on at profit," he said.

"Bosman happened, players could move on a lot more easily and for peanuts, and it seemed every transfer window a key player or three were injured. If we'd have managed to get fees in for these players, maybe some of them would have paid for themselves and it would have ended differently.

"Zura, for example, a 20-year-old Georgian international with 20-plus caps, that was a million pound-plus player even by 2003 standards. He went to Rangers for zilch. But despite all of the wonderful play and exciting times, I still believe we massively underachieved with the talent we had at our disposal."

Jim Duffy eventually took over from Ivano and Dundee finished the season in the Scottish Cup Final at Hampden in his first season which was watched by Giovanni di Stefano.

Graham said: "This guy appears, claiming to be a lawyer who'd represented Saddam Hussein and was a friend of Arkan. He made various other outlandish claims but nobody could actually prove he was a lawyer – as it eventually turned out, neither could he, and he was put away for a long stretch at Her Majesty's pleasure."

Just when Dundee fans thought Caniggia was a never-to-be repeated signing, the club were suddenly being linked with a move for Fabrizio Ravanelli.

"I think a few years previously we'd have thought there was no chance," he said. "But, given what had gone before, there was hardly anything left to surprise us. It was absolutely unreal."

Graham said Ravanelli's place in Dundee folklore is assured following his sensational League Cup hat-trick heroics in the unlikely setting of Clyde.

He said: "It was 1-1 after five minutes and in truth, we made much harder work of it than we should have – it's the Dundee way after all! Lee Wilkie scored a wonder goal but we couldn't shake Clyde off. In fairytale style the White Feather came off the bench and strolled on to the park. Suddenly it was 5-2 and he'd scored a hat-trick inside seven minutes. What an impact!

"He even hit the post in injury time to be denied his fourth. He only played a handful of games for us but he did play at Tannadice so the United fans got to see another world-class player, which I'm sure they appreciated."

But after all the highs it all went up in smoke.

Graham said: "I don't think we'd sold anyone since Caniggia and the money wasn't coming in. Administration was announced in the November. It seemed our world had come crashing down.

"Sara, Nemsadze, Caballero, Ravanelli – all these great players left – but with them there was a fair number of the club staff too, which was a tragedy. These were desperate times. But you often learn a lot about people in times of adversity and this was no different. The then Dundee Supporters Association board formed Dee4Life and galvanised the fans, and as a unit we set about saving our club.

"After a phenomenal effort from the fans, players and staff – and it has to be said the administrators too – we got ourselves to relative safety, albeit still carrying a substantial debt to the bank. Jim Duffy had been a legend as a player, and the way he conducted himself and represented the club while it was all falling apart was incredible. What a real top guy he is.

"Was it all worth it?

"I don't think it's possible to answer 'yes' to that question. People lost their jobs, not just players but office staff and the like who had no influence on the situation we found ourselves in. We nearly lost our club and for all the wonderful football and the world class players, we didn't finish any higher than sixth place.

"But will I ever forget it?

"Never.

"Caniggia, Ravanelli, Nemsadze, Caballero, Artero, Carranza, Speroni, Rab Douglas, Steven Tweed, Gavin Rae, Willie Falconer… and Barry Smith too.

"What a time to be alive."

CHAPTER TWENTY-ONE
A Wise Man Once Said

It was the best of times, it was the worst of times, it was the age of wisdom, it was the age of foolishness, it was the epoch of belief, it was the epoch of incredulity, it was the season of light, it was the season of darkness, it was the spring of hope, it was the winter of despair.

Charles Dickens, A Tale of Two Cities

IT is perhaps fitting that our tale ends just as it started by making reference to Charles Dickens' famous tale of love and revolution.

Despite his reputation as the world's greatest storyteller, the grand old writer might well have struggled to script the Marr brothers' era in Dundee.

By any measure, Dundee Football Club signing Claudio Caniggia in early October, 2000, was phenomenal. Put simply, it stunned the entire footballing world. The transfer would make front page headlines in Caniggia's native Argentina, and Dens Park then attracted mass media attention from across the globe.

That this player was a World Cup runner-up just 10 years previously made it even more remarkable. A generation had watched Caniggia explode on the world scene in arguably the greatest-ever World Cup for stars – yes he was remembered for that tackle from Massing; but he was also remembered for rising to the top in what was a tournament littered with star names.

That's what made Italia 90 so special – it might not have been the greatest tournament in terms of football, but it featured the best collection of talent.

At the time big signings were regularly coming to Scotland, with astounding transfer fees being paid for them. So it wasn't unusual for a former World Cup star of such stature to grace our game.

But it was his final destination that caused such shock.

Celtic and Rangers were breaking the bank to win the league and compete on the European stage in the Champions League. Ronald de Boer, Andrei Kanchelskis and Chris Sutton were here on megabucks.

Celtic were soon to sign Neil Lennon for £6 million. Tore Andre Flo would complete a record-breaking £12 million move to Rangers just a month after

Caniggia's arrival in Dundee. Flo's record transfer fee has still never been broken in Scotland.

That merely emphasises the kind of time it was – certainly in Rangers' case. The level of spending would eventually create huge problems for the Glasgow club.

Celtic played to 60,000 crowds while Rangers turned out in front of 50,000 every week. The Old Firm giants trained on state-of-the-art pitches and their top earners could expect up to £40,000 a week. Put this into contrast with Dundee, whose average gate the season previously was just 6,900 and whose players trained on public parks which were often quagmires.

But Dundee did get their man and excitement reached fever pitch. Those of us whose usual beat was the news pages now found ourselves writing about the goings-on at Dens, as Dundee went from the sports pages to the front pages. There was a genuine sense of excitement across the city. This was a player most of us had grown up watching and now here he was in the Hilltown.

Blonde wigs sold out, Caniggia masks did a roaring trade, and it was fairly unusual to see a replica Dundee top with anything else than 'Caniggia 33' on the back at that time. Luckily, the stock was replenished in time to send one to Caniggia's best mate Diego Maradona who had requested one. That was just another one of the "pinch yourself" moments that transpired.

Dundee games against the likes of Dunfermline and Hibs were now being shown across the world and crowds at Dens went up by 3,000 on average. What it also did was get the next generation to watch Dundee and it also brought those fans back through the turnstile that hadn't gone since the days of Billy Steel. Suddenly the fans had a new idol to worship and didn't have to travel to Glasgow to see world-class stars. It also brought football fans from far and wide – who didn't even support Dundee to Dens – all wanting a glimpse of a guy they'd watched terrorise defences at Italia 90.

A reputation is one thing but delivering is something else. Caniggia didn't disappoint for the Dark Blues and proved on a weekly basis that he was still at the top of his game. He also showed genuine affection for the club and its fans, which endeared him further to the Dens masses. He was polite and courteous and would give away his shirts to good causes and regularly appear at functions and prize-giving ceremonies to hand out gongs.

Interest from elsewhere wasn't slow in coming with such exploits on the pitch. With a dream of making the 2002 World Cup, Dundee fans probably knew it was always likely he'd be pulled away when the big guns came calling. The soap opera which followed Rangers' pursuit of the player's signature saw sparks fly but ultimately his time was up and he left.

The fact he spent less than a season at Dens, but was eventually inducted into the club's inaugural hall of fame, spoke volumes for his impact.

The club described it as "a season when entertainment almost seemed more important than results". It was a brief stay but full of so many fond memories.

By the time Fabrizio Ravanelli arrived in the City of Discovery in 2003, the man who signed Caniggia – Ivano Bonetti – was long gone. But Dundee were still throwing cash around and The White Feather, just like Caniggia in 2000 – had found himself without a club.

Ravanelli's capture was the biggest signing since Caniggia. The White Feather had played for Italy, scored in a Champions League final for Juventus and just seven years previously was the English Premier League's top scorer. His shirt-over-the-head celebration was almost as famous as his unmistakeable grey hair.

Manager Jim Duffy summed it up perfectly when he stated: "To say it's an exciting time for the club is an understatement, and it's also an understatement to say that we are delighted to see a player of this quality here."

Don't forget, this was a time when nothing could surprise Dundee fans.

He took an age to get fit but the moments of magic were just that. Ravanelli played just under six games for the club but in less than 10 minutes at Broadwood he wrote his name into Dundee folklore. The league-cup hat-trick in front of less than 2,000 fans after coming off the bench was almost unbelievable.

That financial matters would overtake football matters and spell the end for Ravanelli (and almost the club) so shortly afterwards was incredibly sad.

The days of big wages and superstar names are gone now at Dens. But the club remains in existence which is ultimately the most important thing.

Dundee fans will never forget the memories of the time these two Gods of the game graced the ground whose fastest performers used to be greyhounds.

It might have been short but it was certainly never dull.

Football blogger Gaby McKay later said: "Sometimes I remember that Fabrizio Ravanelli and Claudio Caniggia both played for Dundee. It's still mental."

The prose is unlike Dickens, perhaps, but within those words there is a nail firmly hit upon the head.

These days Dundee is a world away from the city Caniggia and

Ravanelli arrived in. The changes – even in such a relatively short time – have been dramatic. The new waterfront and the construction of the V&A means that the attention and flash bulbs of the world's media is once again focused on Dundee.

But this time it is thanks to an international star whose vision and skill was just as impressive as anything that was served up by Dundee's two footballing megastars – the acclaimed Japanese architect Kengo Kuma; the man behind the V&A.

Aye, the boy Kengo done good. But could he cut it on a cold Wednesday night, away to Clyde?

The Bird & The Feather

Tale Of The Tape
Dundee And Caniggia's 2000-2001 Season

Caniggia plays all/part of game   *Scores in game

Date	Competition	Result	Venue	Attendance	
Sat Jul 29 2000	SPL	Motherwell 0-2 Dundee	Fir Park	6,161	
Sat Aug 5 2000	SPL	Dundee 3-0 Dunf. Ath.	Dens Park	7,152	
Sat Aug 12 2000	SPL	Hibernian 5-1 Dundee	Easter Road	12,075	
Sat Aug 19 2000	SPL	St Mirren 2-1 Dundee	Love Street	5,165	
Wed Aug 23 2000	Lg Cup	Dundee 3-0 Montrose	Dens Park	2,635	
Sun Aug 27 2000	SPL	Dundee 1-1 Hearts	Dens Park	6,779	
Tue Sep 5 2000	Lg Cup	St Mirren 3-0 Dundee	Love Street	3,571	
Sat Sep 9 2000	SPL	Dundee 1-1 Rangers	Dens Park	10,439	
Sat Sep 16 2000	SPL	St Johnst. 0-0 Dundee	McDiarmid	5,055	
Wed Sep 20 2000	SPL	Dundee 3-0 D. United	Dens Park	9,838	
Sat Sep 23 2000	SPL	Celtic 1-0 Dundee	Celtic Park	59,634	
Sat Sep 30 2000	SPL	Dundee 0-0 Killie	Dens Park	6,170	
Sat Oct 14 2000	SPL	Aberdeen 0-2 Dundee	Pittodrie	16,035	*
Sat Oct 21 2000	SPL	Dundee 1-2 M'well	Dens Park	7,344	*
Sat Oct 28 2000	SPL	Dunf. Ath. 1-0 Dundee	East End Pk	6,397	
Sun Nov 5 2000	SPL	Dundee 1-2 Hibernian	Dens Park	6,604	
Sat Nov 11 2000	SPL	D. United 0-2 Dundee	Tannadice	11,454	*
Sat Nov 18 2000	SPL	Dundee 5-0 St Mirren	Dens Park	6,333	**
Sat Nov 25 2000	SPL	Hearts 3-1 Dundee	Tynecastle	11,539	
Sat Dec 2 2000	SPL	Dundee 1-1 St Johnst.	Dens Park	7,014	
Sun Dec 10 2000	SPL	Dundee 1-2 Celtic	Dens Park	10,763	
Sat Dec 16 2000	SPL	Killie 2-3 Dundee	Rugby Park	6,573	
Sat Dec 23 2000	SPL	Dundee 2-2 Aberdeen	Dens Park	9,093	
Tue Dec 26 2000	SPL	M'well 0-3 Dundee	Fir Park	6,183	
Tue Jan 2 2001	SPL	Hibernian 3-0 Dundee	Easter Rd	12,379	
Sat Jan 27 2001	Scot. Cup	Dundee 0-0 Falkirk	Dens Park	6,395	

Wed Jan 31 2001	SPL	Dundee 2-3 D. United	Dens Park	11,724	*
Sat Feb 3 2001	SPL	St Mirren 2-1 Dundee	Love Street	4,197	
Mon Feb 12 2001	S. Cup (R)	Falkirk 0-2 Dundee	Brockville	6,168	*
Sat Feb 17 2001	S. Cup	Hearts 1-1 Dundee	Tynecastle	9,970	
Wed Feb 21 2001	SPL	Dundee 0-1 Dunf. Ath.	Dens Park	6,113	
Sat Feb 24 2001	SPL	Dundee 0-1 Rangers	Dens Park	9,778	
Sat Mar 3 2001	SPL	St Johnst. 2-3 Dundee	McDiarmid	5,064	
Wed Mar 7 2001	S. Cup (R)	Dundee 0-1 Hearts	Dens Park	6,947	
Wed Mar 14 2001	SPL	Rangers 0-2 Dundee	Ibrox	45,035	*
Sun Mar 18 2001	SPL	Dundee 0-0 Hearts	Dens Park	7,327	
Sat Mar 31 2001	SPL	Dundee 2-2 Killie	Dens Park	6,719	
Wed Apr 4 2001	SPL	Celtic 2-1 Dundee	Celtic Park	59,562	
Sat Apr 7 2001	SPL	Aberdeen 0-2 Dundee	Pittodrie	12,005	
Sat Apr 21 2001	SPL	Dundee 0-3 Rangers	Dens Park	10,687	
Sun Apr 29 2001	SPL	Dundee 0-2 Hibernian	Dens Park	6,659	
Sat May 5 2001	SPL	Dundee 2-1 Killie	Dens Park	6,261	
Sun May 13 2001	SPL	Celtic 0-2 Dundee	Celtic Park	59,435	
Sun May 20 2001	SPL	Hearts 2-0 Dundee	Tynecastle	13,544	

Tale Of The Tape
Dundee And Ravanelli's 2003-2004 Season

Ravanelli plays all/part of game   *Scores in game

Sat Aug 9 2003	SPL	Motherwell 0-3 Dundee	Fir Park	6812
Thu Aug 14 2003	UEFA Q1	Vllaznia Shkoder 0-2 Dundee	Loro Borici	11,000
Sun Aug 17 2003	SPL	Dundee 0-2 Dunf. Ath.	Dens	7750
Sat Aug 23 2003	SPL	Dundee 2-1 Livingston	Dens	5815
Thu Aug 28 2003	UEFA Q1	Dundee 4-0 Vllaznia Shkoder	Dens	8254
Sun Aug 31 2003	SPL	Kilmarnock 1-1 Dundee	Rugby P.	5973
Sat Sep 13 2003	SPL	Dundee 0-1 Celtic	Dens	10,647
Sat Sep 20 2003	SPL	Dundee 2-0 Aberdeen	Dens	7887
Wed Sep 24 2003	UEFA R1	Dundee 1-2 Perugia	Dens	9911
Sat Sep 27 2003	SPL	Rangers 3-1 Dundee	Ibrox	49,548
Sat Oct 4 2003	SPL	Hearts 2-2 Dundee	Tynecastle	11,348
Wed Oct 15 2003	UEFA R1	Perugia 1-0 Dundee	Renato Curi	8685
Sat Oct 18 2003	SPL	Dundee 1-0 Partick Thistle	Dens	6497
Sun Oct 26 2003	SPL	Dundee United 1-1 Dundee	Tannadice	12,767
Wed Oct 29 2003	Lg Cup	Clyde 2-5 Dundee	Broadwood	1701
Sat Nov 1 2003	SPL	Dundee 1-1 Hibs	Dens	7032
Sat Nov 8 2003	SPL	Dundee 0-1 Motherwell	Dens	6374
Sat Nov 22 2003	SPL	Dunf. Ath. 2-0 Dundee	E. E. Park	5490
Sat Nov 29 2003	SPL	Livingston 1-1 Dundee	Almondvale	4625
Wed Dec 3 2003	Lg Cup	Dundee 1-0 Hearts	Dens	7130
Sat Dec 6 2003	SPL	Dundee 1-2 Kilmarnock	Dens	6954
Sat Dec 13 2003	SPL	Celtic 3-2 Dundee	Celtic Park	57,573
Sat Dec 20 2003	SPL	Aberdeen 2-2 Dundee	Pittodrie	10,354
Sun Dec 28 2003	SPL	Dundee 0-2 Rangers	Dens	10,948
Tue Jan 6 2004	SPL	Dundee 1-2 Hearts	Dens	6387
Sat Jan 10 2004	Scot. Cup	Aberdeen 0-0 Dundee	Pittodrie	11,012

***

Sat Jan 17 2004	SPL	Partick 1-2 Dundee	Firhill	4690
Wed Jan 21 2004	S. Cup (R)	Dundee 2-3 Aberdeen	Dens	5857
Sun Jan 25 2004	SPL	Dundee 2-1 Dundee United	Dens	10,747
Sat Jan 31 2004	SPL	Hibs 1-1 Dundee	Easter Rd	8023
Tue Feb 3 2004	Lg Cup Semi	Dundee 0-1 Livingston	Easter Rd	7231
Wed Feb 11 2004	SPL	Motherwell 5-3 Dundee	Fir Park	4247
Sat Feb 14 2004	SPL	Dundee 0-1 Dunf. Ath.	Dens	5643
Sat Feb 21 2004	SPL	Dundee 1-0 Livingston	Dens	6108
Sat Feb 28 2004	SPL	Kilmarnock 4-2 Dundee	Rugby Pk	5454
Sat Mar 13 2004	SPL	Dundee 1-1 Aberdeen	Dens	6839
Wed Mar 17 2004	SPL	Dundee 1-2 Celtic	Dens	8593
Sat Mar 20 2004	SPL	Rangers 4-0 Dundee	Ibrox	49,364
Sat Mar 27 2004	SPL	Hearts 3-1 Dundee	Tynecastle	10,491
Sat Apr 3 2004	SPL	Dundee 2-1 Partick Th.	Dens	5084
Sun Apr 11 2004	SPL	Dundee United 2-2 Dundee	Tannadice	9571
Sat Apr 17 2004	SPL	Dundee 2-2 Hibs	Dens	5508
Sat Apr 24 2004	SPL	Partick Th. 0-1 Dundee	Firhill	2727
Sat May 1 2004	SPL	Hibs 1-0 Dundee	Easter Rd	6180
Sat May 8 2004	SPL	Dundee 2-0 Killie	Dens	4942
Wed May 12 2004	SPL	Dundee 2-0 Livingston	Dens	4954
Sat May 15 2004	SPL	Aberdeen 1-2 Dundee	Pittodrie	7878

The Bird & The Feather

About the author

GRAEME STRACHAN was born in Dundee and joined DC Thomson in 1999. He has covered local news for The Courier and The Evening Telegraph and worked through the Caniggia and Ravanelli years when sport started to move to the front pages.

He has covered news stories at home and abroad. He has also covered league matches, cup finals and Scottish international matches for the sports pages.

He also played a key role in the successful fight for Frank's Law, a Courier-backed campaign to stop the age discrimination which exists for people in Scotland under the age of 65.

The team's coverage of the campaign – named in memory of former Dundee United defender Frank Kopel – won a UK Regional Press Award in 2016 and Scottish Press Award in 2018.

Graeme is a keen football fan and has watched matches across the world.

He has witnessed many of the modern game's greats in the flesh, including Lionel Messi, Gheorghe Hagi, Ronaldinho and Paul Gascoigne. But he rates Claudio Caniggia as one of the best he's seen.

Graeme lives in Dundee with his family.

DC Thomson Media
Heritage Books
2019
www.dcthomsonshop.co.uk